ENVIRONMENTAL MANAGEMENT SYSTEMS

Environmental Management Systems

Principles and Practice

DAVID HUNT and CATHERINE JOHNSON

McGRAW-HILL BOOK COMPANY

London · New York · St Louis · San Francisco · Auckland
Bogotá · Caracas · Lisbon · Madrid · Mexico · Milan
Montreal · New Delhi · Panama · Paris · San Juan
São Paulo · Singapore · Sydney · Tokyo · Toronto

Learning Resources
Centre

Published by
McGraw-Hill Book Company Europe
Shoppenhangers Road, Maidenhead, Berkshire SL6 2QL, England
Telephone 01628 23432
Fax 01628 770224

British Library Cataloguing in Publication Data

Hunt, David
  Environmental Management Systems:
  Principles and Practice
  I. Title II. Johnson, Catherine
  658.408

ISBN 0–07–707910–8

Library of Congress Cataloging-in-Publication Data
Hunt, David,
  Environmental management systems : principles and practice/ David
Hunt and Catherine Johnson.
    p. cm.
  Includes bibliographical references.
  ISBN 0–07–707910–8 (hardback) : alk. paper)
    1. Industrial management–Environmental aspects–European Union
countries.   2. Environmental law–European Union countries.
3. Environmental protection–Standards–European Union countries.
4. Environmental auditing–European Union countries   I. Johnson.
Catherine.   II. title.
HD30.255.H86   1995   95–20986
658.4′08–dc20   CIP

1 2 3 4 5 BL 9 8 7 6 5

Typeset by Keyword Typesetting Services Ltd, Wallington, Surrey
Printed and bound in Great Britain by Biddles Ltd, Guildford, Surrey

Printed on permanent paper in compliance with ISO Standard 9706

Contents

Foreword

Managing for the environment is not a new idea but systematic approaches to it are only now, in the very late twentieth century, being developed. This book draws together the evolution of the concept and, from a mainly UK standpoint, reviews the development of concerns for the environment. It also summarizes legislative requirements.

The authors, who are involved with much of the work, assisted in the development of the approach advocated by the British Standards Institution in BS 7750: 1992 (now BS 7750: 1994). They have a background in providing consultancy and advice to a range of organizations on environmental management issues, and are thus well placed to offer their experience and knowledge through this book.

The use of a systems approach, firstly to quality and then to environment, is discussed and helpful tips and suggestions given.

The book is easy to read and understand and should be of assistance to those considering environmental management for the first time, as well as those already involved.

Oswald A. Dodds, MBE
Chairman UK (BSi) Technical Committee
on Environmental Standards
Chairman of ISO/TC 207/SCI
Director of Contract Services
Northampton Borough Council

Preface

Less than five years ago, the Environmental Management System (EMS) concept was new to many — but not all — organizations. Its subsequent development has been very rapid: BS 7750 was first published by the British Standards Institution in 1992, and the basic approach has since been adopted by the EU Eco-Management and Audit Scheme, and by the International Organization for Standardization in ISO/CD 14001.

We have been privileged to play a part in that development through our work for client companies, and for BSI on the drafting, development and revision of BS 7750 itself. Experiencing the reactions of a wide range of organizations makes us aware that the EMS concept engenders both enthusiasm and concern. The enthusiasm reflects a recognition that an EMS provides a framework within which they can actively and coherently address environmental issues. The concern focuses primarily on a perceived lack of specific guidance, and on the potential demands upon small and medium enterprises.

Given this background, we were pleased to accept the invitation to write this book. Its purpose is to help managers and others who are considering, or already embarking upon, the development and implementation an EMS — possibly, but not necessarily, in conformity with one of the above-mentioned models. While we hope that it may prove particularly helpful to the smaller company, it is written without specific regard to size or sector. Our aim has been to offer guidance and suggestions which are potentially applicable to all types and sizes of organization.

We extend our gratitude to Mr O. A. (Ossie) Dodds, for his kindness in writing the Foreword; his unique contribution to the development of EMS standards is widely appreciated, both within the UK and internationally.

We also thank the companies who provided details of their environmental policies and initiatives — Bayer, British Airways, Ciba-Geigy, Glaxo, ICI, Mobil, National Westminster, Norsk Hydro, Shanks and McEwan, and SmithKline Beecham.

Our Consultancy, **WRc alert**, provided general support and word-processing facilities, and we have had the benefit of stimulating discussions with, and assistance from, numerous colleagues and clients. We also acknowledge the help of the staffs of the WRc Standards and Legislation Group, and Library.

We are grateful to McGraw-Hill not only for for the invitation to write the book, but also for the skill and patience of its staff in bringing it to publication. We also acknowledge the helpful observations on the manuscript made, at various stages, by its reviewers.

Finally, without the encouragement and forbearance of our families — Mair, Angharad and Catrin, and Jim and Fiona — nothing would have been accomplished. We owe them our heartfelt thanks.

D.T.E.H., C.A.J.
WRc alert
Marlow
Bucks, UK

1

Introduction

1.1 Business and the Growth of Environmental Concern

We live in a time of great public and institutional concern about the environment. While the roots of such concern can be traced back at least to the last century, it has grown enormously since the Second World War, fuelled by a mixture of issues, incidents, governmental and international initiatives, and influential publications. The reasons for this growth — and for fluctuations in the level of concern from time to time — are discussed in more detail in Chapter 2, but it is clear that the underlying views of society about environmental issues have changed dramatically in recent decades.

Moreover, the change appears to be irreversible. Thus, while it is well known that environmental concern on the part of the public at large tends to wax and wane with economic circumstances, and that the present recession has seen some decline in the poll ratings of the environment as a general issue, there are a number of factors which maintain its prominence, including:

- Scientific evidence of specific aspects of environmental damage.
- Increasing public awareness of environmental issues.
- Greater satisfaction of basic needs.
- Increasingly stringent pollution control measures.
- The trend to internalize environmental costs through taxes and charges.
- Growing emphasis on environmental matters in education.

The attitudes of industry and commerce have themselves evolved as public concerns have developed and crystallized: from defensiveness, through acceptance, to a recognition of the need for environmental probity as a prerequisite for organizational survival and success.

To chart in this way the evolution of business thinking about the environment is not to decry or castigate business management. Business functions within the framework of society at large, and it is unreasonable to expect that over long periods of years its attitudes will — or indeed can — outstrip those of the communities within which it operates. Ultimately, it is society which determines, whether by laws, taxes or purchasing decisions, what it expects of business;

1

individual companies can anticipate society's attitudes and demands, but can lead public expectations only within the limits of commercial prudence.

Nevertheless, so far as can be judged at any particular point in time, society has reached a settled view that it expects high environmental standards from companies large and small, and is prepared to pay — within limits, of course — a price, directly or indirectly, in terms of increased costs of goods and services.

At the same time, however, businesses of all kinds face increasing competition, fuelled by the reduction or removal of trade barriers, the relentless search for improved efficiency, the impact of easier communication and transport and the growing sophistication and awareness of consumers. Whether some of these stimuli are themselves damaging to the environment is a much debated issue; we shall not add to that debate here, but simply note that business has to deal with environmental concerns alongside a host of other pressures of ever-increasing intensity.

Thus, no company mindful of future success can afford to ignore environmental concerns, however pressing other business considerations may be in the short term. Indeed, organizations of all kinds, in both the private and public sectors, now accept that their environmental performance will be scrutinized by a wide range of 'interested parties' — in Government, in Regulatory Agencies, in the work-place, in the site neighbourhood, in the financial community, in the market-place, in the media and in pressure groups — as well as by the public at large.

For a specific organization, each group of relevant interested parties will have its own particular concerns and expectations. However, it is possible to make some broad generalizations about the nature of the environmental pressures on different business sectors, as shown in the profile–vulnerability matrix of Figure 1.1.

This identifies two major drivers of environmental pressure — regulatory and public interest — and shows how different industrial and commercial sectors are affected by them, according to their inherent environmental 'vulnerability' and their public profile (in the general, not the environmental, sense). While the positioning of individual sectors within the matrix is a subjective judgement, such that different positions might be assigned by different observers, the matrix serves to demonstrate that sectors with high vulnerability but low profile are most strongly influenced by regulation, whereas those with low vulnerability but high profile are most heavily affected by public interest. Of course, those with both high vulnerability and high profile are heavily influenced by both drivers, which are themselves not unconnected, as regulation is itself partly driven by public concern.

The matrix does not show explicitly the pressure which may be exerted by financial factors, but insofar as it follows both regulatory and public interest pressures it acts on all types of organization according to the dominant conditions of the time.

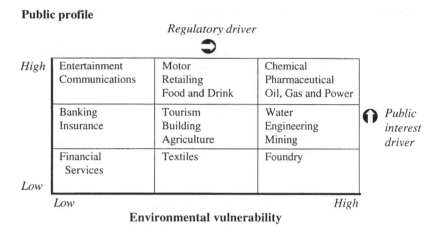

Figure 1.1   The profile–vulnerability matrix

1.2 The Importance of Good Environmental Performance

Table 1.1 identifies the benefits to be gained from good environmental performance, and from a sound, forward-looking and confident approach to environmental issues within an organization which seeks to meet the reasonable expectations of interested parties. The penalties of failing to achieve such performance and develop such an approach may readily be inferred.

Organizations of all kinds are increasingly recognizing the importance of these issues, though the relative importance of the different potential benefits — and penalties — will vary depending upon such factors as the nature of the business, its positioning in the market-place with respect to environmental issues, and the expectations of its interested parties. For some, the pressure to meet legislative and regulatory requirements in an efficient and cost-effective manner may be of basic importance to the survival of a profitable business. For others, new or modified products and services will be seen to offer opportunities for enhanced market share and profitability. For most businesses, however, many or all of the potential benefits will be recognized as significant, to a greater or lesser degree.

A few examples, from a range of industry sectors, will suffice to illustrate these issues. The Chairman of the Board of Management of Bayer AG has stated that: '. . . the future success of the chemical industry . . . depend[s] on its being as environmentally compatible and safe as possible.'[1] Similarly ICI, recognizing that '. . . the chemical industry does not currently enjoy a favourable reputation on its environmental performance . . . ',[2] has clearly noted (in an

Table 1.1   The potential benefits of sound environmental performance and attitudes

Area	Potential benefits
Legal	Avoidance of litigation, fines and legal costs, clean-up costs, civil liabilities.
Image	Enhanced organizational pride, corporate image/PR and attractiveness as employer.
Financial	Increased confidence of regulators, investors and insurers.
Management	Improved 'peace of mind', consistency on issues and time utilization.
Business	Enhanced performance from product differentiation, 'Eco-label' recognition, improved market share, improved margins, sound and opportune investment, improved cost control and sound acquisition and divestment.

awareness programme for employees[3]) that the ability to meet the expectations of potential employees, investment institutions, customers and the community is a significant determinant of business success.

In the waste management industry, which has historically also been perceived to have a poor environmental reputation, there are significant opportunities arising from the general increase in environmental awareness, but corporate success in meeting those opportunities will depend upon public confidence and the avoidance of legal and financial liability through sound environmental management; see, for example, remarks by the Shanks and McEwan Group.[4]

Although the recession in the UK in the 1990s has undoubtedly seen some downturn in the relative importance attached by the general public to environmental issues (see Chapter 2), in relation to more traditional concerns about such issues as economic performance and employment, environmental matters remain important features in the market-place. Thus, as an example, even in the depressed and price-sensitive conditions which prevailed in the UK car market in the late summer of 1992, environmental issues featured strongly in the advertising strategies of some manufacturers. For instance, Saab sought to give considerable, and essentially equal, emphasis to personal safety and environmental issues in a major eight-page advertisement[5] with *The Times* newspaper in September 1992.

Again, several major retail chains have for a long time taken strong positions on environmental issues. For example, the Body Shop's stance on the environment is perceived as a strong differentiating factor within the personal care sector.[6] Similarly, the DIY retailer B&Q has given much attention to the impacts of its products, and recently took a double page spread in *The Times*[7] to describe its work to reduce or eliminate them.

Thus, while changing economic conditions may from time to time raise or lower the level of general concern about environmental issues, there is by now a very wide recognition that they are well established in the assemblage of factors to be addressed in the planning and management of industrial and commercial activities. There is also an increasing awareness that a reactive approach to such concern, and to changing legislative and regulatory requirements, is unlikely to place companies (in any sector) in the most favourable position to achieve business success into the twenty-first century. Here, as elsewhere in the field of environmental management, there are clear parallels with quality management: recognition of the importance of which, in an increasingly competitive world, has been a dominant feature of business thinking in the 1980s and 1990s.

1.3 The Purpose and Structure of this Book

The concept of the Environmental Management System (EMS) has developed in response to this recognition that environmental pressures upon organizations need to be addressed in an integrated and proactive manner.

Begun by individual organizations, the development received considerable impetus from the work of the British Standards Institution (BSI) in producing (in 1992) and subsequently revising (in 1994) the world's first EMS standard, BS 7750.[8] Further impetus was provided by the adoption of the principles and practices of that standard within the then draft of the European Union's Eco-Audit Regulation, later to become the Eco-Management and Audit (EMA) Regulation.[9] Subsequently, other national and international initiatives, particularly by the International Organization for Standardization (ISO), have continued the work (see, for example, the latest ISO drafts[10,11] on EMS).

Whether within the framework of a specific standard or scheme, or as an independent initiative within a specific organization, the EMS concept is proving to be a major influence on business thinking and attitudes to the management of environmental matters. Figure 1.2 (modified from a similar diagram in ISO[11]) shows the basic nature of the EMS approach.

The purpose of this book is to provide the general reader — especially, but not exclusively, within business — with an overview of the development and continuing evolution of the Environmental Management System concept and approach, and specific guidance on the implementation of an EMS within his or her own organization.

While the text, for convenience, frequently refers to BS 7750 as an EMS model, it is just as relevant to those seeking to follow the requirements of the European Union's EMA scheme, of other national standards, or of the requirements of the draft international EMS standard, ISO/CD 14001, all of which typically follow BS 7750 quite closely. It is also relevant to an organization seeking to develop an EMS to its own specific model and requirements.

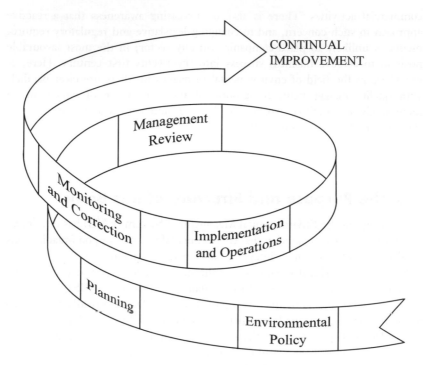

Figure 1.2   Basis of the EMS approach

References

1 H. J. Strenger (Chairman, Bayer AG), 'Guiding Principles of Bayer's Environmental Policy', in *Bayer's Perspective on the Environment — II*, Bayer Communication Centre, Leverkusen, 1991.

2 ICI, 'An Introduction to the Issue Bulletins', *ICI Public Affairs*, London, May 1992.

3 ICI, *Environmental Actions*, ICI Group Personnel, London, 1992.

4 Shanks and McEwan Group plc, *Corporate Environmental Policy* (undated).

5 Saab advertisement, 'We didn't invent the automobile. We've concentrated on perfecting it', *The Times*, London, September 1992.

6 Numerous news items and letters on Body Shop International and its environmental policies and performance, *Financial Times*, August and September 1994; see also D. Wheeler, 'Auditing for Sustainability: Philosophy and Practice of The Body Shop International', *Eco-Management and Auditing*, vol. 1, 10–16, 1993.

7 B&Q advertisement, 'The more environmental problems we solve the more we find worth solving', *The Times*, London, October 1994.

8 British Standards Institution, BS 7750: 1992 (now revised as BS 7750: 1994), *Environmental management systems*, BSI, London, 1992 (1994).

9 European Union, 'Council Regulation (EEC) No. 1836/93 of 29 June 1993 allowing participation by companies in the industrial sector in a Community eco-management and audit scheme', *Official Journal of the European Communities*, L168/1–18, 10 July 1993.

10 ISO, Committee Draft of ISO 14001, 'Environmental Management Systems — Specification with guidance for use', October 1994.

11 ISO, Committee Draft of ISO 14000, 'Environmental Management Systems — General Guidelines on principles, systems and supporting techniques', October 1994.

2

The History of Environmental Concern

2.1 The Broad Development of Environmental Consciousness

The effects of human activities in shaping the environment are not confined to modern times. The earliest human beings were nomadic hunter–gatherers, and their way of life accounted for all but the last few thousand years of man's two million years of existence;[1] it is still pursued by a few. This lifestyle permitted the spread of human beings throughout the world; they inhabited most of it by about 10 000 years ago. The environmental effects of the hunter–gatherer lifestyle would have been limited to those of successful hunting, namely the extinction of species, but this would have been limited by the low numbers of humans and the primitive technology available to them.

The first great transition in the human lifestyle was the development of agriculture, about 10 000 years ago. Settlements developed concurrently, and human populations increased and provided pressure for land to be cleared and brought into agricultural production by ever more intensive methods. As agriculture spread and populations increased, deforestation followed, not only to provide agricultural land but also because the trees were felled to provide fuel and timber. The consequences have been permanent; little of the forest which once covered Europe, for example, still exists, and of course very little of the landscape has escaped the influence of agriculture or industry.

The problems of deforestation, overgrazing and soil erosion were understood by the ancient Greeks. Plato wrote:

> 'What now remains compared with what then existed is like the skeleton of a sick man, all the fat and soft earth having wasted away, and only the bare framework of the land being left ... there are some mountains which now have nothing but food for bees, but they had trees not very long ago ...'[1]

In Europe, at least, after the spread of Christianity, attitudes could be summed up by two perspectives contained in the Judaeo-Christian tradition (whether attitudes were shaped, or justified, by these perspectives is a different issue). The book of *Genesis* tells us:

'So God created man in his own image, in the image of God he created him; male and female he created them. And God blessed them, and God said to them, "Be fruitful and multiply, and fill the earth and subdue it; and have dominion over the fish of the sea and over the birds of the air and over every living thing that moves upon the earth."'

Genesis 1, 27–28, Revised Standard Version

The words 'subdue' and 'dominion' could justify philosophies which saw the earth and its resources as gifts provided by God for exploitation. Later on in *Genesis*, however, the story of the Garden of Eden uses language which is open to a different interpretation:

'The Lord God took the man and put him in the garden of Eden to till it and keep it.'

Genesis 2, 15, Revised Standard Version

Here man is portrayed not as an exploiter, but as a steward. While the garden has been filled with sources of food for man, he is to keep the garden and not to destroy it. These two viewpoints epitomize two extremes of attitude, which have persisted to the present day, towards man's relationship with the earth and other living things .

From the earliest times to the Middle Ages, the prevailing views within this spectrum would have been determined far more by religion, superstition and the teachings of the church than by rational understanding. Our ancestors were largely ignorant of any of what today we would call the environmental sciences; a detailed description of the development of understanding in these areas is given in Bowler.[2] The seventeenth century saw great advances in knowledge and understanding; for instance in physics, chemistry, botany and anatomy; the Royal Society of London was founded at this time.[2] These advances in knowledge were used to justify a view of the world as a mechanical system existing for exploitation by man, as exemplified by the Royal Society's encouragement of the study of animals to determine '. . . whether they may be of any advantage to mankind . . .'.[3] Simultaneously, great voyages of discovery were opening up new parts of the world to Europeans, creating opportunities for such exploitation.

Several writers have concluded that despite the two possible poles of view which could be found in the Judaeo-Christian tradition, it was the former, exploitative one, which dominated before, during and after the scientific revolution.[1,3,4] It would be wrong, however, to attribute the blame for environmental damage to the teachings of the church. It had also the 'stewardship' concept to offer. The exploitative version seems to have been chosen, driven by commercial interests, and the fact that environmental degradation in the form of deforestation, soil erosion and the extinction of species has occurred the world over, where the Judaeo-Christian traditions have had no influence, supports this view.[3]

This exploitation was not, of course, without its environmental impacts, and they were noticed.

Coal was burnt in Britain from the thirteenth century, and was soon recognized as causing air pollution problems. Queen Eleanor visited Nottingham in 1257, and found the air so full of coal smoke that she immediately left, fearing for her health. In London, the problem of smoke was so severe that a Commission was set up to investigate it in 1285. In 1306 a proclamation was issued banning the use of sea-coal, but it appears to have been ignored.[5]

Many communities were dependent on a shared water supply, whether a well or a stream, and records from these times show that practices and regulations had evolved to protect the quality of the water supply for the benefit of all. The history of the village of Foxton, Cambridgeshire, which relied solely on one shared stream, shows the following examples:[6]

> 1492 John Everard, butcher, allowed his dunghill to drain into the common stream of this village, to the serious detriment of the tenants and residents; fined 4d; pain of 10s.

> 1562 All inhabitants are ordered that henceforth they shall not let out their gutters and cess-pits at any time before eight o'clock at night; on pain of 12d.

Deforestation in Britain was extensive due to the demand for timber for shipbuilding and charcoal manufacture, and in 1662 a policy of conservation and replanting was proposed.[2]

On the whole, however, exploitation proceeded with scant regard for environmental consequences, and at this time the earth's resources, if their scale was given any conscious thought, must have seemed inexhaustible.

2.2 The Industrial Revolution and the Nineteenth Century

In the eighteenth century, great changes took place in agriculture, industry and transport in western Europe. This industrial revolution was marked initially by a growth in the use of water power (which had been in use for centuries) but the really significant change was the introduction of steam power in factories, railways and ships. While coal had been burnt previously, it was this new technology which initially gave the impetus for its massively increased exploitation; world production increased some forty-six fold during the nineteenth century.[1] New methods of steel production, and the growing uses for electricity, provided further demand for this non-renewable resource. Oil was first exploited on a commercial scale in the mid-nineteenth century, and the development of oil-burning furnaces and the internal combustion engine provided increasing demand for it. Developments in chemistry gave rise to artificial dyes, fertilizers and textiles.

Table 2.1   Environmental groups formed in the nineteenth century. (Source: based on Cotgrove[8])

Date	Group
1865	Commons, Open Spaces and Footpaths Preservation Society
1877	Society for the Protection of Ancient Buildings
1889	Royal Society for the Protection of Birds
1892	Sierra Club (USA)
1895	National Trust
1899	National Society for Clean Air and Environmental Protection
1899	Town and Country Planning Association

This period in history was characterized by the growth of a way of life almost totally dependent on non-renewable energy, which provided, for some sectors of the population, rapid improvements in their material quality of life. The less fortunate members of society, who joined swelling urban populations and found work in the new industries, worked long hours in dangerous or unhealthy conditions, and lived in overcrowded and insanitary homes. Eventually, of course, the new technologies and increased productivity benefited all, but this took time.

The problems of the expanding urban environment attracted the attentions of the famous social reformers of the Victorian Age, and in the latter part of the nineteenth century there was a discernible trend in environmental concern. Such concern had been voiced earlier (see Section 2.1) but it was in 1865 that the first British environmental group was formed,[7] and others soon followed (Table 2.1).

These groups gave voice to a feeling that the preservation of historic buildings, wildlife and natural beauty should be contrived rather than left to chance. At a time when state intervention in everyday life was much less than it is now, the cause of environmental damage could be said to be due as much to uncontrolled exploitation as to the new technologies, and most of the groups listed in Table 2.1 were concerned to protect open spaces and buildings of historic interest for public enjoyment.[8] John Muir, a Scottish emigrant to America and a naturalist, mountaineer and writer, was influential in arguing for the need for national parks. He wrote:

'Thousands of tired, nerve-shaken, over-civilised people are beginning to find out that going to the mountains is going home; that wildness is a necessity; and that mountain parks and reservations are useful not only as fountains of lumber and irrigating rivers, but as fountains of life.'[9]

He founded the Sierra Club, which was especially concerned that the sale of public land and the destruction of forests was threatening to destroy the few remaining recreational areas in the USA. The world's first national park, Yosemite, was created in the late nineteenth century, and views like Muir's are again much-voiced during the upsurge in environmental concern during the late twentieth century (see Section 2.4). The Romantic Movement in the arts at this time encouraged the exploration of wild and remote areas, and this was a pronounced change in fashion, for earlier generations had found uncultivated areas offensive;[4] a detailed description of this change of attitude is given in Thomas.[3]

The great industrial development of the late nineteenth century brought increased prosperity and opportunities for education, travel and leisure. Consequently there was among the public increased awareness of human activities upon the environment, and concerned people supported the proliferating environmental groups and societies (there were many more at the local level). Despite the benefits it brought, industrial expansion was not wholeheartedly welcomed, and the economic depression of the 1880s brought, in some sectors of society, doubts about the wisdom of unrestrained industrialization.[7]

Of the groups listed in Table 2.1, The National Society for Clean Air (or the Coal Smoke Abatement Society, as it then was) is the exception in type, as it was concerned to encourage public authorities in enforcing existing legislation relating to smoke pollution. The value of its work was recognized in a leading article in *The Lancet* in 1902, which noted:

> 'The Coal Smoke Abatement Society is a most useful institution ... the work upon which this Society is engaged is worthy of support, for the part that is played in pathology by the murky atmosphere of London and other of our great cities can hardly be exaggerated.'[10]

The problem of smoke pollution in urban areas had been recognized for years (see Section 2.1). In 1845 the Health of Towns Commission published a report which identified as 'nuisances' firstly, 'evils arising from defective drainage and cleansing' and, secondly, smoke pollution.[11] In the days before environmental regulatory agencies were established, or national pollution control legislation existed to be enforced, efforts to introduce a clean air Act were widely resisted; six such Bills were defeated during the middle years of the nineteenth century, meeting fierce opposition from industrialists.[5,11] However, during the latter half of that century various pieces of legislation provided for smoke control, and it was these that the Coal Smoke Abatement Society was anxious to see enforced.

The growing alkali industry, likewise unregulated at this time, was a new and additional source of air pollution in the form of hydrochloric acid. Its effects were described by *The Times* in 1862: 'Whole tracts of country, once as fertile as the fields of Devonshire, have been swept by deadly blights till they are as barren as the shores of the Dead Sea.'[11] It was known that simple scrubbers would control hydrochloric acid emissions, but individual industrialists had no incentive to install or operate such devices. In 1862 a campaign was conducted by Lord Derby (whose estate was a few miles east of the alkali works at St Helens) and encouraged by others including landowners whose estates were suffering damage, which led to the first Alkali Act being passed in 1863. A new Alkali Inspectorate (the predecessor of today's Pollution Inspectorate) was set up to enforce this new legislation.[5,11]

Water, too, was becoming increasingly polluted during this time, as a result of increasing urban populations and industrial effluent, in the same way that air was being polluted by the smoke from domestic fires as well as emissions from the new industries.

At this time few homes had either piped water or sanitation, and outbreaks of cholera and typhoid were common, but understanding of the role of contaminated water in transmitting disease dawned only slowly.

In 1847 it became an offence to foul drinking water supplies, and legislation made it easier for municipalities to provide piped water. As towns developed sewers, to deal with used water, human waste and industrial effluent as well as surface run-off, the condition of rivers, into which the sewers discharged directly, became unacceptable. By the 1870s the smell from the River Thames was so bad that sometimes Parliament was only able to sit when sheets soaked in disinfectant had been hung at the windows.[6] Various items of legislation passed in the latter half of the nineteenth century gave local authorities increased powers to provide utility services. The Rivers Pollution Prevention Act of 1876 was particularly significant in that it made pollution of rivers a criminal offence, but its effectiveness was limited because a polluter could escape prosecution by demonstrating the use of 'best practicable and available means' to render the discharge harmless. At this time, technologies for treating sewage and other effluents were in their infancy, and the legislation was unsophisticated in that it did not allow for consideration of the total load of pollutants to be borne by the river.

Thus it was that the technological developments of the industrial revolution, after an initial period of unrestrained activity during which their polluting capabilities were demonstrated, gave rise to the type of legislation and regulation which have come to be taken for granted in the twentieth century.

2.3 The First Half of the Twentieth Century

The technological developments and increases in productivity continued into the twentieth century, bringing with them widespread increases in material standards of living; at the same time, the concerns of the 'environmental movement' remained and more environmental groups were formed (see Table 2.2). While the aims of most of the groups were still preservation of threatened land, species and buildings, the Ramblers' Association differed in type. It was formed as a federation of local rambling clubs with the aim of improving rights of access to the countryside for ordinary people, for they now had more leisure time, even if it was unemployment that provided this for some.

Table 2.2 Environmental groups formed in the first half of the twentieth century. (Source: partly based on Cotgrove[8])

Date	Group
1912	Royal Society for Nature Conservation
1924	Ancient Monuments Society
1926	Council for the Protection of Rural England
1931	National Trust for Scotland
1935	Ramblers' Association

The first half of the twentieth century brought new evidence of the capabilities of the new technologies to cause large-scale damage to the environment. Unsustainable agricultural practices caused the 'dust-bowl' in the Great Plains of the USA, when so much soil was lost in storms that countless farms were abandoned and the area extensively depopulated.

The science of ecology, meaning the study of the interactions between organisms and their environment, was only identified at the very end of the nineteenth century,[2] but was increasingly pursued in the early twentieth century. The first Ecological Society was founded in Britain in 1913. There were no clear links between this new science and the continuing environmental movement; on the contrary, early ecologists hoped the results of their improved understanding of natural processes would enhance man's abilities to exploit resources with maximum efficiency.[2]

While the development of the field of environmental economics has seen an upsurge in the 1980s and 1990s, it is possible to trace its origins as far back as the 1920s. At this time the economist Pigou proposed that a system of taxes or subsidies should be used to correct the distortions introduced to the allocation of resources by the fact that organizations or individuals could use common property (e.g. clean air or water) without paying for their consumption, or pollution, of these resources.[12]

2.4 The Post-war Period

Even as Europe struggled with the aftermath of the Second World War, Government initiatives were taken to ensure nature conservation. The first national parks in Britain were established in the 1940s, a Wild Life Conservation Special Committee was set up to identify sites for conservation, and in 1949 the Nature Conservancy was established.[2]

There were few new initiatives during the 1950s, but the 1960s were a time of protest by the young against established values, originally in the anti-war and civil rights movements, but spreading to encompass a backlash against the material values of industrialized society. This protest movement persisted in the form of the environmental movement into the 1970s. New environmental groups continued to be formed during the post-war period (see Table 2.3), but

Table 2.3   Environmental groups formed in the post-war period (Source: partly based on Cotgrove[8])

Date	Group
1946	Soil Association
1961	World Wildlife Fund
1966	Conservation Society
1971	Friends of the Earth
1971	Greenpeace
1973	Ecology Party
1987	Whale and Dolphin Conservation Society

Table 2.4   Some significant milestones in the development of environmental awareness 1950–1979

1950–1960	Mercury poisoning at Minamata, Japan
1952	London smog kills 4000
1957	Fire at Windscale nuclear reactor causes radioactive release
1962	Publication of Rachel Carson's *Silent Spring*
1966	Aberfan disaster
1967	Torrey Canyon oil tanker disaster off the Scillies
1968	Publication of Paul Ehrlich's *The Population Bomb*
1970	Establishment of US Environmental Protection Agency
1970	UK establishes Royal Commission on Environmental Pollution
1970	European Conservation Year
1972	Publication of *Limits to Growth*
1972	UN Stockholm Conference on the Human Environment
1972	European Community decides to adopt an environmental policy
1976	Publication of Gerald Foley's *The Energy Question*
1979	Near-meltdown at Three Mile Island nuclear power station

the 1970s were characterized by the establishment of a new breed of pressure group, more vociferous and radical than its predecessors.

Concern also reached less radical sectors of society and brought government initiatives in the form of new agencies to address environmental concerns and introduce a new era of regulation. Some of the significant developments of this period are listed in Table 2.4, along with some of the more notorious incidents of environmental damage, and the more influential publications, which served to keep the issue in the public mind.

It has been argued that the environmental movement waned in the latter half of the 1970s and early 1980s, in the face of economic recession precipitated by the oil price shock of 1973. Much of the concern in the 1960s and early 1970s was, however, prompted by fears that mankind faced a crisis not so much due to pollution of the environment but due to the exploitation of non-renewable resources at such a rate that they would soon become too scarce for the industrial lifestyle to continue. This concern (though not that about expanding populations) has abated in recent years. In the Western world, at least,

Table 2.5 Some significant milestones in the development of environmental awareness 1980–1993

1980	US establishes 'Superfund' following Love Canal incident
1982	10–year moratorium agreed on commercial whaling
1984	Accident kills over 2000 at Union Carbide plant at Bhopal, India
1984	Liquefied natural gas plant explosion kills 452 in Mexico City
1985	Greenpeace ship *Rainbow Warrior* blown up by French agents
1985	World population passes 5 billion
1986	Chernobyl nuclear power station disaster
1986	Lead-free petrol available in UK
1986	Sandoz warehouse fire, Basel, pollutes Rhine
1987	Publication of *Our Common Future* (Brundtland)
1987	European Year of the Environment (EYE)
1988	Chico Mendes, defender of rainforest, assassinated
1988	Publication of the *Green Consumer Guide*
1989	*Exxon Valdez* tanker accident
1990	Shell fined £1million for oil pollution of Mersey
1992	Publication of BS 7750
1992	UN Conference on Environment and Development, Rio, Brazil
1993	*Braer* tanker accident

industries have become less energy and resource intensive and exploitable reserves seem greater than ever. Rather it is the pollution or destruction of resources which ought, in principle, to be renewable, which is now the main focus of concern.

The late 1980s in particular saw a phenomenal growth in environmental concern. No doubt historians will debate the reasons for this. Perhaps it was the drought in the USA in the late 1980s which suddenly prompted fears outside of the scientific community that global warming may be a reality, and perhaps it was Lady (then Mrs) Thatcher's famous speech to The Royal Society in 1988, when she said 'It may be that we have unwittingly begun a massive experiment with the system of the planet itself' that made it fashionable to appear to be concerned for the environment. No doubt advances in understanding of environmental science, and increased material prosperity, have played their part, combined with the continuing series of environmental accidents exemplified in Table 2.5, together with further responses of governments and other bodies.

The 1980s saw a spectacular growth in membership of UK environmental groups; Table 2.6 shows that the combined membership of the listed groups almost doubled. Of course the total number of individuals concerned will be less than this total, because there will be much overlap between the groups, but Figure 2.1 shows the rise in membership of Friends of the Earth and Greenpeace during this period.

This latest upsurge in environmental concern has been characterized by phenomena not previously seen. The word 'green' came to be indiscriminately applied not only to individuals involved with environmental campaigns but to

Table 2.6 Membership of UK environmental groups

Group	Membership
British Trust for Conservation Volunteers	71 000
Council for the Protection of Rural England	45 000
Friends of the Earth	226 000
Greenpeace	384 000
National Trust	2 065 000
Royal Society for Nature Conservation	215 000
Royal Society for the Protection of Birds	680 000
World Wide Fund for Nature	250 000
Total*	3 936 000

*The total in 1980 was about 1 800 000

any product or idea remotely concerned with protection of the environment. These new phenomena have included:

- 'Green' consumerism
- 'Green' advertising
- 'Green' investment
- Environmental reporting
- Environmental economics
- Increased interest in 'sustainable development'

2.4.1 'Green' consumerism

The 1980s saw a growth in 'green' consumerism (which in turn gave rise to 'green' advertising: see below) i.e. discrimination on the part of the consumer in favour of environmentally preferable or 'green' products, services or suppliers.

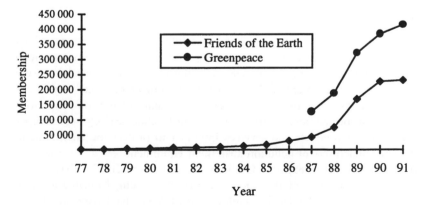

Figure 2.1 Membership of Friends of the Earth and Greenpeace

If consumers really are prepared to pay more for 'greener' products and services, this provides opportunities for those companies whose products or services have perceived environmental advantages. While this willingness to pay more may well fluctuate with economic conditions, even if it is replaced with a preparedness to avoid those products and services believed to be environmentally damaging, a new element of competition has entered the market-place, as shown by the success of *The Green Consumer Guide*[13] and similar publications.

2.4.2 'Green' advertising

In the late 1980s, manufacturers and advertisers began to exploit consumers' environmental concern by making claims in advertising. Among the claims for products with genuine environmental benefits compared to rivals, others appeared which ranged from the meaningless to the misleading. Friends of the Earth responded by launching an annual 'Green Con' award. The Advertising Standards Authority has received a steady stream of complaints, many of which have been upheld, for a variety of reasons, including:

- Absolute claims that a product is 'environmentally safe' or 'environmentally friendly'.
- Statements such as 'working for the environment' with no indication of what this meant.
- References to the use of recyclable material when the suppliers were not themselves engaged in recycling the material.
- Exaggeration of the environmental benefits of using (for example) recycled paper, rechargeable batteries.

In 1991 guidance on acceptable environmental claims in advertising was published by the Incorporated Society of British Advertisers Ltd.[14]

2.4.3 'Green' investment

'Green' investment is an extension of the principle of ethical investment, which seeks to avoid investment in certain sectors, and to encourage investment in socially beneficial sectors. In the UK, 29 ethical investment products were launched between 1986 and 1990.[15] 'Green' investment products vary in the ways in which their investments are selected; some aim to avoid companies with a known or suspected poor environmental record, others actively seek companies engaged in products and services intended to protect the environment, such as manufacturers of pollution abatement equipment.

In the USA, in 1989, the Coalition for Environmentally Responsible Economies, an offshoot of the Social Investment Forum, launched a set of principles called the Valdez Principles (named after the tanker which ran aground off Alaska). These form a corporate code of conduct regarding the environment; they were launched in the UK in November 1989. The 10 principles can be summarized as follows:

1 Protection of the biosphere
2 Sustainable use of natural resources
3 Reduction and responsible disposal of waste
4 Wise use of energy
5 Risk reduction
6 Marketing of safe products and services
7 Damage compensation
8 Public disclosure of environmental information
9 Appointment of environmental directors and managers, and commitment of management resources
10 Assessment and annual audit

They have been followed by an Environmental Investment Code launched in the UK. This code calls on companies to commit themselves to environmental excellence, to set targets for improvement and to provide detailed reports to shareholders on their long-term environmental strategy.[15]

2.4.4 Environmental reporting

Environmental reporting by European companies is, at the time of writing, slowly but steadily increasing. This is partly in response to demands for greater availability of information and partly because legislation such as the UK's Environmental Protection Act 1990 provides for public registers of information, including details of releases to the environment. The precedent was set in the USA some years earlier, and additional pressure has been provided by American companies operating in Europe, who wish to adopt a uniform practice world-wide for disclosure of information, but are reluctant to do so until their European competitors adopt similar practices. Some examples of the reports that are now being issued to the public are those of companies such as Norsk Hydro (who published what was probably the first report of its type in the UK in 1990; the background to this innovative step is described in Duff[16]), British Airways, BT, BP, ICI and National Power. Many of these give details of environmental objectives and targets set, and the rate of progress towards them. (Environmental reporting is discussed further in Sections 7.9 and 7.18.)

2.4.5 Environmental economics

After over a decade of increasingly free market economic policies pursued throughout much of the world, it is not surprising that economic theories favouring pollution charges have found increased favour among politicians. The developments in pollution control described earlier in this chapter, and in Chapter 3, amounted to a 'command and control' approach, relying on inspection by relatively small numbers of personnel. Penalties have historically been imposed infrequently and at levels which provided no financial incentives to operators to avoid pollution. On the contrary, it was often, in the past, financially preferable for an organization to continue polluting, paying occasional modest fines, than to mend its ways.

The weaknesses of such systems have been acknowledged, but finding alternatives has not been easy and the search has given rise to a new speciality in the field of economics. In the 1970s the OECD (Organization for Economic Co-operation and Development) defined the 'Polluter Pays Principle' which states that 'the polluter should bear the expenses of carrying out the (pollution prevention and control) measures decided by public authorities to ensure that the environment is in an acceptable state'. The Polluter Pays Principle might logically be extended to require payment by the polluter for the damage caused to the environment which the authorities have decided is acceptable, but this was not intended by the OECD to be part of their meaning.[17] The adoption of the OECD meaning can be seen in UK policy, where, for instance, HMIP is intended to be self-supporting, recouping its costs from the organizations which it regulates.

Economists, however, are attempting to integrate the environment into classical economical thinking. The idea of taxing pollution, described by Pigou in the 1920s (see Section 2.3) was elaborated by Beckerman in 1975[12] but the idea was not popular, to the extent that Beckerman's views were expressed in a minority report to the Third Report of the Royal Commission on Environmental Pollution, of which he was a member. However, the idea that the environment constitutes a finite resource, just as labour, capital and raw materials do, and thus its use (or pollution) should incur charges, was forcefully argued in *Blueprint for a Green Economy*[18] (popularly known as the Pearce Report), and market-based instruments are now seen as an important device for protecting the environment, although examples of their adoption in the UK are still rare.

The reasons for the slow rate of implementation are numerous and complex, and beyond the scope of this book. They include, however, the difficulty of assigning values to publicly owned assets such as unpolluted air or a pleasant view, and hence the charges which should be levied on organizations (or individuals) who pollute the air or spoil the view. Another difficulty concerns allowance for future benefits, for classical economists discount the future heavily, to the extent that benefits to be realized just a few decades hence are practically worthless in today's terms. Although it is well known that individuals do not always think in this way[19] — for example, they save for their old age or invest in their children's futures — integrating the future value of unpolluted ground or saved species with conventional economic ideas is not straightforward.

There is a second impetus for attempting to assign financial values to environmental resources, and that is to find better measures of wealth and development, to aid in policy decision-making. Conventional measures of a nation's wealth, such as GNP, make no allowance for the growth or depletion of this resource-base, and thus a nation could appear to be growing wealthier while causing irreversible damage to its (or others') environment. The concept of sustainable development recognizes that more meaningful measures of 'development' are needed, as was argued in the Pearce Report.[18]

At the time of writing, however, there is yet little evidence to suggest that the conventional methods of national accounting are being modified in this way. There is real pressure, though, for this to change, because of rapid increase in acknowledgement of the need to find means of sustainable development.

2.4.6 Sustainable development

The World Commission on Environment and Development (the Brundtland Report[20]) did not invent the concept of sustainable development, but it did give the idea wide popularity. It used the following definition:

Sustainable development is development that meets the needs of the present without compromising the ability of future generations to meet their own needs.

It is notable that the Brundtland Report gave this idea such a high profile, not because an unspoilt environment is inherently desirable, but because the ability of the developing countries to improve their standards of living is highly dependent on the availability to them of natural resources, such as clean water, fertile soil and sustainable forests to supply timber and fuel. In other words, economic growth can only be achieved if the environment is protected. The idea has found wide support; the UK government stated its intention to develop policies consistent with the concept in 1988.[21]

2.5 The Durability of Environmental Concern

It has been argued that environmental concern is largely confined to the 'middle classes', a view apparently substantiated by characteristics of the upsurge in environmental concern in the late twentieth century. Certainly the sudden fashion for 'green consumerism' can be seen as a middle-class interest, for often the 'environmentally-friendlier' consumer goods — organic vegetables, cars with catalytic converters — are privileges available only to the better-off in Western society. Research published by MORI[22] shows that the age group 25–44 and social classes AB are the most likely to let environmental considerations influence their purchasing behaviour. It might be claimed that green consumerism was a spin-off of the boom years of the 1980s, and that it

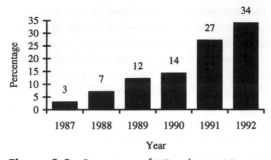

Figure 2.2 Percentage of MPs selecting 'Conservation and the Environment' from a list, in response to the question 'which of these subjects do you receive the most letters about or receive most approaches about from individuals in clinics or in other ways?' The description of the subject has varied slightly over the years. In 1987 and 1988 it was 'Conservation and Ecology', in 1989 it was 'Environment and Pollution' and since 1990 it has been 'Conservation and the Environment'.

would diminish under the impact of the economic recession of the 1990s. There is evidence, however, that this time attitudes are persisting. For instance, Figure 2.2 shows the percentage of Members of Parliament who reported that the environment was amongst the most frequent issues raised in the letters they received.

Research conducted by MORI[22] investigated the nature and behaviour of 'Green Activists', i.e. those who have undertaken five or more from a defined list of eleven activities demonstrating concern for the environment. The findings show that the proportion of Green Activists rose from 14 per cent of the adult population in 1988 to 31 per cent in 1991, and fell back somewhat to 23 per cent in 1992.

There is evidence, however, that environmental concern has subsequently risen back to the levels of the late 1980s. A survey carried out for the UK Department of the Environment in 1993 was reported in the May 1994 issue of ENDS.[23] In 1989, 30 per cent of interviewees spontaneously cited the environment or pollution as being among the most important issues the Government should be dealing with. By 1993, this figure had fallen to 22 per cent, but this issue was still the third most important (it had been second in 1989). The environment/pollution was still a greater concern than education, the economy in general or crime/law and order.

Finally, the argument so clearly put forward by the Brundtland Report (see Section 2.4), that protection of the environment is a prerequisite of economic growth, has dispelled the idea that environmental concern is something only the wealthy can afford.

Businesses have, of course, already begun to respond to these influences. In the early 1990s many companies have, for the first time, appointed

Table 2.7 Environmental components of the national curriculum

Origins of waste products and their fates
Sources and implications of pollution, and possible ways of preventing it
Processes that affect water purity
Scientific principles associated with major changes in the biosphere
Environmental impacts of technological innovations
Renewable and non-renewable resources
Sustainable development

environmental managers, whose roles often extend beyond ensuring regulatory compliance to establishing Environmental Management Systems.[24]

In the 1990s understanding of the relationships between man's activities and the environment is proceeding apace, as is evidence that damage is accelerating and, in some cases, permanent. This evidence, combined with improved understanding on the part of the public, will ensure that the environment remains a major issue for organizations of all kinds. In the UK, the national curriculum for school students now includes environmental issues, as listed in Table 2.7. The recipients of this knowledge may only be school students today, but before long they will themselves be customers, neighbours and employees, and they will have lasting expectations of the behaviour of organizations.

References

1   C. Ponting, *A Green History of the World*, Penguin, London, 1991.
2   P. J. Bowler, *The Fontana History of the Environmental Sciences*, Fontana, London, 1992.
3   K. Thomas, *Man and the Natural World: Changing Attitudes in England 1500–1800*, Allen Lane, London, 1983.
4   D. Pepper, *The Roots of Modern Environmentalism*, Croom Helm, London, 1984.
5   P. Brimblecombe, *The Big Smoke. A History of Air Pollution in London since Medieval Times*, Methuen, London, 1987.
6   D. Kinnersley, *Troubled Water. Rivers, Politics and Pollution*, Hilary Shipman, London, 1988.
7   P. Lowe and J. Goyder, *Environmental Groups in Politics*, George Allen and Unwin, London, 1983.
8   S. Cotgrove, *Catastrophe or Cornucopia. The Environment, Politics and the Future*, Wiley, New York, 1982.
9   T. Gifford, *The Great Outdoors*, vol. xv, no. x, 'John Muir', October 1992, 20–22.
10   National Society for Clean Air, *Clean Air. 90 Years of Progress 1899–1989*, National Society for Clean Air, Brighton, 1989.
11   E. Ashby and M. Anderson, *The Politics of Clean Air*, Clarendon Press, Oxford, 1982.
12   W. Beckerman, *Pricing for Pollution*, 2nd edition, Institute of Economic Affairs, London, 1990.

13 J. Elkington and J. Hailes, *The Green Consumer Guide*, Victor Gollancz, London, 1988.

14 Incorporated Society of British Advertisers Ltd, *Environmental Claims in Advertising. A Single Guide to All the Applicable Advertising Codes*, produced by the Incorporated Society of British Advertisers Ltd in conjunction with the DTi, London, 1991.

15 A. Simpson, *The Greening of Global Investment. How the Environment, Ethics and Politics are Reshaping Strategies*, The Economist Publications Limited, Special Report No. 2108, London, 1991.

16 C. Duff, 'Norsk Hydro's Environmental Report', *Long Range Planning*, vol. 25, no. 4, 1992, 25–31.

17 A. Markandya and J. Richardson (Eds), *The Earthscan Reader in Environmental Economics*, Earthscan Publications Ltd, London, 1992.

18 D. Pearce, A. Markandya and E. B. Barbier, *Blueprint for a Green Economy*, Earthscan Publications Ltd, London, 1989.

19 F. Cairncross, *Costing the Earth*, Business Books Ltd, London, 1991.

20 World Commission on Environment and Development, *Our Common Future*, Oxford University Press, Oxford, 1987.

21 Her Majesty's Government, *Our Common Future: a Perspective by the UK on the Report of the World Commission on Environment and Development*, HMSO, London, July 1988.

22 MORI, personal communication.

23 ENDS Report 232, May 1994.

24 ENDS Report 225, October 1993.

3

An Overview of Environmental Legislation and Regulations

3.1 Introduction

One of the primary objectives of environmental management is, of course, the achievement of compliance with legislative and regulatory requirements. Indeed, as we shall see, an early step in the establishment of an Environmental Management System (EMS) is the development of a mechanism by which the organization can maintain an awareness of the current and projected environmental legislation with which it must, or may in future need to, comply.

The requirements of such a mechanism are considered in Section 7.10. By contrast, this chapter summarizes the environmental legislative and regulatory framework, and the structure and interrelations of the environmental regulatory agencies, within the UK. It does not purport to be a comprehensive description of environmental legislation, nor a definitive statement of legal principles as they apply to the environment; still less should it be taken as a source of legal advice. Rather, it paints a broad picture of environmental laws and regulations, and the means of their implementation, for managers and specialists responsible for, or involved in, the development or maintenance of an EMS.

While this chapter is primarily concerned with the UK situation, the importance of European Union* legislation to the development of UK environmental law is such that attention must of necessity be paid to EU environmental legislation. While this should also assist readers in other EU Member States, the authors would remind them of the importance of establishing the mechanisms by which EU environmental laws are given effect within their own national jurisdiction.

Finally, it should be noted that, because UK and EU environmental laws and regulations are now both numerous and increasing, a number of specialist products are available to provide the non-specialist with an overview of their applicability and requirements, many as loose-leaf or computer-based systems which are periodically updated. Some examples of these systems are cited in Section 7.10.

---

*The Maastricht Treaty has, of course, created the European Union (EU). For consistency, however, we have used the term 'EU' to apply to all EU *and* EC legislation.

Table 3.1   Principal components of the UK environmental regulatory system

Secretary of State for Environment Department of Environment			
Her Majesty's Inspectorate of Pollution	Local Authorities	National Rivers Authority	Health and Safety Commission/ Executive
The most polluting industrial processes	*Air Pollution Control for less polluting industrial processes*	*Discharges to water of less harmful substances*	*Work-place health and safety*
Integrated Pollution Control (IPC) and Best Available Technology Not Entailing Excessive Costs (BATNEEC)	*Planning legislation Statutory Nuisance Noise Clean Air Acts Contaminated land*	*Water quality and monitoring Flood protection and land drainage Fisheries Water resources Navigation Conservation and recreation*	
Drinking Water Inspectorate	Waste Regulation Authorities	Sewerage Undertakers	Nuclear Installations Inspectorate
Drinking water quality	*Issue of Waste Management Licences*	*Issue of consents for trade effluents to sewer*	*Nuclear issues*

3.2 The UK Environmental Regulators

Within the UK, responsibility for the enforcement of environmental legislation and regulations falls to a number of different agencies. The broad position in England and Wales is summarized in Table 3.1; in Scotland and Northern Ireland, somewhat different (albeit broadly parallel) arrangements apply.

Overall supervision of environmental legislation rests with the Department of the Environment (DoE) and the Secretary of State (in Wales, with the Welsh Office and the Secretary of State for Wales), to whom appeal can be made regarding the conditions set by specific regulatory agencies.

Her Majesty's Inspectorate of Pollution (HMIP) is the regulatory agency dealing with the most polluting industrial processes, those covered by Integrated Pollution Control (IPC). Formed in 1987, HMIP evolved from a number of existing Inspectorates, including the Industrial Air Pollution Inspectorate, the Radiochemical Inspectorate and the Hazardous Waste Inspectorate. In Scotland, the equivalent agency is Her Majesty's Industrial Pollution Inspectorate (HMIPI).

Local authorities have a number of environmental regulatory roles. They operate Air Pollution Control for the less polluting industries, control smoke under the Clean Air Acts, and are also responsible for the control of statutory nuisances. As Planning Authorities, they are responsible for requiring environmental assessment of major planning applications, and as Waste Regulation

Authorities (WRAs) they are responsible for various aspects of the control of wastes, including the issue of waste management licences.

The National Rivers Authority (NRA), established in 1989 as a consequence of the privatization of the water industry, regulates discharges to water from the less polluting industrial processes; it is also consulted by HMIP in relation to such discharges from processes subject to IPC. The NRA also has responsibilities in relation to water quality and its monitoring, flood protection and land drainage, fisheries, water resources, navigation (on some water bodies), and conservation and recreation. In Scotland, the River Purification Boards undertake many of the pollution control functions undertaken by the NRA in England and Wales.

Sewerage undertakers (principally the Water Utility Companies set up as a consequence of privatization of the water industry in England and Wales, and local authorities in Scotland) have responsibilities in relation to public sewers and sewage treatment and disposal. The Drinking Water Inspectorate within DoE exercises regulatory control of drinking water quality, and as such deals primarily with the Water Utility Companies.

The Health and Safety Executive (HSE), reporting to the Health and Safety Commission (HSC), is the principal regulator for health and safety and enforces the health and safety provisions of the Health and Safety at Work etc. Act 1974. The Nuclear Installations Inspectorate (a part of HSE) is, as its name indicates, the principal regulatory body for nuclear installations.

It is the Government's intention to bring together many environmental regulatory functions in England and Wales under a new Environment Agency (EA), and in Scotland under a Scottish Environment Protection Agency (SEPA). Part of a parliamentary bill to establish these agencies was published in October 1994 (the Environment Agencies Bill 1994).

The Agency, it is proposed, will bring together the activities of HMIP, NRA and the WRAs. Thus, it will not embrace the environmental planning function exercised by local government, despite the wish of some environmental campaigners for it to do so. (In Scotland, SEPA would bring together the roles of the equivalent organizations, but would also take over the air pollution control functions of local authorities under Part I of the Environmental Protection Act 1990.) Some environmental campaigners would also have included other environmental responsibilities — in the area of planning, for example — but this has been rejected.

It is possible that additional environmental regulatory functions will be transferred to these agencies after their establishment. In the meantime, the passage of the bill through Parliament is likely to engender considerable debate about the nature and activities of these proposed new bodies. Particular attention is likely to be focused on any perceived weakening of the regulatory mechanism, and on the proposed obligation upon the new agencies to take costs and benefits into account when carrying out their duties.

Table 3.2 EU legislation relating to environmental regulatory systems and related matters

Number and reference*	Title and comments
1210/90 OJEC, L120/1, 11 May 1990	**Regulation on the establishment of the European Environmental Agency and the European Environmental Information and Observation Network** Establishes a body to supervise environmental data gathering within the EU.
91/692/EEC OJEC, L377/48, 31 Dec 1991	**Directive standardizing and rationalizing reports on the implementation of certain Directives relating to the environment** Specifies information to be submitted, and reporting frequency.

*In this and subsequent similar tables, and elsewhere in this chapter, OJEC refers to the *Official Journal of the European Communities*.

While this section has been concerned with UK environmental regulatory bodies, it is appropriate also to note here that, under an EU Regulation of 1990 (Table 3.2), a European Environment Agency (EEA) has recently been established to obtain information on the current and future state of the EU environment. This data-gathering role of the EEA is, however, to be reviewed after it has been operative for a period, at which time wider responsibilities (including monitoring the implementation of EU environmental legislation) might be assigned to it. The EEA is based in Copenhagen, and will be supported in its work by a network of 'national focal points' for collecting relevant data.

3.3 Environmental Legislation in the UK and EU

3.3.1 UK environmental legislation

In its broadest sense, environmental legislation — if we include laws to protect the rights of individuals to clean water, for example — has a long history in most countries. In the UK, however, the history of legislation to protect the health and well-being of the environment and the population *in general* extends at least to the nineteenth century, which saw the formation of the Alkali Inspectorate and the first Alkali Act (1863), the first legislation to protect birds (1869), the first Public Health Act (1875) and the first Rivers Pollution Prevention Act (1876).

Partly, one presumes, as a result of the two World Wars and the economic depression of the 1930s, relatively few environmental laws were enacted in the first half of the twentieth century. While more was passed in the period from 1950 to 1975, growth in UK environmental legislation has been particularly great since 1975, in response to:

- Concern on the part of the public, media and pressure groups.
- Directives and other instruments enacted by the EU (which the UK joined in 1973).

- International conventions, agreements and protocols on environmental matters.

Before proceeding to consider specific areas of legislation in detail, it is worth examining some of the broad trends which have emerged, and the basic principles which now underpin UK environmental law. Many of these can be traced to the recommendations of such bodies as the Royal Commission on Environmental Pollution and the House of Commons Select Committee on the Environment, and to the influence of the EU; they include:

- A move towards specific, numerical standards, and away from general notions of 'harm'.
- Treatment of the environment as a whole, rather than on a compartmental basis.
- Separation of regulatory and operational activities, e.g. in the waste and wastewater areas.
- Consolidation of environmental legislation, and of the enforcing regulatory bodies.
- Requirements for potential polluters to apply for permission to operate, discharge or emit.
- Requirements for operators to demonstrate fitness to operate processes.
- Requirements for operators to demonstrate the use of specific techniques.
- Application of the 'Polluter Pays Principle' to the costs of control and clean-up.
- Growing use of public registers, and greater 'transparency' of pollution control measures.
- Increases in fines, and the sanction of custodial sentences for responsible individuals.
- Increased monitoring, especially on the part of process operators.

3.3.2 EU environmental legislation

As noted above, the EU exercises a major influence upon the environmental legislative framework of its Member States: a process which began in 1973, when the European Union agreed its first Environmental Action Programme. The current programme (the Fifth: 'Towards Sustainability') sets out the broad approach which the Community will take on environmental matters up to the millennium.

Previous programmes have set out proposals for areas requiring legislation; the Fifth is more general, addressing the need to use a range of measures to complement conventional regulation, to consider environmental matters alongside economic and social issues, and to ensure that responsibility for working towards sustainable development is shared by governments, industries and the public at large. Thus, for example, specific proposals for legislation relating to civil liability for damage caused by waste have been put aside while consideration is given to more general aspects of civil liability for environmental damage at large, possible measures to address which are discussed in a Commission Green Paper on the Repair of Environmental Damage.[2]

Early EU environmental legislation was developed under general provisions of the Treaty of Rome, but revisions to the Treaty in 1987 introduced specific provision for environmental law-making. At the same time, Qualified Majority Voting (QMV) in Council (see below) was introduced for issues related to the development of the single internal market. Although this has affected few aspects of EU environmental legislation to date, the Maastricht Treaty has very considerably extended the coverage of QMV in the environmental sphere.

Legislative proposals are initiated by the Commission, the European Union's 'Civil Service'; those on environmental matters are the responsibility of Directorate General XI for Environment, Nuclear Power and Civil Protection. The European Parliament comments on proposed items of environmental legislation, and has effected amendments to many of them; its influence was extended by the Single European Act and has been further enhanced by the Maastricht Treaty. Legislation is ultimately passed by the Council—the relevant Ministers from the Member States—and its application is overseen by the Court of Justice, consisting of judges appointed by the Member States.

EU legislation, including environmental legislation, takes one of three principal forms:

- Regulations: these apply directly, without national legislation by the States.
- Directives: these set out the required outcome, but leave the means to the States.
- Decisions: these are binding upon those to whom they apply.

For environmental matters, Directives have been most frequently used, although it seems that the use of Regulations in the environmental sphere is increasing. Decisions have been used to give effect to the requirements of international conventions.

3.4 Types of Environmental Regulatory Instrument

Numerous types of regulatory instrument can be applied to protect the environment. Historically, controls in the form of regulatory standards (e.g. levels of releases not to be exceeded) have been most commonly used, together with more general control of new developments through the planning process (see Section 3.11). In recent years, however, there has been seen an increasing tendency to complement such standards and controls with other types of instrument, involving direct financial incentives or deterrents, so-called 'Market Based Instruments'.

There is also a growing trend towards the development of voluntary schemes under which organizations or products meeting specific criteria may be registered, giving indirect financial and other benefits (e.g. in marketing) through the consequent ability to use special logos and statements of participation. These schemes include requirements to make environmental information available to the public and other interested parties. The importance of the availability of environmental information is recognized by other initiatives that are explicitly addressing this issue.

3.4.1 Regulatory standards

There are many kinds of environmental standards, and they are best classified according to the position in the pathway from source to target at which they apply (see Figure 3.1).

Virtually all the different types of environmental standard have been used by the UK and EU, and examples of the different types in EU legislation are shown in Table 3.3.

A major recent development in UK environmental regulation is Integrated Pollution Control (IPC). The purpose of IPC, which is applied by Her Majesty's Inspectorate of Pollution (HMIP) to the most polluting processes, is to consider, in an integrated manner, environmental impacts upon all media (i.e. air, water and land). The application of IPC is considered in more detail in Section 3.5.

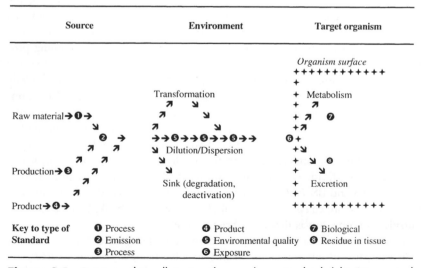

Figure 3.1 Points on the pollutant pathway where standards/objectives may be set. (Modified from Fig. 47 in Holdgate.[3])

Table 3.3 EU Directives embodying different types of standard

Type	Number and reference	Subject
Product	73/404/EEC OJEC, L347/51, 17 Dec 1973	Biodegradability of surfactants in detergents
Process	83/477/EEC OJEC, L263/33, 24 Sep 1983	Protection of workers from asbestos
Emission	88/609/EEC OJEC, L336/1, 7 Dec 1988	Large combustion plant emissions to atmosphere
Environmental Quality	85/203/EEC OJEC, L87/1, 27 Mar 1985	Sets limits on nitrogen dioxide concentration in air
Exposure	80/778/EEC OJEC, L229/11, 30 Aug 1980	Quality of water for human consumption
Biological	82/605/EEC OJEC, L247/12, 23 Aug 1982	Lead in blood for worker protection

3.4.2 Market-based and other instruments

As noted above, growing use has been made in recent years of financial measures to complement conventional regulatory standards in bringing about desired environmental improvements. These are the so-called 'Market Based Instruments' (MBI), examples of which include: differential taxation on leaded and unleaded petrol, to encourage use of the latter, and recycling credits, to foster recycling schemes by passing back the reduced landfill costs to the operators of the schemes, and the proposed EU carbon tax (see below).

With regard to more general environmental control of developments, the technique of Environmental Assessment (sometimes known as Environmental Impact Assessment) is applied to ensure that the significant potential environmental impacts of proposed projects are considered during the planning process.

Further measures for environmental protection and improvement include voluntary schemes in which companies meeting certain standards of environmental probity (in their products, services and/or activities) can participate, with a view to gaining marketing and other advantages. These include the EU 'Eco-Labelling Scheme' and the EU 'Eco-Management and Audit Scheme' (EMA) (Table 3.4), and certification to the British Standard BS 7750, which provides a specification for an Environmental Management System (EMS).

The EMA and BS 7750 approaches, being both concerned with the application of EMSs, are considered in detail elsewhere in this book; Eco-Labelling is outside its scope, but is discussed briefly here.

The concept of Eco-Labelling developed, in part, as a response to the increasing use of environmental claims in advertising by manufacturers and retailers. While many claims were made cautiously and responsibly, others were, whether intentionally or not, misleading. Notorious examples included

Table 3.4 Summary of some major items of EU legislation relating to general environmental initiatives

Number and reference	Title and comments
90/313/EEC OJEC, L158/56 23 Jun 1990	**Directive on the freedom of access to information on the environment** Requires public bodies to provide access to environmental information held by them.
880/92 OJEC, L99/1 11 Apr 1992	**Regulation on a Community Eco-Label award scheme** Provides for the establishment, by EU Member States, of an Eco-Labelling scheme to highlight products with reduced environmental impact.
1836/93 OJEC, L168/1 10 July 1993	**Regulation allowing voluntary participation by companies in the industrial sector in a Community eco-management and audit scheme** Provides for the establishment, by EU Member States, of an Eco-Management and Audit (EMA) Scheme under which industrial and other sites could be registered, subject to their developing an EMS, conducting environmental audits and producing a verified, public statement of performance.

the claim by a car manufacturer that the ability of its models to run on unleaded petrol would benefit the ozone layer, and statements that household products did not contain particular substances, when no product of the type concerned had ever done so.

Thus Eco–Labelling has the principal objectives of:

- Giving consumers the information needed for informed purchasing choices.
- Spurring manufacturers to provide products with less adverse environmental impact.

It places considerable emphasis upon the ability to assess the impact of products in production, use and disposal (i.e. from 'cradle to grave'), which is a difficult and challenging task. Eco–Labelling is the subject of an EU Regulation to establish a Union-wide scheme (Table 3.4) and, in the UK, implementation of it is the responsibility of the UK Eco-Labelling Board (UKEB).

However, at the time of writing the EU Eco-Labelling scheme appears to be in some disarray. The European Commission has proposed that reponsibility for the scheme be transferred to the European standards body, CEN, but has in turn been instructed by the Environment Council to resume implementing the scheme itself.[4]

Finally, with regard to the public availability of environmental information, it should be noted that a recent EU Directive on freedom of access to such information (Table 3.4) requires public bodies (such as regulatory agencies) to provide access to environmental information which they acquire and hold as a result of their environmental protection and other duties. In the UK, this Directive is given effect, under the European Communities Act 1972, through the Access to Environmental Information Regulations 1992.

(Note that a recent decision of the High Court that a privatized water company is an 'emanation of the state' in respect of EU law *may* have the effect of extending the coverage of the Directive to utilities.[5])

3.5 Integrated Pollution Control

The new regime of Integrated Pollution Control (IPC), which was provided for under the Environmental Protection Act 1990, supersedes much former pollution control legislation and introduces new requirements. These include:

- The need to minimize pollution with regard to Best Practicable Environmental Option (BPEO).
- The need to control emissions using Best Available Techniques Not Entailing Excessive Costs (BATNEEC).
- An increase, from £2000 to £20 000, in the maximum fine for a pollution offence which can be imposed in a magistrates' court.
- The ability of HMIP to seek, in the High Court, enforcement orders against persistent polluters.
- The empowerment of HMIP to issue prohibition notices for a prescribed process in certain circumstances.

The concept of BPEO marks a fundamental change in the regulatory approach of the UK, in that previously there was no mechanism for considering the environment as a whole.

The processes to be controlled under the new systems introduced by the Environmental Protection Act 1990 fall into two categories: Parts A and B, as described in the Environmental Protection (Prescribed Processes and Substances) Regulations 1991 and subsequent amending Regulations. Part B processes are controlled under the system of Local Authority Air Pollution Control, which is described in Section 3.7. Part A processes are those subject to Integrated Pollution Control, and they have been included in Part A on the basis of their potential to discharge Red List Substances to water[6] (see Table 3.5), to discharge prescribed substances to land (see Table 3.6) or discharge prescribed substances to air (see Table 3.7). The IPC system requires that prescribed processes use BATNEEC for:

'... preventing the release of substances prescribed for any environmental medium into that medium or, where that is not practicable by such means, for reducing the release of such substances to a minimum and for rendering harmless any such substances which are so released ...'

All operators of Part A processes, once these are brought under the IPC system, need to apply for an authorization to operate. The application should provide HMIP with the following information:

- A description of the prescribed process and the way it is operated, including a mass balance of materials used and any aspects which can cause releases to the environment.
- Plans to reduce malfunctions that may have an effect on the environment and any associated maintenance and test procedures.
- Arrangement for materials handling.
- A list of substances which might cause harm if released to the environment and which will be used in connection with the process.
- A description of techniques to be used for preventing releases to the environment.
- An assessment of the consequences of proposed releases to the environment, including an assessment of how they will be transported through the environment and how they will affect ecosystems.
- Details of proposals for monitoring releases to the environment.
- How the BPEO and BATNEEC requirements will be met.
- In the case of existing plant, plans for upgrading it to BATNEEC standards, usually within four years of the process first falling under IPC control.

Table 3.5 Release to water: prescribed substances (the Red List)

Mercury and its compounds	1,2-dichloroethane
Cadmium and its compounds	Trichlorobenzene
All isomers of hexachlorocyclohexane	Atrazine
All isomers of DDT	Simazine
Pentachlorophenol and its compounds	Tributyltin compounds
Hexachlorobenzene	Triphenyltin compounds
Hexachlorobutadiene	Trifluralin
Aldrin	Fenitrothion
Dieldrin	Azinphos-methyl
Endrin	Malathion
Polychlorinated biphenyls	Endosulfan
Dichlorvos	

Table 3.6 Release to land: prescribed substances

Organic solvents
Azides
Halogens and their covalent compounds
Metal carbonyls
Organo-metallic compounds
Oxidizing agents
Polychlorinated dibenzofuran and any congener thereof
Polychlorinated dibenzo-p-dioxin and any congener thereof
Polyhalogenated biphenyls, terphenyls and naphthalenes
Phosphorus
Pesticides, that is to say, any chemical substance or preparation for destroying any organism harmful to plants or wood or other plant products, any undesired plant or harmful creature
Alkali and alkaline earth metals and their oxides

Table 3.7 Release into air: prescribed substances

Oxides of sulphur and other sulphur compounds
Oxides of nitrogen and other nitrogen compounds
Oxides of carbon
Organic compounds and partial oxidation products
Metals, metalloids and their compounds
Asbestos, glass fibres and mineral fibres
Halogens and their compounds
Phosphorus and its compounds
Particulate matter

It should be noted that the 'techniques' to be identified in this application refer not only to hardware but also to the way the process is managed, the training of staff, etc., and that HMIP's guidance states that these management techniques themselves need to be monitored for effective implementation.

The IPC system incorporates novel (in the UK) provisions for public access to information, in that the applications for authorizations are placed on public registers, and the public then have the opportunity to make representations to HMIP. Authorizations subsequently issued, and details of monitoring results provided to HMIP in order to comply with the authorization, are likewise placed on the public registers. If the operator has grounds for believing that some of the information required by HMIP is of a commercially sensitive nature there is provision for this to remain confidential (i.e. disclosed to HMIP only) and should the need for this be disputed, there is an appeals procedure.

Only one process consent for emissions to the different environmental compartments (air, water, land) will be required. The consent will be issued by HMIP in consultation with the Health and Safety Executive, and with the following other statutory consultees, not all of whom will always be consulted, depending on the location and nature of the process:

- National Rivers Authority
- Ministry of Agriculture, Fisheries and Food
- Secretary of State for Wales (for processes carried on in Wales)
- Sewerage undertaker
- Appropriate Nature Conservation body (see Section 3.12)
- Harbour authority

Should the operator wish to make changes to the nature of the prescribed process, these may necessitate the prior approval of HMIP, in which case the applicant needs to apply for a variation to the existing authorization. Applications relating to substantial changes to the process are themselves the subject of further public consultation. Conversely, HMIP has the power to vary the conditions of an authorization, and has a duty to do so if it considers that changes in understanding of environmental risk, or developments in technology which redefine BATNEEC, mean that the conditions it considers appropriate differ from those in the existing authorization. Authorization conditions shall in any case be reviewed every four years.

HMIP has a duty not to issue an authorization if it has grounds to believe that the operator will not be able to comply with the conditions it contains. Once an authorization has been issued, HMIP has a number of powers to enforce the conditions contained in it. If HMIP believes that an operator is, or is likely to, contravene authorization conditions, it can issue an enforcement notice. This would specify remedial measures to be taken, over a specified timescale.

If HMIP believes that there is a risk of serious pollution occurring, it has a duty to serve a prohibition notice, which would again specify remedial measures to be taken, over a specified timescale, but additionally would suspend the authorization for those parts of the process causing the risk, and operation without an authorization, or contravention of the conditions in an authorization, are offences.

Implementation of IPC began in April 1991 for new processes, for substantial changes to existing processes, and for large combustion plants. All other existing processes will be brought within IPC by 1996. During the transition period, earlier legislation, such as the Health and Safety at Work etc. Act 1974, continues to apply.

3.5.1 EU legislation

The drawbacks of legislation aimed solely at controlling emissions to a single medium, in that it provides an incentive to transfer pollution from one medium to another, have been recognized by the EU, which has issued a proposal for a Directive on Integrated Pollution Prevention and Control, IPPC (COM (93) 423 final, OJEC, C311/6, 17 November 1993). The proposal has similarities to the UK IPC system, in that it would aim to prevent emissions of substances to the environment or reduce them to a minimum through the application of Best Available Technology (BAT), defined as '…industrially feasible, in the relevant sector, from a technical and economic point of view' and thus equivalent to the UK BATNEEC.

Each member state would be able to determine the emission limits defining BAT. These would not be the only consideration, however; if more stringent emission limits were needed to achieve compliance with environmental quality standards, then these more stringent limits would apply. Conversely, if environmental quality standards could be met by the application of less stringent emission limits than those defining BAT, then these less stringent emission limits may be permissible; but the circumstances in which this would be permitted are restricted by a number of qualifications.

Institutional arrangements for enforcing the system would be left to member states. As in the existing UK system, provision would be made for public access to information, in that applications submitted by operators, and permits issued to them, would be made available for public inspection. The proposal defines the types and sizes of installation to which the IPPC regime would apply, but Member States would be free to apply its provisions to others.

At the time of writing, negotiations on the proposed Directive are proceeding slowly. Issues under debate include the requirement for co-ordinated issuing of permits and the possible relaxation of emission standards in relatively unpolluted areas.[7]

3.6 Water

3.6.1 Introduction

Environmental legislation pertaining specifically to water is contained primarily (but not exclusively) within the Water Industry Act 1991 and the Water Resources Act 1991, which have consolidated much of the legislation relating to water pollution control, and establishing the responsibilities and powers of the NRA, contained in the Control of Pollution Act 1974 and/or the Water Act 1989.

Following water industry privatization in England and Wales, regulatory responsibility for pollution control and water resources lies with the NRA (save where HMIP is the controlling authority under IPC), and for drinking water quality with the Drinking Water Inspectorate. Water supply and sewerage services are provided by the water service plcs, which have specific duties placed upon them by the Water Industry Act 1991 in relation to these activities.

3.6.2 Discharges to surface waters

Under the Water Resources Act 1991 it is a criminal offence to cause or knowingly permit the entry into controlled waters, of any poisonous, noxious or polluting matter or any solid waste matter, trade or sewage effluent, without a consent. Thus, accidental spillages and unconsented discharges of such material constitute the basis of an offence.

Controlled waters include territorial waters, coastal waters, inland waters and groundwaters. Applications for consents to discharge are made to the NRA; they must be advertised and the NRA must consider any resulting written representations. Charges are imposed by the NRA to recover its costs in dealing with applications, and in monitoring and regulating discharges for which consents are granted.

Consent conditions are normally based on Environmental Quality Standards (EQSs), which are standards for specific substances, groups of substances or other determinands developed to protect the quality of water for specified uses, set by the DoE or EU. Consent conditions take into account such factors as river flows and the contributions to the receiving waters of other discharges and of diffuse sources, and are typically set in terms of maximum permitted concentrations, flows and loads; they may also address the design of discharge outlets, the periods of discharge and the facilities for sampling and metering. Monitoring frequencies depend upon such factors as the importance of the discharge (e.g. its contribution to the concentrations of substances of concern in the receiving waters) and the extent to which those concentrations approach the relevant EQSs.

For important discharges of complex composition, increasing use is likely to be made in future of consents incorporating a condition relating directly to effluent toxicity, as measured by specified procedures under closely controlled conditions. The use of such 'Toxicity-Based Consents' (as an adjunct to, not a replacement for, traditional chemical controls) has advantages in controlling pollution in cases where discharges contain a wide and perhaps varying range of substances, for many of which EQSs have not been set or for which inadequate ecotoxicological data are available to establish a safe receiving water concentration.

Fines for polluting controlled waters are unlimited in the Crown Court, and to a maximum of £20 000 in the Magistrates' Court. Since the formation of the NRA, both the frequency of prosecution and the levels of fines imposed have increased; the highest fine imposed to date was £1million against a major oil company for an oil spillage to the River Mersey. Additionally, the NRA may recover the costs, reasonably incurred, of preventative, remedial and restorative work, and overall 'clean-up' costs to the polluter may greatly exceed the fine itself.

Discharges to controlled waters of prescribed ('Red List') substances, or from prescribed processes, are controlled by HMIP, which is obliged to consult the NRA, the requirements of which are to be incorporated in any authorization granted (or if necessary varied). HMIP must not authorize a discharge which would cause, or contribute to causing, breach of a water quality objective.

3.6.3 Discharges to sewers

Under the Water Industry Act 1991, the water service plcs have responsibility for controlling discharges to sewer through the granting of trade effluent consents. (Their discharges of treated effluent to controlled waters are in turn consented by the NRA.) The Act also makes it an offence to discharge any matter into a public sewer which is likely to damage the sewer or treatment process, or endanger the staff of the water service plc.

Table 3.8 Substances which must be notified if present in the effluent for which a consent to discharge to sewers is applied

---

Mineral oils
Alkalis
Metals and their compounds
Iron, aluminium, antimony, arsenic, beryllium, chromium, copper, lead, nickel, selenium, silver, tin, vanadium, zinc, cadmium, mercury
Cyanides or compounds containing cyanide
Salts including: nitriles, chlorates, fluorides, sulphates, hypochlorites, nitrates, nitrites, perchlorates, sulphides, carbides
Phenols, cresols and simple derivatives
Tar and tar oils
Mineral acids
Oil emulsions
Grease
Ammonia or ammoniacal compounds
Paint wastes (as sludges)
Pharmaceuticals including steroids and hormones
Surface active agents
Organohalogen compounds, including pesticides and degreasing agents
Organosulphur compounds containing nitrogen
Organophosphorus or organosilicon compounds
Acrylonitrile
Formaldehyde
Carbohydrates
Yeast
Petroleum or any other substances capable of producing flammable or toxic vapours including calcium carbide and carbon disulphide
Solvents including: alcohols and nitration products, ketones, esters, ethers, hydrocarbons including benzene, toluene and xylene and their industrial equivalents
Cooling water
Boiler blowdown
Scrubbing water
Any other substance known to be toxic or hazardous

To apply for a consent to discharge to sewer, the intending discharger has to indicate if any of the substances shown in Table 3.8 are contained in his effluent. The consent conditions imposed will depend on the ability of the treatment works to deal with the substances involved, and upon the dilution available in the sewage treatment works and in the receiving water. They may also be related to constraints on the disposal of the sewage sludge: for example, to quality standards applicable to certain metals in sludge used in agriculture.

The charge levied for a consented discharge by the water service plcs depends, *inter alia*, upon its volume and composition ('strength'), and upon the type of treatment applied.

Discharges to sewer containing prescribed ('Red List') substances, from Part A processes, are regulated by HMIP under IPC. Discharges of prescribed substances from other processes will be regulated by HMIP under the Water Industry Act 1991.

3.6.4 Other aspects of marine pollution control

Oil pollution of UK territorial waters is an offence under the Prevention of Oil Pollution Act 1971, and the UK is signatory to a number of international conventions dealing with marine oil pollution generally. The Merchant Shipping (Salvage and Pollution) Act 1994 has imposed strict liability upon owners of ships (other than loaded oil tankers) for coastal oil pollution.

The dumping of waste at sea is controlled by the Food and Environment Protection Act 1985, which makes unlicensed dumping or incineration in UK waters and fisheries, or from British vessels, an offence. Licensing is undertaken by the Ministry of Agriculture, Fisheries and Food (MAFF), which takes into account protection of the sea and legitimate uses thereof, marine ecosystems and human health. Dumping of industrial wastes at sea is being phased out under the London Dumping Convention.

3.6.5 Potable water

As noted above, the water service plcs are under a duty to supply wholesome water for domestic use. Compliance with UK regulations, giving effect to EU legislation on the quality of water for domestic use and for food processing, is regulated by the Drinking Water Inspectorate.

3.6.6 EU legislation and international conventions

Much of the recent UK legislation referred to above gives effect to EU Directives and other legislation relating to water quality and pollution control. While it is beyond the scope of this chapter to describe such EU legislation in detail, some of the more important items are summarized in Table 3.9.

The planned revision of the 1976 Directive on bathing water quality is raising questions about a number of important issues, some with potentially large financial implications. Discussions have centred on the proposed limits for enteroviruses and faecal streptococci, and on the degree of protection which it is reasonable to afford against relatively minor illnesses. Sampling and measurement methodologies and quality control procedures will also be subject to revision.

Another long-standing Directive to be revised is that of 1980 on the quality of water for human consumption (the 'drinking water Directive'). It is likely that particular attention will be focused on limits for pesticides (currently subject to a blanket $0.1 \, \mu g \, l^{-1}$ limit, applicable to all regardless of toxicity) and lead, among others.

With regard to the 1976 framework Directive on dangerous substances, it appears that further 'daughter' Directives on individual 'Black List' and 'Grey

Table 3.9 Summary of some major items of EU legislation relating to water

Number and reference	Title and comments
73/404/EEC OJEC, L347/51 17 Dec 1973	**Directive on the approximation of the laws of the Member States relating to detergents** Sets requirements for biodegradability; supported, amended and extended by 73/405/EEC, 82/242/EEC, 82/243/EEC.
75/440/EEC OJEC, L194/26 25 Jul 1975	**Directive concerning the quality required of surface water intended for the abstraction of drinking water in the Member States** Sets standards for raw water used for potable supply, with methods/frequencies of measurement set in a companion Directive (79/869/EEC, OJEC, L271/44, 29 Oct 1979).
76/160/EEC OJEC, L31/1 5 Feb 1976	**Directive concerning the quality of bathing waters** Sets out microbiological and other standards to be met in fresh and salt waters designated as bathing waters by Member States.
76/464/EEC OJEC, L129/23 18 May 1976	**Directive on pollution caused by certain dangerous substances discharged into the aquatic environment of the Community** A 'framework' Directive, under which subsequent 'daughter' Directives provide specific Emission and Environmental Quality Standards for a range of 'List I' substances (e.g. selected pesticides, organochlorine compounds and heavy metals). Standards for less dangerous ('List II') substances set by individual Member States.
77/795/EEC OJEC, L334/29 24 Dec 1977	**Decision on a common procedure for the exchange of information on the quality of surface fresh water in the Community** Sets out procedures for exchanging information on the quality of rivers and lakes at points designated by Member States.
78/659/EEC OJEC, L222/1 14 Aug 1978	**Directive on the quality of fresh waters needing protection or improvement in order to protect fish life** Sets out standards to be met in waters designated as fisheries by Member States.
79/923/EEC OJEC, L281/47 10 Dec 1979	**Directive on the quality required of shellfish waters** Sets out standards to be met in waters used for the production of edible shellfish.
80/68/EEC OJEC, L20/43 26 Jan 1980	**Directive on the protection of groundwater against pollution caused by certain dangerous substances** A 'framework' Directive placing general duties on Member States to protect the quality of groundwater.
80/778/EEC OJEC, L229/11 20 Aug 1980	**Directive on the quality of water for human consumption** Sets standards and minimum sampling frequencies for drinking water quality, covering some 60 parameters.
82/176/EEC OJEC, L81/29 27 Mar 1983	**Directive on limit values and quality objectives for mercury discharges by the chlor-alkali electrolysis industry** Sets specific Emission and Environmental Quality Standards for mercury, a 'List I' substance, arising from chlor-alkali plant.
83/513/EEC OJEC, L291/1 24 Oct 1983	**Directive on limit values and quality objectives for cadmium discharges** Sets specific Emission and Environmental Quality Standards for cadmium, a 'List I' substance.
84/156/EEC OJEC, L74/49 17 Mar 1984	**Directive on limit values and quality objectives for mercury discharges by sectors other than the chlor-alkali electrolysis industry** Sets specific Emission and Environmental Quality Standards for mercury, a 'List I' substance.

Table 3.9 (cont.)

Number and reference	Title and comments
84/491/EEC OJEC, L274/11 17 Oct 1984	**Directive on limit values and quality objectives for discharges of hexachlorocyclohexane** Sets specific Emission and Environmental Quality Standards for hexachlorocyclohexane (Lindane), a 'List I' substance.
86/280/EEC OJEC, L181/16 4 Jul 1986	**Directive on limit values and quality objectives for discharges of certain dangerous substances included in List I of the Annex to Directive 76/464/EEC** Sets specific Emission and Environmental Quality Standards for the pesticide DDT, for carbon tetrachloride and for pentachlorophenol, as 'List I' substances.
88/347/EEC OJEC, L158/35 25 Jun 1988	**Directive amending Annex II to Directive 86/280/EEC on limit values and quality objectives for discharges of certain dangerous substances included in List I of the Annex to Directive 76/464/EEC** Sets specific Emission and Environmental Quality Standards for hexachlorobenzene (HCB), hexachlorobutadiene (HCBD), chloroform, and the 'Drins' (Aldrin, Dieldrin, Endrin, Isodrin), as 'List I' substances.
90/415/EEC OJEC, L219/49 14 Aug 1990	**Directive amending Annex II to Directive 86/280/EEC on limit values and quality objectives for discharges of certain dangerous substances included in List I of the Annex to Directive 76/464/EEC** Sets specific Emission and Environmental Quality Standards for 1,2 dichloroethane, trichloroethane, perchloroethane and trichlorobenzene, as 'List I' substances.
91/271/EEC OJEC, L135/40, 30 May 1991	**Directive concerning urban waste water treatment** Sets minimum levels of waste water treatment according to effluent volume in 'person equivalents' and sensitivity of receiving waters.
91/676/EEC OJEC, L375/1, 31 Dec 1991	**Directive on the protection of waters against pollution caused by nitrates from agricultural sources** A Directive dealing with nitrate pollution from fertilizer application.
COM(93) 680 final OJEC, C222/6, 10 Aug 1994	**Proposal for a Council Directive on the ecological quality of surface waters** Would require Member States to take steps to improve the ecological quality through establishing classification and monitoring systems, pollution inventories, targets and timetabled programmes for improvement.
COM(94) 36 final OJEC, C112/3 22 Apr 1994	**Proposal for a Council Directive concerning the quality of bathing waters** Would amend requirements of existing Directive on bathing water quality (76/160/EEC, see above); further details are given in the text.

List' substances are now unlikely, as EU attention shifts to sector controls to be introduced through IPPC.

A major new initiative, awaited for some years, has been the recent publication of a draft Directive concerning the ecological quality of surface waters. This would require Member States to establish classification and monitoring systems, pollution inventories, targets and timetabled programmes for improving water quality to permit aquatic ecosystems to be self-sustaining. The UK's Statutory Water Quality Objective (SWQO) approach and evolving application of biological assessment (RIVPACS) may go far towards meeting the proposed requirements. However, this is a complex proposal, addressing difficult areas and raising issues of subsidiarity and consistent application, and it is likely that discussions will continue for some time.

Furthermore, the EU is party to a number of international conventions addressing various aspects of water pollution control, most notably (from a UK viewpoint) the Oslo Convention, dealing with marine pollution by dumping from ships and aircraft, and the Paris Convention, dealing with marine pollution from land-based sources. Ministerial Conferences on the Protection of the North Sea have also had a major impact on the pollution control practices of Member States bordering that Sea.[8]

3.7 Air

3.7.1 Introduction

The Environmental Protection Act 1990 (EPA) brought into being two complementary systems of air pollution control: that under IPC for the most potentially polluting (Part A) industrial processes (see Section 3.5), and Local Authority Air Pollution Control (LAAPC) for those (Part B) processes having a lesser potential to cause pollution. These will replace many of the previous air pollution controls. Other air pollution controls are furnished by the Clean Air Act 1993. This provides for the control of smoke, dust and grit in the case of processes which are not prescribed under the Environmental Protection Act 1990, the approval of chimney heights and the creation of smoke control areas.

The EPA also provides for improved control of atmospheric pollution not otherwise controlled but constituting a statutory nuisance. Regulations made under this Act control straw and stubble burning.

3.7.2 Emissions from industrial sources

The same basic duties and procedures apply under LAAPC as under IPC, with local authorities (typically district councils and London borough councils) rather than HMIP acting as Regulatory Agencies. They have similar powers to those of HMIP in relation to authorization and enforcement, and the appeal and public register systems are also similar. However, because LAAPC deals only with emissions to air, the concept of Best Practicable Environmental Option (BPEO) will not be applied, any water pollution and waste issues being subject to the normal, separate control systems applicable outside IPC. The fee system is similar to that for IPC, but without variation according to the number of process components.

The concept of applying Best Available Techniques Not Entailing Excessive Cost (BATNEEC) to prevent, reduce to a minimum and render harmless releases of prescribed substances, and for rendering harmless other releases, applies under LAAPC as under IPC. Guidance Notes, including Process Guidance Notes for a number of affected processes, have been published giving information on requirements (including limits, standards and objectives). While these Notes provide guidance, and the regulators must have regard to their contents in determining applications, their requirements can be varied in specific circumstances according to local conditions and scientific and technological developments. All Part B processes fell under local authority control before or during 1992.

3.7.3 Emissions from motor vehicles

These are of growing importance, and are addressed in two ways: by control of fuel composition, and by specifying maximum permitted emissions from vehicles. Both of these modes of control have been adopted by the EU. EU Directives specify the lead content of petrol and the sulphur content of gas oil (which includes diesel among other fuels) and are given effect by regulations made under the Control of Pollution Act 1974.

The EU has issued a number of Directives specifying emission limits from vehicles, and these are given effect by regulations made under the Road Traffic Acts.

In addition to EU requirements, the UK has set emission limits for older vehicles, in regulations that require emissions from certain types of vehicle to be checked as part of the annual road worthiness test.

3.7.4 Emissions due to energy use

The EU has begun to address carbon dioxide emissions by proposing energy efficiency standards for refrigerators and freezers, requiring them to be labelled with details of their energy consumption, and requiring energy efficiency programmes to be established for buildings.

3.7.5 Emissions from other sources

The Clean Air Act 1993 provides local authorities with powers to deal with smoke pollution from domestic and other premises by declaring smoke-free zones. It also prohibits the emission of dark smoke from industrial or trade premises, and prohibits the use of furnaces whose chimney heights have not been approved by the local authority.

3.7.6 EU and other international initiatives on air pollution

Because air pollution in particular often transcends national boundaries, there are numerous items of EU legislation addressing its control. Many of these are intended to address those air pollution concerns which are regional, continental or even global in scale. For instance, within Europe the issue of acidification needs to be tackled at the regional level, because every country suffers from

Table 3.10 Summary of some major items of EU legislation relating to air

Number and reference	Title and comments
80/779/EEC OJEC, L229/30 30 Aug 1980	**Directive on air quality limit guides and guide values for sulphur dioxide and suspended particulates** Sets guide and limit values and specifies measurement methods.
89/427//EEC OJEC, L201/53 14 July 1989	**Directive amending the above** Amends the guide and limit values and the specified measurement methods.
82/884/EEC OJEC, L378/15 31 Dec 1982	**Directive on a limit value for lead in the air** Sets a limit value on annual mean concentration and specifies a measurement method.
84/360/EEC OJEC, L188/20 16 July 1984	**Directive on the combating of air pollution from industrial plants** Requires authorization of certain categories of industrial plants, and the use of BATNEEC to prevent air pollution by certain specified substances.
85/203/EEC OJEC, L87/1 27 Mar 1985	**Directive on air quality standards for nitrogen dioxide** Sets guide and limit values and specifies a measurement method.
88/609/EEC OJEC, L336/1 7 Dec 1988	**Directive on the limitation of emissions of certain pollutants into the air from large combustion plants** Sets emission limits, primarily for new power stations, and specifies emission reduction programmes for existing plant.
94/66/EC OJEC, L337/83 24 Dec 1994	Council Directive amending the above. Sets new SO_2 emission limits for certain categories of coal-fired plant.
89/369/EEC OJEC, L163/32 14 Jun 1989	**Directive on the prevention of air pollution from new municipal waste incineration plants** Specifies combustion conditions and emission limits for new municipal waste incinerators.
89/429/EEC OJEC, L203/50 15 Jul 1989	**Directive on the reduction of air pollution from existing municipal waste incineration plants** Requires the upgrading of old municipal waste incinerators according to specified time-scales.
94/67/EC OJEC, L365/34 31 Dec 1994	**Directive on the incineration of hazardous waste** Specifies combustion conditions and emission limits for new and existing incinerators.

Table 3.10 (cont.)

Number and reference	Title and comments
COM(92) 226 final OJEC, C196/1 3 Aug 1992	**Proposal for a Council Directive introducing a tax on carbon dioxide emissions and energy** Would set harmonized taxes on fossil fuels.
94/63/EC OJEC, L365/24 31 Dec 1994	**Directive on the control of VOC emissions resulting from the storage of petrol and its distribution from terminals to service stations (the so-called 'Stage I' Directive)** Would specify maximum losses permitted and technologies to be used for achievement of this objective.
93/12/EEC OJEC, L74/81 27 Mar 1993	**Council Directive relating to the sulphur content of certain liquid fuels** Would reduce the permitted sulphur content of certain fuels.
3093/94 OJEC, L333/1 22 Dec 1994	**Council Regulation on substances that deplete the ozone layer** Controls ozone-depleting substances, including CFCs, halons, carbon tetrachloride, 1,1,1-trichloroethane, methyl bromide, HBFCs and HCFCs.
COM(94) 109 final OJEC, C216/4 6 Aug 1994	**Proposal for a Council Directive on ambient air quality assessment and management** Would harmonize air quality assessment, and provide for further Directives addressing various pollutants.

acid deposition contributed by more than one of its neighbours. Some of the more important EU Directives controlling air pollution are summarized in Table 3.10.

The global nature of many air pollution issues, including acidification, the depletion of the ozone layer in the stratosphere, and the generation of ground-level ozone in the troposphere, has led to their being addressed by a number of international agreements. Some of these are outlined below.

Montreal Protocol

The Montreal Protocol is an agreement on the phase-out of substances which deplete the ozone layer. In the face of increasingly clear evidence that depletion of the ozone layer was accelerating, the original agreement was made more stringent in 1990 and again in November 1992. Signatories are now committed to:

- Phasing out 15 CFCs completely by the year 1996
- Banning halons by 1994
- Banning methyl chloroform by 1996
- Phasing out HCFC production by 2030

EU Member States have agreed in certain respects to act more quickly.

UNECE Convention on Long-range Transboundary Air Pollution

The UNECE (United Nations Economic Commission for Europe) includes Western, Central and Eastern European countries and Canada and the USA. A number of protocols have been agreed under this convention, specifying emission reduction programmes. Although the UNECE has no enforcement powers, signatories make certain commitments and provision for meeting them in their national legislation. The protocols to which the UK is a party are:

- The protocol concerning the control of emissions of nitrogen oxides or their transboundary fluxes, usually referred to as the Sofia Protocol, which commits parties to freeze national emissions at 1987 levels by 1994.
- The protocol concerning the control of emissions of volatile organic compounds (VOCs) or their transboundary fluxes, which commits parties to reduce VOC emissions by 30 per cent from 1988 levels by 1999.
- The protocol concerning the control of emissions of sulphur dioxide, which commmits the UK to reduce its emissions by 80 per cent by 2010, using 1980 as a baseline. Different targets are set for different countries, according to their contribution to exceedances of 'critical loads'.

UN Framework Convention on Climate Change

The UK is a party to this convention, by which it is committed to return emissions of greenhouse gases to 1990 levels by the year 2000. The convention is due to be reviewed in 1995.

3.8 Waste Management

3.8.1 Introduction

The Environmental Protection Act 1990 (EPA) now regulates waste management in the UK, and supersedes many of the earlier provisions (contained in The Control of Pollution Act 1974). The EPA defines:

- The responsibilities of agencies involved in regulation and provision of waste disposal facilities.
- The requirements for licensing those involved in waste disposal.
- The conditions required for the issue of, and surrender of, site licences.
- The Duty of Care imposed on anybody involved in waste production, storage, transfer or disposal.

The Act covers household, commercial and industrial waste, collectively known as 'controlled waste' (Controlled Waste Regulations 1992). The term 'special waste' is used to denote that subset of controlled wastes which are especially hazardous, or which require special treatment.

3.8.2 The Regulatory System

The Act creates a regulatory regime, in which the following are defined:

- Waste Regulation Authorities (WRAs), usually county councils, who operate the licensing system and prepare waste disposal plans, which are encouraged to give priority to recycling waste.
- Waste Disposal Authorities (WDAs), usually county councils, who are responsible for making sure, by arrangement with contractors, that controlled waste collected in their area is disposed of, and that places are provided where the public can dispose of household waste. The arrangements are such that the WDAs are functionally separate from WRAs.
- Waste Collection Authorities (WCAs), usually district councils or London boroughs, who are responsible for collection of household waste and commercial waste when requested to do so. The WCA may also, if licensed to do so, collect industrial waste.
- Waste Disposal Contractors (WDCs), either Local Authority Waste Disposal Companies (LAWDCs) or private companies, who collect, keep, treat or dispose of waste. In the case of LAWDCs, they must be at arm's length from the WDA function.

3.8.3 The Waste Management Licensing System

Waste Management Licences (WMLs) authorize the licensee to deposit, treat, keep or dispose of controlled waste under specified conditions, and conducting such operations without a WML, or breaching the licence conditions, is an offence. (There are certain exemptions to these licensing requirements for Part A and Part B processes; see Section 3.5.) WMLs are issued by the WRA.

Applications for WMLs must provide a working plan describing the site and the manner of intended operation, the proposed pollution prevention systems, and details of the applicant. The WRA must consult, and consider the responses of, the NRA and the HSE; the NRA may request that a licence not be granted, or seek to impose additional conditions. The WRA may reject an application:

- If it is not satisfied that the applicant is a fit and proper person (i.e. technically and financially competent, and free from relevant public health or pollution convictions).

- To prevent environmental pollution, harm to human health or serious detriment to local amenity.

Appeal lies to the Secretary of State for the Environment. The WML and its conditions remain in force until surrendered, revoked, suspended or varied by the WRA. It may be transferred to another fit and proper person, with the approval of the WRA.

An application to surrender must contain information on the holder of the licence, the site, the activities involved, the quantities and types of waste handled, and details of the site condition (e.g. in the case of landfill, details of geology and hydrology, of stability, of gas and leachate generation, and of groundwater quality). Surrender of the WML is only possible with the acceptance of the WRA (which must consult the NRA); such acceptance will not be given if the WRA is not satisfied that the condition of the site is unlikely to cause pollution or harm. Acceptance of surrender leads to issue by the WRA of a Certificate of Completion, when the WML formally ceases.

The WRA is responsible for supervising the activities covered by the WML, and an officer of the authority may, if necessary, carry out emergency action and recover the costs thereof from the licence-holder. Failure of the operator to comply with the conditions of the licence will result in the WRA requesting compliance within a specified period, and revoking or suspending the licence if the operator fails to do so. Breach of a condition of a WML is a criminal offence.

Most provisions of the Waste Management licensing system came into force in 1994.

3.8.4 Definition of types of waste

The definition of 'waste' in the Environmental Protection Act 1990 has been amended (in the Waste Management Licensing Regulations 1994) to bring it into line with the definition used in the amended EU framework Directive on waste (see Table 3.11).

With regard to the more hazardous types of waste, the Control of Pollution (Special Waste) Regulations 1980 define a class of special wastes, by reference to their inflammability, corrosivity and toxicity to human life, but not specifically to their broader environmental effects. This definition will again need to be revised to bring it into line with the definition of hazardous waste provided by the EU Directive on hazardous waste (Table 3.11). This Directive is supported by the European Waste Catalogue, which lists wastes by industrial sector.

Table 3.11 Summary of some major items of EU legislation relating to waste

Number and reference	Title and comments
75/442/EEC OJEC, L194/39 25 Jul 1975	**Directive on Waste** Framework Directive requiring safe disposal of waste, competent authorities to plan waste disposal, and encouragement of prevention and recycling of waste.
91/156/EEC OJEC, L78/32 26 Mar 91	**Amending Directive 75/442/EEC on waste** Strengthens the requirements and specifies permit requirements for waste disposal operators.
75/439/EEC OJEC, L194/23 25 Jul 75	**Directive on the disposal of waste oils** Requires regeneration or safe destruction or disposal of waste oils, which are defined.
76/403/EEC OJEC, L108/41 26 Apr 76	**Directive on the disposal of polychlorinated biphenyls and polychlorinated terphenyls** Prohibits uncontrolled emission and requires Member States to define proper disposal.
78/176/EEC OJEC, L54/19 25 Feb 78	**Directive on waste from the titanium dioxide industry** Promoting the prevention and reduction of wastes arising from the production of titanium dioxide pigment (Amended by 83/29/EEC).
82/883/EEC OJEC, L54/19 31 Dec 1982	**Directive on procedures for the surveillance and monitoring of environments concerned by waste from the titanium dioxide industry** Addresses monitoring of all media, covering determinands, sampling frequencies and methods of measurement.
87/101/EEC OJEC, L42/43 12 Feb 87	**Amendment of the above** Specifies more detailed requirements including atmospheric emission limits for combustion of waste oil in plant >3MW.
84/631/EEC OJEC, L326/31 13 Dec 84	**Directive on the supervision and control within the European Community of the transfrontier shipment of hazardous waste** Requires systems for control of movement of waste both within and entering and leaving the EU. Amended by 85/469/EEC, 86/279/EEC, 87/112/EEC, 90/170/EEC, but to be superseded in 1994 by 259/93.
86/278/EEC OJEC, L181/6 4 Jul 1986	**Directive on the protection of the environment, and in particular of the soil, when sewage sludge is used in agriculture** Sets limits on the heavy metals contents of sludge, and prohibits its application to certain crops.
COM(88) 624 final OJEC, C307/9 2 Dec 1988	**Proposed Directive amending in respect of chromium Directive 86/278/EEC on the protection of the environment, and in particular of the soil, when sewage sludge is used in agriculture** Would set limits for the chromium content of sludge.
COM(89) 282 final OJEC, C251/3 4 Oct 89	**Proposal for a Directive on civil liability for damage caused by waste** Would make producers of waste liable for damage to the environment caused by the waste, irrespective of fault. Amended by COM(91) 219 final, but in abeyance pending outcome of consultations regarding environmental liability in general.
COM(93) 275 final OJEC, C212/33 5 Aug 1993	**Amended proposal for a Council Directive on the Landfill of Waste** Would specify the types of waste which could be landfilled, and means of constructing and operating landfills so as to avoid environmental damage.
91/689/EEC OJEC, L377/20 31 Dec 1991	**Council Directive on Hazardous Waste** Requires separate collection of, and proper transport and storage of, hazardous waste, which it defines.

Table 3.11 (cont.)

Number and reference	Title and comments
91/157/EEC OJEC, L78/38 26 Mar 1991	**Directive on batteries and accumulators containing certain dangerous substances** Prohibits marketing of batteries of certain composition and requires separate collection and disposal of specified types of batteries and accumulators.
94/62/EEC OJEC, L365/10 31 Dec 1994	**Directive on packaging and packaging waste** Would require various measures to reduce packaging waste.
259/93 OJEC L30/1 6 Feb 1993	**Regulation on the supervision and control of shipments of wastes within, into and out of the European Community** Specifies notification and consignment note requirements and role of authorities.

3.8.5 The Duty of Care

The Act imposes a 'Duty of Care' on all disposers, carriers, holders, importers and producers of waste not to permit the waste to be deposited, released to the environment or transported in an illegal manner. A Code of Practice on the Duty of Care has been issued, summarizing how the Duty can be met. Regulations require that those subject to the Duty of Care keep appropriate documentation.

3.8.6 Developments in European Union legislation

The major items of European Union legislation relating to the minimization, transport and disposal of waste are summarized in Table 3.11 (see also Table 3.10 for items relating to waste incineration). The European Commission has also established a project to address four priority waste streams: used tyres, chlorinated solvents, redundant vehicles and health care wastes.

3.8.7 Potential issues related to past and current disposal practices

It is accepted that landfills containing putrescible wastes are likely to continue to degrade actively for many years, possibly decades, after completion of tipping, and to produce significant quantities of both leachates (which can potentially contaminate water resources) and landfill gas (which can migrate and cause an explosion hazard) during that time.

Concern about these dangers has resulted in a number of trends in waste management emerging over the last several years, in response both to the increasing stringency of European Union legislation, and to the rise of environmental issues in the public's consciousness. The principal thrusts of change may be summarized as:

- More stringent definition of waste types
- Greater isolation of wastes from the environment until rendered innocuous
- Increased professionalism within the waste management industry
- Reduction in volumes of waste at source
- Greater sorting, recycling and reclamation of wastes.

3.9 Contaminated Land

3.9.1 Background

Contaminated land may be regarded as land that has been degraded by human activity, thereby potentially restricting the use to which it may be put. Contamination can arise from a wide range of industrial and commercial activities, the main contaminants of concern being acids, alkalis, heavy metals and organic compounds (including fuels). The main routes by which land or groundwater become contaminated include leakage or spillage from pipes and tanks, storage of solid raw materials or products, on-site disposal of wastes, and deposition of airborne contamination (e.g. from chimneys).

While the fact that land available for redevelopment may have been contaminated by earlier uses does not necessarily make it unsafe or unusable, the contamination must be taken into account by buyers, sellers, developers and planning authorities. Remedial measures may need to be applied before redevelopment, depending on the nature and extent of the contamination and the intended future uses.

Contaminated land became a major issue of concern in Europe and the USA during the 1980s and 1990s, the main reasons being:

- The pressure to redevelop urban and inner city land, left by a gradual run-down of basic industries, rather than develop 'green field' sites. (It has been estimated that over 50 per cent of all development in the UK occurs on previously used land.)
- Contamination of groundwater used for drinking water supply. (Extremely small quantities of certain chemicals may contaminate large quantities of groundwater to levels greater than those permitted by drinking water standards.)
- The need for urgent action at certain sites presenting a hazard or causing environmental damage.

These concerns have led to an increased demand for accurate site investigation techniques to identify the nature and scale of the contamination, and suitable technologies to effect the remediation of the site. There is also an increased awareness of the potential of site disturbance to pollute further the soil and groundwater. Finally, because of the operation of the *caveat emptor* (buyer beware) principle, increasing concern about land contamination led to calls either to change the conveyancing rules or to maintain public registers of contaminated sites.

3.9.2 Definition of contaminated land

The Interdepartmental Committee on the Redevelopment of Contaminated Land (ICRCL) has set 'trigger values' that relate the concentration of chemical contaminants to be achieved in soils to particular end-uses, and which provide the basis of the current definition of contaminated land.[9] The *Threshold* Trigger Level is the concentration below which soil can be considered as uncontaminated for the intended after-use. A soil concentration in excess of the (higher) *Action* Trigger Level indicates that remediation work is required.

Although the Government seems intent on retaining some type of trigger level approach, this raises a number of questions. For example, what is an uncontaminated soil, when some natural, uncontaminated soils can exceed the ICRCL Trigger Levels? In addition, although the ICRCL gives guidance on what constitutes contamination when land is being redeveloped, this is explicitly stated not to be applicable to land in its current use.

3.9.3 Legislation controlling contaminated land

Section 143 of the Environmental Protection Act 1990 sets out to address the concerns about contaminated land, by requiring local authorities to compile and maintain public registers of land subject to potentially contaminative uses. Because it would be prohibitively expensive to investigate every potentially contaminated site to determine its actual degree of contamination, an extensive list of contaminative uses (42) to which sites may have been put was published in May 1991.

This elicited a large number of comments, particularly from the property industry. Concern was expressed about:

- Potential blight affecting large areas of land, including many sites urgently in need of redevelopment.
- The absence of clear evidence of actual contamination as a requirement for listing.
- The lack of provision for de-listing on the basis of investigation or remediation.

Postponement of the process was announced in March 1992 and, in July 1992, DoE published new draft regulations in which the list of potentially contaminative uses was reduced to eight uses, shown in Table 3.12, focusing on the types of activity most likely to cause contamination. The revised list was estimated to reduce by 85–90 per cent the area of land which the registers would cover, but it was estimated that up to 100 000 sites could still have been

Table 3.12 Section 143 registers (EPA 1990): specified contaminative uses

1	Manufacture of gas, coke or bituminous material from coal.
2	Manufacture or refining of lead or steel or an alloy of lead or steel.
3	Manufacture of asbestos or asbestos products.
4	Manufacture, refining or recovery of petroleum or its derivatives, other than extraction from petroleum-bearing ground.
5	Manufacture, refining or recovery of other chemicals, excluding minerals.
6	Final deposit in or on land of household, commercial or industrial waste (within the meaning of section 75 of the Environmental Protection Act) other than waste consisting of ash, slag, clinker, rock, wood, gypsum, railway ballast, peat, bricks, tiles, concrete, glass, other minerals or dredging spoil; or where the waste is used as a fertilizer or in order to condition the land in some other beneficial manner.
7	Treatment at a fixed installation of household commercial or industrial waste (within the meaning of section 75.
8	Use as a scrap metal store, within the meaning of section 9(2) of the Scrap Metal Dealers Act 1964.

involved. Under the revised proposals, the registers were to have been split into two parts: Part A, covering sites which had not been investigated or treated, and Part B, covering sites which had been investigated and/or treated for any contamination found. This was intended to enable prospective purchasers to gain access to reports of investigation and remedial work, so that the effects of treatment and the degree of remediation achieved could be assessed. Other changes in the proposed regulations included:

- An obligation on local authorities to inform those interested in a site two months before it was registered.
- The introduction of limited rights to challenge the reasons for register entry.

Although compilation of the registers had begun, with a view to publication by April 1994, continuing concerns about their impact on land values and on development led to the modified proposals being withdrawn early in 1993.

Now, the Bill to establish the Environmental Agency (see Section 3.2) contains new proposals for dealing with the issue of contaminated land. In summary, the proposed approach would involve:

- Repeal of section 143 of the Environmental Protection Act 1990.
- A definition of contaminated land based on harm to man, property and the environment.
- Identification of contaminated sites by local authorities, and the issue of remediation notices upon those responsible for the contamination, or the owner or occupier of the land (under a system of guidance to be provided by the Secretary of State for the Environment). Appeal against such notices would lie to the magistrates' court.
- A separate system for closed landfills, involving their notification by local authorities to the Environment Agency, which would designate those likely

to cause serious harm as 'special sites'. 'Remediation statements' describing the remedial actions necessary would be prepared for all closed landfills (by local authorities or, for special sites, by the Agency). Appeal against remediation notices issued by the Agency would lie to the Secretary of State for the Environment.

- Fines and powers for the enforcing authority to carry out, and recover through 'charging notices' the costs of, remediation in the event of non-compliance.
- Public registers of remediation notices and statements, and of appeals against notices.

These proposals, based on the legal concept of 'nuisance' (see Section 3.10), are clearly intended to avoid many of the problems which beset implementation of section 143 of the Environmental Protection Act 1990. However, the complexities of the subject and the potential financial implications of legislation in this area should ensure that the relevant clauses of the Bill will receive close scrutiny by Parliament. For a further discussion of potential areas of concern, see ENDS Report 238.[10]

3.9.4 Other relevant legislation

Other existing legislation covering related areas can have a bearing on the contaminated land issue, in particular that dealing with:

- Planning for land use change and development control
- Building regulations
- Public health
- Environmental protection and pollution control
- Responsibilities of land owners or occupiers in relation to health and safety issues

Thus, for example, the Town and Country Planning Act 1971 requires local authorities to develop structure plans for their areas, which become statutory frameworks for development. Although the Act does not address redevelopment of contaminated land specifically, a number of DoE Circulars offer guidance on the topic to the authorities. Again, waste disposal by landfilling is a potentially contaminating practice, the controls placed on which have been described above.

3.10 Nuisance and Litter

3.10.1 Introduction

Nuisance consists of unlawful interference with the enjoyment of land or other property, and is actionable at common law: a remedy available to aggrieved individuals and companies. Public nuisance is a form of nuisance affecting a class of persons, rather than an individual.

3.10.2 Statutory nuisances

These are defined by the Environmental Protection Act 1990 and include the following when prejudicial to health or a nuisance:

- The general state of premises, the emission from them of smoke, fumes, gas or noise, and the arising on them of dust, steam, smell or other effluvia.
- Any accumulation or deposit.
- The keeping of animals.

The Act requires local authorities to *anticipate* nuisance by conducting inspections and, where necessary, deal with any statutory nuisance (actual or likely) encountered by serving an abatement notice with time-scale for compliance; they can also seek an injunction in the High Court. Individuals can also take action on statutory nuisances in the magistrates' court, to which appeal against an abatement notice also lies. A failure by a company to comply with an abatement notice could lead to a fine of up to £20 000.

Additional local authority powers to control noise are conferred by the Control of Pollution Act 1974, which addresses noise on the street, on construction sites, and from plant and machinery; the Act also enables authorities to designate Noise Abatement Zones. Further powers are conferred upon local authorities and private individuals by the Noise and Statutory Nuisance Act 1993.

3.10.3 EU legislation

In the areas covered by the concept of 'nuisance', this consists primarily of legislation on permitted noise levels and methods of measurement relating to motor vehicles, aircraft and construction equipment, some examples of which are shown in Table 3.13. Enactment of their requirements in the UK is commonly made through the provisions of:

- The Road Traffic Act 1972
- The Civil Aviation Act 1982

and of Regulations made under these Acts.

3.10.4 Litter

Part IV of the Environmental Protection Act 1990 greatly strengthened the legal position regarding litter control. It places a statutory duty upon local

Table 3.13. Summary of some major items of EU legislation relating to noise

Number and reference	Title and comments
70/157/EEC OJEC, L42/16 23 Feb 1970	**Directive on the approximation of laws in the Member States relating to the permissible sound level and the exhaust system of motor vehicles** Sets limits, and equipment and procedures for measurement. (Amended by: 73/350/EEC, 84/424/EEC.)
78/1015/EEC OJEC, L349/21 13 Dec 1978	**Directive relating to the permissible sound level and exhaust system of motorcycles** Sets limits, and equipment and procedures for measurement. (Amended by: 87/56/EEC, 89/235/EEC.)
92/14/EEC OJEC, L76/12 23 Mar 1992	**Directive limiting aircraft noise** Requires Member States to apply relevant requirements of Chicago Convention on subsonic aircraft.
84/532/EEC OJEC, L300/11 19 Nov 1984	**Directive relating to common provisions for construction plant and equipment: 'framework' Directive** Sets out framework to avoid barriers to trade. Daughter Directives address noise from a wide range of types of plant and equipment, including compressors (84/533/EEC), tower-cranes (84/534/EEC), welding generators (84/535/EEC), power generators (84/536), concrete-breakers and picks (84/537), excavators, dozers and loaders (86/662).
84/538/EEC OJEC, L300/171 19 Nov 1984	**Directive on the approximation of the laws of the Member States relating to noise emitted by lawn mowers** (Amended by: 88/180/EEC and 88/181/EEC.)

authorities (the 'Principal Litter Authorities') to maintain open land and roads which they control free of litter and refuse, a duty which extends to statutory undertakers and transport providers, and to certain educational establishments and national parks.

The Litter Control Areas Order 1991 enables local authorities to designate as Litter Control Zones areas of land to which the public has access (e.g. land under the control of statutory bodies and undertakings, car parks, shopping centres, industrial estates, recreational areas, camping and caravan sites). A statutory Code of Practice on Litter and Refuse gives advice on standards of cleanliness ('Grades') for particular types of area ('Zones'), and the time-scales within which freedom from litter and refuse ('Grade A') should be achieved. The public can apply to the magistrates' court for a litter abatement order to be served, failure to comply with which can lead to a maximum fine of £1000 and fines of up to £50 per day for continuing offence after conviction, and the Principal Litter Authority may serve a litter abatement notice, failure to comply with which can also lead to a fine.

Other sections of the Act are enforced through the Street Litter Control Notices Order 1991, under which local authorities may issue Street Litter Control Notices (failure to comply with which can result in a fine) to various types of premises (e.g. banks and building society branches with external cash machines, take-away food operations, service stations). Notices can specify the street area covered, the number of litter bins to be provided and the frequency of emptying and cleaning operations.

3.11 Environmental Assessment and Planning

3.11.1 Introduction

Under UK planning regulations, which give effect to EU legislation (see Table 3.14), certain types of proposed development project (both private and public) require formal Environmental Assessment (EA: not to be confused with Environmental Audit, also abbreviated to EA) or, as it is sometimes known, Environmental Impact Assessment (EIA). The relevant planning applications must be accompanied by an Environmental Statement (ES) describing the results of the EA.

The EA requirement is implemented through a complex regulatory framework, the single most important element of which is the Town and Country Planning (Assessment of Environmental Effects) Regulations 1988 (SI 1199). The requirements of the Directive have, however, been implemented through a range of Regulations and Orders (about 20 in all), because certain types of project affected lie outside the scope of planning legislation.

3.11.2 Types of project affected

The Regulations originally required that an Environmental Statement accompany planning applications for types of Projects listed in Schedule 1 (also called 'Annex I' projects, in which they are listed in the Directive), including, among others: chemical plant, motorways, oil refineries, waste disposal facilities and power stations.

Table 3.14 EU legislation relating to environmental aspects of planning

Number and reference	Title and comments
85/337/EEC OJEC, L175/40 5 Jul 1985	**Directive concerning the assessment of the environmental effects of certain public and private projects** Requires provision of an Environmental Statement and assessment of environmental effects before planning permission is granted.
COM (93) 575 final OJEC, C130/8 12 May 1994	**Proposal for a Council Directive amending Directive 85/337/EEC on the assessment of the effects of certain public and private projects on the environment** See text for details of main proposed amendments.

Similarly, projects of the types listed in Schedule 2 (also called 'Annex II' projects, again because of the Directive) *may* require an EA, if their size, location and nature is such that they are likely to have significant effects upon the environment. Such project types originally included, among others: holiday villages and hotel complexes, oil and gas pipelines, flood relief work, wastewater treatment facilities, food industry and agricultural developments, as well as modifications to existing Schedule 1 projects.

The range of project types for which EA *may* be required (i.e. Schedule 2 projects) has since been extended (in England and Wales by the Town and Country Planning (Assessment of Environmental Effects) (Amendment) Regulations 1994, SI 677) to include: motorway service areas, coast protection schemes and wind generators. Privately financed toll roads have also been included under 'Schedule 1' provisions.

The opinion of the relevant planning authority on whether or not an EA is required can be sought before submission of a planning application; appeal lies to the Secretary of State for the Environment.

3.11.3 Practical application and problems

It has been estimated that, in the UK, about 300 Environmental Statements have been published every year under these regulations, the vast majority (about 90 per cent) for Schedule 2 projects.[11] Reviews of the application of the Directive, both in the UK and throughout the EU, have revealed a number of problems (see, for example, ENDS Report 221[11] and Coles *et al.*,[12] and literature cited therein). With regard to the UK, it has been observed that:

- EA/ES quality has often been poor, although it has improved as experience has grown.
- Application across different local authorities has been patchy.

The Institute of Environmental Assessment (IEA) has developed review criteria against which EA/ES quality may be assessed, based on those of Lee and Colley,[13] and addressing the essential ES elements shown in Table 3.15. The Institute, which has pressed for independent scoping and review of EAs, has found that common quality problems include: poor prediction of impact magnitude and assessment of significance, lack of quantification of residuals and baseline conditions, inadequate examination of alternatives, and biased presentation of information.

Similarly, the EU-wide review undertaken for the Commission has concluded that:

- The extent of application across Member States has been very variable, especially for Annex II projects. The use of quantitative criteria for determining which require assessment, and the criteria themselves, differ greatly

Table 3.15 The essential elements of an Environmental Statement, from the Review Criteria of the Institute of Environmental Assessment (IEA)

1   Description of the development, the local environment and the baseline conditions
1.1 Description of the development
1.2 Site description
1.3 Residuals (i.e. waste, energy and residual materials)
1.4 Baseline conditions
2   Identification and evaluation of key impacts
2.1 Identification of impacts
2.2 Prediction of impact magnitude
2.3 Assessment of impact significance
3   Alternatives and mitigation
3.1 Alternatives
3.2 Mitigation
3.3 Commitment to mitigation
4   Communication of results
4.1 Presentation
4.2 Balance
4.3 Non-technical summary

across the Union. Some countries do not require any assessment for entire types of Annex II project.

- In some cases, large numbers of assessments have been made, for relatively small projects, such that quality may suffer, and resources not be used to best effect.
- The coverage of specific environmental issues required by the Directive is not always implemented in national legislation, and only a minority of countries have made statutory provision for the 'scoping' of assessments, and for information on alternatives to the proposed development to be provided.
- Arrangements for the public to access, and to comment on, Environmental Statements vary, and are often unsatisfactory; and the findings of assessment are not always taken into proper account in final decisions on projects.
- ES quality has been poor, as a result of inadequate scoping and quality control.

The EU-wide review concluded that, as a result of such deficiencies, the environmental benefits of the assessment process have not been fully realized. Undertaking an EA and preparing an ES typically adds about 1 per cent to total costs, and was not considered to result in significant delays to projects.

The UK Government has recently published further guidance on EA/ES good practice, to help overcome some of the problems observed.[14] The guide addresses the scoping of assessments, recommending procedures to identify key issues, advocating the involvement of planning authorities and statutory consultees in defining terms of reference, and advising early discussions with the public. Guidance is also given on methods of impact prediction, on making

Table 3.16 Summary of some major items of EU legislation on nature conservation

Number and reference	Title and comments
79/409/EEC OJEC, L103/1 25 Apr 1979	**Directive on the conservation of wild birds** Requires Member States to protect, by various means, all species of wild birds and their habitats.
3626/82 OJEC, L384/1 31 Dec 1982	**Regulation on the implementation in the Community of the Convention on international trade in endangered species of wild flora and fauna** Provides framework for application of the Convention on International Trade in Endangered Species (CITES); much amended to keep abreast of changes in CITES.
2078/92 OJEC, L215/85 30 Jul 1992	**Regulation on agricultural production methods compatible with the requirements of the environment and the maintenance of the countryside** Establishes an aid scheme to promote less polluting farming practices, upkeep of abandoned farmland, etc.
3907/91 OJEC, L370/17 31 Dec 1991	**Regulation on the action by the Community relating to nature conservation** Provides for the EU to grant financial support for the maintenance or re-establishment of certain defined habitats.
92/43/EEC OJEC, L206/7 22 Jul 1992	**Directive on the conservation of natural habitats and of wild fauna and flora** Requires a network of special areas of conservation to be established, in order to ensure biodiversity; the habitat types to make up the network are listed.

clear the limitations of knowledge and uncertainties in predicted impacts, and on alternatives to, and needs for, the proposed development.

3.11.4 Proposed revision of the Directive

The proposed revision of the Directive (see Table 3.14) seeks to address problems in its implementation revealed by an EU study, and covers — among other things — the issues of screening and scoping.

For Annex II (UK–Schedule 2) projects, a formal screening procedure would be required to determine whether or not they required assessment. Such assessment would be mandatory for Annex II projects likely to have a significant impact on specially protected areas, presumed to be, at a minimum, those designated under the 1992 Directive on conservation of natural habitats and wild fauna and flora (see Table 3.16). The planning authority would also have to publish its decision on the need or otherwise for an EA to be performed.

An additional scoping stage is also proposed, to ensure that the information required in the assessment is defined at the outset, through agreement between the planning authority and statutory consultees.

The proposed revision also includes reference to examination of alternatives to the proposed development, and to the reasons for the final choice of approach. (It also makes explicit that statutory consultation should address the information to be provided by the developer, as well as the application itself, and that the public should be consulted before planning consent is granted, rather than before work on the development is started.)

The planning authority would be explicitly required to take into account the findings of the EA and the opinions of statutory consultees and the public in reaching its decision, and to publish the decision with their reasons and considerations.

The proposed amendments would also revise procedures for consultation *between* Member States in respect of the effects of relevant projects, in accordance with the 1991 Espoo Convention on transboundary environmental impact assessment.

Finally, the proposed amendments include changes regarding the types of development to be covered. Regarding Annex I, nuclear fuel reprocessing facilities and facilities for the temporary storage of nuclear waste would be added, and the definition of integrated chemical installations clarified. Regarding Annex II, changes are proposed to the agriculture, tourism and leisure, and infrastructure categories.

3.11.5 The issue of 'Strategic EA'

The EU has also separately considered[11,15] extension of the EA approach from specific projects to cover also the environmental impacts of policies, plans and programmes on the broader scale ('Strategic EA'). The UK (among other Member States) opposed this development, believing that Directive 85/337/ EEC provides a poor model for incorporating environmental factors in decision-making at the policy level.[16] Further EU initiatives in this area will await a review of practices in the Member States.[11]

3.12 Nature Conservation

There is a long history of UK legislation relating to nature conservation, but EU legislation in this area is a comparatively recent development (Table 3.16 and Section 3.6 on water for details of the proposed Directive on the ecological quality of surface waters).

The UK Government agency responsible for nature conservation is English Nature, EN (formerly the Nature Conservancy Council, NCC), and that responsible for landscape and countryside protection is the Countryside Commission, CC. In Wales and Scotland these functions are the responsibility of the Countryside Council for Wales and Scottish National Heritage, respectively.

Much earlier UK legislation was consolidated in the Wildlife and Countryside Act 1981 which — among other things — provides for the protection of many plant and animal species, and for the designation of areas as Sites of Special Scientific Interest (SSSIs) on the basis of their wildlife or landscape features. Certain environmental aspects of agricultural practice are addressed through legislation dealing with agriculture (e.g. designation of Environmentally Sensitive Areas under the Agriculture Act 1986), and control of international trade to protect endangered species (through a licensing system administered by the Department of the Environment) is covered by the Endangered Species (Import and Export) Act 1976.

Additional protection for hedgerows is expected, as an element in the Environment Agencies Bill discussed previously.[17]

3.13 Other Controls on Hazardous Processes and Materials

3.13.1 Introduction

A number of regulations address diverse aspects of the operation of hazardous processes and the use of hazardous substances. Some of the relevant items of EU legislation are listed in Table 3.17.

3.13.2 Control of Industrial Major Accident Hazard (CIMAH) and Related Regulations

The UK CIMAH Regulations came into force in 1985, to give effect to the EU Directive known informally as the 'Seveso Directive', introduced following the explosion in 1976 at a chemical factory in the Italian town of that name (see Table 3.17). These were amended by The Control of Industrial Major Accident Hazards (Amendment) Regulations 1994, which extended coverage to waste management facilities.

They require operators of sites producing, storing or using certain hazardous substances (having explosive, flammable or toxic characteristics, e.g. liquid and gaseous fuels) to submit to the HSE a safety report demonstrating their assessment of risks and their adoption of safety management systems to prevent, and control the consequences of, accidents. The relevant local authority (typically the county council) is also required to draw up an emergency plan for the locale, and the operator to notify neighbours of the site of its existence and of the actions to be taken in emergency.

The requirements laid down vary according to the magnitude of the hazard, and advice on the environmental (as opposed to safety) aspects of the

Regulations is provided by DoE and NRA, though this would be provided by the proposed Environmental Agency after its creation.

In addition, the Planning (Hazardous Substances) Act 1990, implemented through the Planning (Hazardous Substances) Regulations 1992, requires that the consent of the relevant local authority (the 'Hazardous Substances Authority') be obtained — through an authorization system analogous to that of IPC — for the storage of certain hazardous substances above specified quantities.

The operation of the 'Seveso' Directive has been reviewed, and a proposed replacement (see Table 3.17) would substantially amend its provisions and requirements.

3.13.3 Other regulations relating to hazardous substances

The principal UK regulatory instrument is the Control of Substances Hazardous to Health Regulations 1988 (amended 1991), widely known as the COSHH Regulations. These Regulations apply to all places of work and hazardous substances, and require employers to assess risks to health, introduce and maintain appropriate risk prevention and control measures, comply with specified exposure limits, inform and train employees, and monitor their exposure and health.

Although concerned with occupational health and safety, rather than with more general environmental protection, the COSHH Regulations provide all organizations affected by them with a convenient listing of materials potentially hazardous to the wider environment, which they hold or use.

In the UK, the Chemicals (Hazard Information and Packaging) Regulations 1993 (the CHIP Regulations) and the Notification of New Substances Regulations 1993 implement several EU Directives on hazardous substances in Table 3.17.

3.13.4 Pesticides

The EU has enacted a number of Directives relating to pesticides. These include controls on residues in foodstuffs to protect consumers, prohibitions on the marketing and use of products containing certain active ingredients, and measures to harmonize pesticide registration procedures across the European Union. These are enforced in the UK primarily through the Food and Environmental Protection Act 1985, and various Regulations made under it (and associated Codes of Practice relating to pesticide supply, and safe use). Other relevant UK legislation includes the Environmental Protection Act 1990 and the Water Resources Act 1991 (relating to the disposal of waste pesticides and pesticide containers), and the Health and Safety at Work etc. Act 1974 and

Table 3.17   Summary of some major items of EU legislation relating to hazardous processes and materials

Number and reference	Title and comments
82/501/EEC OJEC, L230/1 5 Aug 1982	**Directive on the major accident hazards of certain industrial activities ('Seveso Directive')** Sets out requirements for a notification system relating to hazardous substances and installations, including requirements for the provision of information to workers and neighbouring populations.
87/216/EEC OJEC, L85/36 23 Mar 1987	**Amendment to 82/501/EEC** Reduces trigger levels of certain materials for notification.
88/610/EEC OJEC, L336/14 7 Dec 1988	**Amendment to 82/501/EEC** Broadens the coverage of the system and clarifies public information requirements.
COM(94) 4 final OJEC, C106/4 14 Apr 1994	**Proposal for a Council Directive on the control of major accident hazards involving dangerous substances (COMAH)** Intended to provide for a more effective system than that of 82/501.
79/831/EEC OJEC, L259/10 15 Oct 1979	**Directive amending for the sixth time Directive 67/548/EEC on the approximation of the laws, regulations and administrative provisions relating to the classification, packaging and labelling of dangerous substances** Introduced requirement to test for potential environmental hazards before marketing new chemicals. (Directive 67/548/EEC and its first five amendments dealt only with protection of human, and especially worker, health and safety.) Subsequently adapted to technical progress on a number of occasions (80/1189/EEC, 81/957/EEC, 82/232/EEC, 83/467/EEC, 84/449/EEC, 86/431/EEC, 87/432/EEC, 87/302/EEC, 88/490/EEC, 90/517/EEC, 91/325/EEC, 91/326/EEC, 91/410/EEC, 91/632/EEC, 92/32/EEC, 92/37/EEC, 92/69/EEC, 93/21/EEC, 93/72/EEC, 93/101/EEC).
92/32/EEC OJEC, L154/1 5 Jun 1992	**Directive amending for the seventh time Directive 67/548/EEC** Introduced concept of risk assessment.
90/219/EEC OJEC, L117/1 8 May 1990	**Directive on the contained use of genetically modified micro-organisms** Establishes notification, consent and emergency systems.
90/220/EEC OJEC, L117/15 8 May 1990	**Directive on the deliberate release into the environment of genetically modified organisms** Harmonizes protection measures across the European Union.
87/18/EEC OJEC, L15/29 17 Jan 1987	**Directive on harmonization of laws, regulations and administrative provisions concerning good laboratory practices and the control of their application for tests on chemical substances** Applies the principles of the Organization for Economic Co-operation and Development (OECD) to the testing of chemicals under 79/831/EEC.
76/769/EEC OJEC, L262/201 27 Sep 1976	**Directive relating to restrictions on the marketing and use of certain dangerous substances and preparations** Restricts uses of certain substances; list extended through amendments: 79/663/EEC, 82/806/EEC, 82/828/EEC, 83/264/EEC, 83/478/EEC, 85/467/EEC, 85/610/EEC, 89/677/EEC, 89/678/EEC, 91/173/EEC, 91/338/EEC, 91/339/EEC, 91/659/EEC.

Table 3.17 (cont.)

Number and reference	Title and comments
79/117/EEC OJEC, L33/36 8 Feb 1979	**Directive prohibiting the placing on the market and use of plant protection products containing certain active substances** Bans marketing and use of pesticides containing certain active ingredients; list extended through amendments: 83/131/EEC, 85/298/EEC, 86/214/EEC, 86/355/EEC, 87/181/EEC, 87/477/EEC, 89/365/EEC, 90/335/EEC, 90/533/EEC, 91/188/EEC.
91/414/EEC OJEC, L230/1 19 Aug 1991	**Directive on the placing of plant protection products on the market** Harmonizes pesticide registration procedures across the European Union.
94/43/EEC OJEC, L227/31 1 Sep 1994	**Directive establishing Annex VI of Directive 91/414/EEC** Would set standards for assessing environmental effects and efficacy.
COM(93) 351 final OJEC, C239/3 3 Sep 1993	**Proposal for a Council Directive concerning the placing of biocidal products on the market** Would harmonize authorization procedures for biocides.
793/93 OJEC, L84/1 5 Apr 1993	**Regulation on the evaluation and control of the risks of existing substances** Describes a programme to establish priority lists of substances for risk evaluation.
93/67/EEC OJEC, L227/9 8 Sep 1993	**Directive on risk assessment of new notified substances** Lays down guidelines on standardized procedures for risk assessment, and specifies labelling and information requirements.
93/112/EC OJEC, L314/38 16 Dec 1993	**Directive amending Directive 91/155/EEC defining and laying down detailed arrangements for the system of specific information relating to dangerous preparations in implementation of Article 10 of Council Directive 88/379/EEC** Specifies environmental information to be included in safety data sheets for substances and preparations.
1179/94 OJEC, L131/3 26 May 1994	**Regulation concerning the first list of priority substances as foreseen under Council Regulation 93/793/EEC** Requires the preparation of priority lists of substances for risk evaluation.
1488/94 OJEC, L161/3 29 Jun 1994	**Regulation laying down the principles for the assessment of risks to man and the environment in accordance with Council Regulation 793/93** Lays down principles to be followed in carrying out risk evaluation.

the COSHH Regulations 1988 (governing aspects of the use of pesticides for both agricultural and non-agricultural purposes).

3.13.5 Genetically modified organisms

Control of genetically modified organisms (GMOs) is the subject of two EU Directives (see Table 3.17), given effect in the UK through a number of regulations made under the European Communities Act 1972, the Health and Safety at Work etc. Act 1974 and the Environmental Protection Act 1990. Among other things, these regulations address the acquisition, use and marketing of GMOs, through their requirements for risk assessment, notification, authorization and registration of activities.

References

1   ENDS Report 226, November 1993, 41.
2   European Commission, Green Paper on the Repair of Environmental Damage, Supplement to *Europe Environment*, No. 407, 30 March 1993.
3   M. W. Holdgate, *A Perspective of Environmental Pollution*, Cambridge University Press, Cambridge, 1979.
4   ENDS Report 237, October 1994, 24.
5   ENDS Report 236, September 1994, 38.
6   Department of the Environment, Agreed 'Red List' of dangerous substances confirmed by the Minister of State (Lord Caithness). *News Release* 194, 10 April 1989, DoE, Marsham Street, London, 1989.
7   ENDS Report 237, October 1994, 35.
8   T. F. Zabel and D. G. Miller, 'Water Quality of the North Sea: Concerns and Control Measures', *Journal of the Institution of Water and Environmental Management*, 1992, vol. 6, Supplementary European Issue, 31.
9   Interdepartmental Committee on the Redevelopment of Contaminated Land, 'Guidance on the Assessment and Redevelopment of Contaminated Land', Department of the Environment, London, 1987.
10 ENDS Report 238, November 1994, 15.
11 ENDS Report 221, June 1993, 20.
12 T. Coles, K. Fuller and M. Slater 'Practical Experience of Environmental Assessment in the UK', in *Proceedings of IBC/IEA Conference on Advances in Environmental Assessment*, IBC, London, October 1992.
13 N. Lee and R. Colley, *Reviewing the Quality of Environmental Statements*, Occasional Paper 24, Department of Planning and Landscape, University of Manchester, 1990.
14 Department of the Environment, 'Draft Guide on Preparing Environmental Statements for Planning Projects', DoE, London, 1994.
15 D. Noble, 'Environmental Assessment and the Commission of the European Communities', in *Proceedings of IBC/IEA Conference on Advances in Environmental Assessment*, IBC, London, October 1992.
16 T. Baldry, 'Environmental Assessment: Current Issues', in *Proceedings of IBC/IEA Conference on Advances in Environmental Assessment*, IBC, London, October 1992.
17 ENDS Report 237, October 1994, 22.

4

The Development of Environmental Auditing and Other Environmental Management Practices

4.1 The Development of Corporate Responses to Environmental Concerns

As noted in Chapter 1, organizations of all kinds, in both the private and public sectors, now readily acknowledge the importance of environmental matters to their activities, and accept the scrutiny of their environmental performance by a wide range of interested parties, as depicted in Figure 4.1.

Corporate responses to these growing pressures to achieve and to demonstrate environmental excellence have typically included:

- The development and publication of environmental policy statements.
- The implementation of programmes to bring about improvements in specific areas of environmental performance.
- The application of 'environmental auditing'.

4.2 Environmental Policies

A number of studies, including one by the Institute of Environmental Assessment (IEA),[1] provide evidence that about 50 per cent of UK companies

Figure 4.1 The interested parties

have a written environmental policy, and many of those without such a policy intend to introduce one in the near future. The Confederation of British Industry (CBI) has published a booklet[2] giving guidelines for the production of environmental policies.

It is common experience — borne out by the results of the IEA study — that there are wide differences between sectors; companies in sectors having clear environmental concerns and vulnerabilities are more likely to have established an environmental policy than are those in less 'sensitive' sectors. It is also well established that policy statements have tended, over the years, to evolve from simple undertakings to comply with legislation to wider commitments to environmentally responsible operation.

4.3 The Evolution of Environmental Auditing

Much has been written on the subject of environmental auditing, including, in addition to numerous articles and conference papers, texts such as those by Greeno et al.,[3,4] Blakeslee and Grabowski,[5] Cahill,[6] Renger[7] and HASTAM;[8] a position paper[9] and a guide[10] from the International Chamber of Commerce; reports by the Canadian Institute of Chartered Accountants[11] and the US Environmental Protection Agency;[12] and a guide by the Confederation of British Industry.[13]

The environmental audit was originally developed, in the 1970s in North America, as a management tool to examine and evaluate the compliance of facilities and operations with (increasingly numerous and complex) environmental laws and regulations.[3] In parallel, however, with the trend of environmental policy statements away from a simple commitment to legal compliance, the concept of the environmental audit itself evolved to address wider issues than just legal and regulatory compliance (Table 4.1).

In fact, the term 'environmental audit' has achieved a very wide currency, and its common usage (confusingly) encompasses a very broad range of activities (Table 4.2).

A commonly used definition of environmental audit is that[9] of the International Chamber of Commerce, ICC, given in Table 4.1 (which, it should be noted, excludes liability or transactional 'audits' by its reference to 'periodic'). In a later publication,[10] ICC noted that 'Companies use different names to describe the application of audit principles to environmental programmes ...' and cited 'review, surveillance, survey, appraisal, evaluation and assessment' as the alternatives to 'audit' which have been applied (sometimes in response to requests from legal or financial staff).

As we shall discuss in more detail in Chapter 6, auditing alone cannot provide company management with the assurance that environmental practices and performance not only have met, *but will also continue to meet*, legislative requirements and sound corporate policy commitments and expectations. A

Table 4.1   Evolution of environmental policies and environmental auditing

Policy	Commitment to legal compliance	→	Proactive: commitment to lead, not follow, opinion.
Audit	Examination of compliance with legal and regulatory requirements	→	'A management tool comprising a systematic, documented, periodic and objective evaluation of how well environmental organization, management and equipment are performing with the aim of helping to safeguard the environment by: 1 facilitating management control of environmental practices; and 2 assessing compliance with company policies which would include meeting regulatory requirements.' (ICC[9])

Table 4.2   Examples of types of environmental audit described

Legislative Compliance Audit
Liability or Transactional Audits
   Pre-acquisition
   Merger
   Divestiture
Minimization Audits
   Waste
   Water
   Emissions
   Energy
Issue Audits
Policy Compliance Audits
Environmental Management System Audits

number of writers on environmental auditing have therefore emphasized the importance of an environmental management system as a basis for sound and optimally effective audits.

For example, the influential ICC guide on environmental auditing[10] observes (in its Figure 2) that audit programmes naturally evolve from identification of problems (which might be thought of as a review, rather than an audit, process), through verification of compliance status, to confirming (presumably checking is meant) management system effectiveness. Again, while Greeno *et al.*[3] suggest that limited attention need be paid to the management system if the purpose of the audit programme is limited to identifying non-compliance situations, the context shows that this observation refers to past, rather than likely future, non-compliance and the same authors elsewhere[4] observe that:

'... audit tests that include verification of the management system can be much more productive than tests that focus strictly on performance of the equipment at the time of the audit.'

and that:

> ⚉ '... future audit programs will shift their focus toward auditing the environmental management systems rather than the facility's compliance status at the time of the audit.'

While the numerous writings on auditing do address many aspects of environmental management systems, there were — certainly before the advent of BS 7750: 1992 — few detailed treatments of the environmental management system concept itself. We are aware of only one text prior to that time devoted specifically to the subject, by Marguglio,[14] (published in 1991), and its author himself observed that it '... fills a void in the environmental literature'.

As the concepts of environmental auditing and management systems have developed, so too has the definition of environmental audit. Thus, a somewhat different (draft) definition from that of the ICC was proposed (broadly following the approach of the Canadian Institute of Chartered Accountants[10]) by the International Standards Organization's Strategic Advisory Group on the Environment (SAGE):

> 'A systematic process of objectively obtaining and evaluating evidence to determine the reliability of an assertion with regard to environmental aspects of activities, events and conditions, as to how they measure to established criteria, and communicating the results to the client.'

Through its reference to systematic gathering of evidence to *test a verifiable assertion*, this draft definition sought to take environmental auditing closer to the traditional concept of auditing. It thereby excluded some activities historically passing under the generic name of 'environmental audit', which do not involve testing a 'verifiable assertion', and which would probably be better identified as 'environmental reviews'.

Later work within ISO Technical Committee TC 207 (see Chapter 8) has further amended the above draft definition:[15]

> 'A systematic, documented verification process of objectively obtaining and evaluating evidence to determine whether specified environmental activities, events, conditions, management systems, or information about these matters, conform with audit criteria, and communicating the results of this process to the client.'

but with essentially the same effect regarding the distinction between audits and reviews.

⚉ These observations should not be taken to mean that reviews are in any sense less important than audits; on the contrary, if a well-established environmental management system is not in place, a review rather than an audit is the appropriate form of investigation to undertake. Rather, it is a reflection of the fact that, as the general subject of environmental management matures and as national and international standards develop, terminology also needs to be refined to distinguish more clearly between related, but different, concepts.

At the time of writing (mid-1994), three principal types of environmental audit have been identified, and are being addressed, by ISO Technical Committee TC 207, namely, Environmental Management System Audits, Compliance/Performance Audits and Audits of Environmental Statements. The Technical Committee has (like its predecessor, SAGE) placed initial emphasis upon the first of these, again emphasizing the importance of an environmental management system to an optimally effective environmental auditing programme. We shall return to the subject of environmental management system auditing in Section 7.15, and conclude the present chapter with a brief description of the development of the European Union (EU) Eco-Management and Audit Regulation.

4.4 Development of the European Union (EU) Eco-Management and Audit Regulation

The definition of environmental audit given in Table 4.1, developed by the International Chamber of Commerce (ICC), has been employed (with some amendment) in the EU Regulation to establish an 'Eco-Management and Audit' (EMA) scheme.[16] Although introduced by an EU Regulation bearing upon the Member States, the scheme is a voluntary one in which participating companies would establish an environmental management system, undertake environmental audits and produce an externally verified and publicly available environmental statement.

From an original emphasis upon the audit process (reflected, for example, in its originally proposed title of 'Eco-Audit' scheme), the Regulation evolved in response to the content of drafts of BS 7750 to give much greater emphasis upon the need for auditing to take place against the background of an established environmental management system (Table 4.3). The basic provisions of the EMA scheme as finally agreed are set out in Figure 4.2.

The EMA scheme and BS 7750 are thus entirely complementary, although some of the terminology used is rather different. For example, as Figure 4.2 shows, the EMA Regulation uses the term 'environmental management system' rather more narrowly than does BS 7750, excluding from it the policy, programme, and audit and review processes. Nevertheless, the essential elements of an EMS as described in BS 7750 are all present.

The relationship between the EMA scheme and BS 7750 is discussed further in Chapters 6, 7 and 8.

Table 4.3 Evolution of the EU Eco-Management and Audit scheme

Version	Principal features
February 1991 (draft)	Emphasized auditing. Audit to 'review' management systems.
July 1991 (draft)	Lengthy details of audit requirements. Listed briefly the requirements for an 'environmental protection system'.
August 1991 (draft)	Inclusion of substantial portions of text from the draft of BS 7750. Emphasized *establishment and maintenance* of procedures.
March 1992 (draft)	Mandated the European standards body, CEN, to develop environmental management system and auditing standards.
July 1993 (final)	Final adoption: includes reference to Economically Viable Application of Best Available Technology (EVABAT)

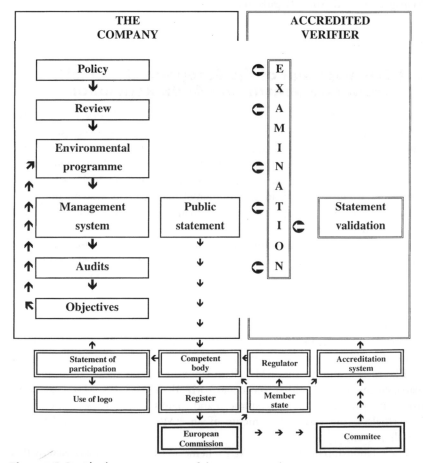

Figure 4.2 The basic provisions of the EU EMA scheme

References

1 D. R. Thomson, *The Growth of Environmental Auditing*, Institute of Environmental Assessment, East Kirkby, 1993.
2 Confederation of British Industry, *Corporate Environmental Policy Statements*, CBI, London, 1992.
3 J. L. Greeno, G. S. Hedstrom, and M. DiBerto, *The Environmental Health and Safety Auditor's Handbook*, Arthur D. Little, Cambridge, MA, 1988.
4 J. L. Greeno, G. S. Hedstrom, and M. DiBerto, *Environmental Auditing: Fundamentals and Techniques*, revised edition, Arthur D. Little, Cambridge, MA, 1988.
5 H. W. Blakeslee and T. M. Grabowski, *A Practical Guide to Plant Environmental Audits*, Van Nostrand Reinhold, New York, 1985.
6 L. B. Cahill (Ed.) with R. W. Kane, *Environmental Audits*, 6th edition, Government Institutes Inc., Rockville, MD, 1989.
7 M. Renger, *Environmental Audit*, The Institute of Chartered Accountants in England and Wales, London, 1992.
8 HASTAM, *Environment Audit*, Mercury Books, London, 1991.
9 International Chamber of Commerce, 'ICC Position Paper on Environmental Auditing', *Industry and Environment*, vol. 11, no. 4, 1988, 14–17.
10 International Chamber of Commerce, *ICC Guide to Effective Environmental Auditing*, ICC Publication No. 483, ICC, Paris, 1991.
11 The Canadian Institute of Chartered Accountants, *Environmental Auditing and the Role of the Accounting Profession*, The Institute, Toronto, 1992.
12 US Environmental Protection Agency National Enforcement Investigations Center, *Multi-Media Compliance Audit Procedures*, EPA Report No. EPA-330/9–87–001–R, US EPA National Enforcement Investigations Center, Denver, CO, 1987.
13 Confederation of British Industry, *Narrowing the Gap. Environmental Auditing Guidelines for Business*, CBI, London, 1990.
14 B. W. Marguglio, *Environmental Management Systems*, Marcel Dekker, New York, 1991.
15 British Standards Institution, 'Guidelines for Environmental Auditing — General Principles of Environmental Auditing', Draft for Public Comment, Document 94/400 413 DC, London, June 1994.
16 Council of the European Communities, Council Regulation (EEC) No. 1836/93 of 29 June 1993 allowing voluntary participation by companies in the industrial sector in a Community eco-management and audit scheme, *OJEC*, No. L168, 10 July 1993, 1–18.

5

The Quality Management Systems Concept

5.1 The Development of the Concepts and Practice of Quality Management

5.1.1 Examples through history

The concept of product quality must surely date back to the first efforts of human beings to fashion tools and implements, for it is difficult to imagine any such efforts not being accompanied by at least some notion of fitness for use. Despite this lengthy history, recent times have seen great changes in the concept of quality and the means used to achieve it, these changes being driven partly by developments in technology and in manufacturing, but also by the need to improve international competitiveness. The following discussion is not intended to be a comprehensive study of this history, but simply to indicate how the need for a Quality Systems standard arose.

Historians have traced the idea of product specifications at least as far back as 3000 BC. In Egypt, at about this time, stone blocks of uniform dimensions were required for the construction of the pyramids. These stone blocks were prepared with remarkable accuracy, and it is believed that the adoption of uniform methods and procedures was the key to this achievement.[1] Another early manifestation of the concept of product quality was the invention of the first coinage, about 700 BC. The earliest coins were small ingots of gold or silver of definite weight and purity, and stamped with a mark guaranteeing their value. Uniform properties, or quality, of coins was essential for trade and commerce and attempts to achieve such uniformity have been a prime concern of rulers throughout history.[2,3]

The concept of fitness for use remained the primary criterion for product quality for many centuries. During the Middle Ages, craft guilds emerged to ensure that craftsmen were trained to produce goods of the required standard, which would be judged by the master who inspected the finished product.[3,4] This system of inspection of all finished products would not survive with the idea that manufactured goods could be advantageously made from a number of interchangeable parts;[4,5] neither would it be adequate after the onset of the industrial revolution and the ability of manufacturing technology to manufacture goods in quantity.

76

Efforts to manufacture interchangeable components were first made in the armaments industry in the eighteenth century. The earliest known example of a demand for such interchangeability is the contract awarded by the US War department in 1813 for 20 000 pistols. The contract specified that 'the component parts of pistols, are to correspond so exactly that any limb or part of one pistol may be fitted to any other pistol of the twenty thousand'.[5]

In order to meet this specification, at first the components of pistol locks were made so that each component could take the place of the corresponding part of a model or pattern lock. Gradually, though, arms manufacturers began to introduce gauges to check the dimensions of parts while they were being made. These were radical ideas in manufacturing, and the goal of interchangeability took years to achieve. It spread from armaments manufacture to the civilian sector, by, for example, the movement of mechanics and other workers from armaments to sewing machine factories. The story is told in detail in Hounshell.[5]

During the nineteenth century gauges came to be widely used to determine if a manufactured component was acceptable or not, and the judgement of an experienced craftsman began to be replaced by the ideas of specifications and tolerances.[4] A further refinement with time was the replacement of physical standards with written ones.

Manufacturing technology developed concurrently with the drive for interchangeability. In the face of the newly achieved mass production, the difficulty of sampling all goods or components became prohibitive, and led to the introduction in the early twentieth century of the concept of sampling inspection, where only a representative number of items from a batch need be subject to inspection. The practice of sampling inspection has been developed by the publication throughout the twentieth century of a number of standards and sampling tables, including several British Standards.[3]

A further development arose from the work of Walter A. Shewart, of Bell Telephone Laboratories, in the 1920s.[4] He had been requested to develop a form of inspection report which would provide the greatest amount of information. In response to this request he formulated the idea that variation in a process, and hence in output, is due to two types of cause: common causes and special causes. Common causes are inherent in the process over time, whereas special causes arise because of specific circumstances. He emphasized the economic importance of investigating special causes only when they do exist, and of not overlooking them on the assumption that they are common causes. Shewart's work was not a substitute for the use of specifications and tolerances, but the control charts named after him provided a means for understanding, and dealing with, process variation.

5.1.2 From inspection to process control

Historically, as described above, attention focused on inspection of products or components. During the latter half of the twentieth century, drawbacks in this method of quality control have become apparent. These include costs incurred in discarding or reworking unfit products, the costs of inspection activities, and the difficulty of competing in a global market-place where quality is increasingly uppermost in the mind of the customer. In recognition of these concerns, quality activities have expanded to include the prevention of weaknesses in products, inspection being subsumed by a much broader discipline called quality assurance.

In 1967 the Government published a White Paper, CMND 3291.[6] At this time, it was common practice in public purchasing for purchasers to engage in detailed design work, with industry being used to conduct the manufacturing process, but with the purchaser undertaking inspection. This inhibited industry from promoting its own designs, and did not encourage self-regulation of quality.[7] The main recommendations of CMND 3291 were:

- Purchasers should allow scope wherever possible for initiative by tenderers.
- Specifications should stipulate purposes and performance required, rather than detailed specifications of a product.
- Greater standardization and reduced variety.
- Preference should be given to products which conform to British Standards.
- The extension of schemes for measuring product quality to provide quality control, to ensure that the whole production of a particular article conforms to minimum requirements, and so that the need for further inspection and testing by the purchaser is removed.
- The establishment of schemes for assessing the performance and reliability of products.

While the existing assessment schemes mentioned clearly referred to products, not manufacturing systems, the penultimate point refers to the *control of production to remove the need for purchaser inspection*, an important change of emphasis.

Following CMND 3291 there were changes to Ministry of Defence procurement procedures, including:[7]

- The introduction of NATO-harmonized quality control requirements.
- The use of Allied Quality Assurance Publications (AQAPs) as requirements in contracts.
- The establishment of a quality management, contractor assessment function for Defence suppliers.

The net effect was a change of emphasis, away from inspection of products and towards the evaluation of a contractor's capability to produce quality products.

5.1.3 Early Quality Management System Standards

The Allied Quality Assurance Publications (AQAPs), referred to above, were not the only quality management system standards. At this time quality surveillance was still conducted by the purchaser, so many large purchasers, such as the MoD and the then CEGB, not only conducted surveillance but also produced their own quality management system standards. Suppliers could thus find themselves having to meet the requirements of a number of similar, but distinct, quality system standards.[7]

To overcome this problem, the Confederation of British Industry (CBI) and other bodies had advocated the production of a national standard. However there was scepticism within British industry about the use of defence-related standards for industry. This was the reason for the British Standards Institution (BSI) publishing BS 5179 *Guide to the Operation and Evaluation of Quality Assurance Systems* (based largely on AQAP material) as a guide, rather than a specification, in 1974.[7]

5.2 The Quality Systems Standard BS 5750/ISO 9000, and the Growth of its Application

Rationalization of the proliferation of standards began with the publication, in 1979, of BS 5750: *Quality Systems*, Part 1, *Specification for Design, Manufacture and Installation*. Certification to the new standard was slow in gaining popularity at first, partly because many of the purchasers who had been operating second party assessment schemes to their own standards saw no reason to cease doing so.

By 1982 the government was concerned about this state of affairs, and gave positive encouragement to the adoption of BS 5750 and certification schemes. A register of manufacturers who had been assessed to BS 5750 was published.

The purpose of BS 5750 was of course purely to improve the quality of products. The register referred to above was to be of *manufacturers* (not firms, companies, organizations or suppliers of services); and the wish for improved quality and reliability was driven by a desire to strengthen the international competitiveness of British goods.

Throughout the 1980s and early 1990s the rate of adoption of BS 5750 right through British industry has been increasing. There has also been a growth in certification bodies. The international version of BS 5750 was published, as ISO 9000, in 1987 (and, in the same year, as a European Standard). The standard was revised in 1994.[8]

The sequence of events described in this chapter is summarized in Table 5.1.

Table 5.1   Developments in the means of achieving product quality through the ages

Date	Development
Middle Ages	Inspection of all goods by master craftsmen.
Early nineteenth century	Product components made to match models.
Early nineteenth century	Product components made to fit gauges.
Late nineteenth century	Numerical specifications begin to replace gauges.
Early twentieth century	Sampling inspection ideas developed.
Early twentieth century	Shewart chart developed.
Post-Second World War	Attention turned towards prevention of weaknesses in products.
1960s	First standards addressing requirements of quality management systems published.
1960s	Quality systems standards proliferate throughout large purchasers.
1974	BS 5179: *Guide to the Operation and Evaluation of Quality Assurance Systems* published.
1979	BS 5750: *Quality Systems*, Part 1, *Specification for Design, Manufacture and Installation* published.
1983	Government quality campaign.
1987	ISO 9000 published.
Early 1990s	BS 5750 begins to be widely adopted in service industries.

5.3 The BS EN ISO 9000 Series ('BS 5750') and its Requirements

BS 5750, now referred to as the BS EN ISO 9000 series,[8] consists of a number of parts, each of which contains either guidance and/or a specification. The parts containing specifications are listed in Table 5.2, together with the numbers of the ISO and European Standard equivalents.

The contents of the three parts varies according to the range of activities undertaken by their users. Thus, BS EN ISO 9001, the most comprehensive, contains 20 clauses, and BS EN ISO 9002 and 9003 contain subsets of these. (BS EN ISO 9002 and 9003 do not contain any material not included in Part 1, so the following discussion will be confined to the contents of BS EN ISO 9001.) The essential elements of a Quality Management System in conformity with the standard are shown in Figure 5.1, which also identifies — for each element — the main requirements.

'Quality' has been defined as:

> The totality of features and characteristics of a product or service that bear upon its ability to satisfy stated or implied needs.

These features and characteristics are often specified by the customer, although sometimes the purpose to which the product is to be put is stated

Table 5.2 The parts of the ISO 9000 series which contain specifications

Former BS 5750 part no.	BS no. following 1994 revision	Title	Applicability
Part 1	EN ISO 9001	Model for quality assurance in design, development, production, installation and servicing	Used by organizations involved in design/development, production, installation and servicing
Part 2	EN ISO 9002	Specification for production, installation and servicing	Used where there is no design activity; the organization manufactures to pre-existing designs
Part 3	EN ISO 9003	Specification for final inspection and test	Used by manufacturers of simple products where quality can be assured by final inspection and test, without specific quality control during the manufacturing stage

instead. The purpose of the quality management system is to enable products to be made either to the specification or fit for their purpose. The BS EN ISO 9000 series specifies what management must do, and in relation to what activities, in order to be confident that this goal will be achieved. It does not, however, specify how they must do it. The BS EN ISO 9000 series contains generic specifications intended to be applicable to any manufacturing activity. Although its scope is stated as relating to '... a supplier's capability to design and supply conforming product ...'[8] its generic nature and lack of detail have led to its being adopted by service industries, to the extent that a guide to its application in such industries has recently been published.[9]

At the time of writing, the International Standards Organization (ISO) is examining general management principles, with a view to revising the ISO 9000 series and addressing all fields of management, not only quality. Three aspects are being examined:

- General management principles (in all fields, including health and safety, environment, etc.)
- Auditing
- Harmonization of document format

This work may result in new, or revised, standards being issued in the late 1990s.

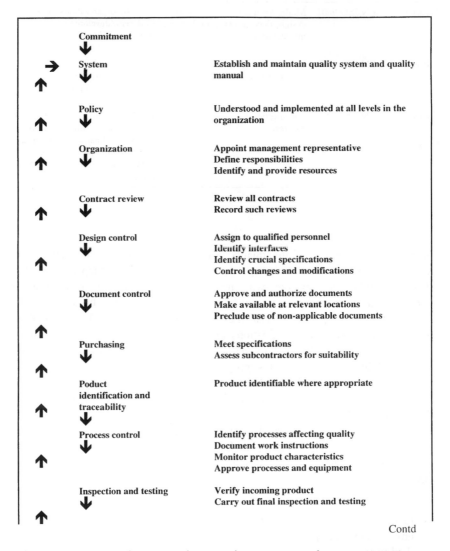

Commitment	
↓	
System	Establish and maintain quality system and quality manual
↓	
Policy	Understood and implemented at all levels in the organization
↓	
Organization	Appoint management representative
↓	Define responsibilities
	Identify and provide resources
Contract review	Review all contracts
↓	Record such reviews
Design control	Assign to qualified personnel
↓	Identify interfaces
	Identify crucial specifications
	Control changes and modifications
Document control	Approve and authorize documents
↓	Make available at relevant locations
	Preclude use of non-applicable documents
Purchasing	Meet specifications
↓	Assess subcontractors for suitability
Poduct identification and traceability	Product identifiable where appropriate
↓	
Process control	Identify processes affecting quality
↓	Document work instructions
	Monitor product characteristics
	Approve processes and equipment
Inspection and testing	Verify incoming product
↓	Carry out final inspection and testing

Contd

Figure 5.1 Basic elements and principal requirements of BS EN ISO 9001

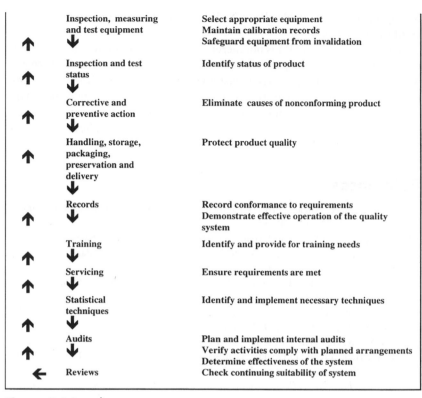

Figure 5.1 (contd)

5.4 Total Quality Management

The spread and development of the concepts described above have been accompanied by a growing interest in Total Quality Management (TQM), sometimes also called Company-Wide Quality. TQM is as concerned with the philosophy of how companies operate as with management tools, and it has many advocates, some of them well-known names (see, for example, DTI[10]) and not all of whom share the same priorities. The driving force behind TQM has been, as was the case with all the developments already discussed, a desire to reduce costs and remain competitive in changing world market-places. While the early ideas of TQM were formulated by Americans, it was in Japan, after the Second World War, that the ideas were first adopted with enthusiasm, in order to build competitive industries in the aftermath of the war. Subsequently TQM has been adopted increasingly in the United States and more recently in Europe. The British Standards Institution has recently published a British Standard (a guide, not a specification) on Total Quality

Management,[11] but, unlike BS EN ISO 9000, this is not supported by a certification scheme.

One of the aims of TQM is not merely to satisfy the customer, but to delight the customer. The concept of customer is also extended, to recognize that as well as the conventional, external customer, the organization has internal customers. While, in the face of consumer concern about protection of the environment, it would then seem logical for environmental management to be a part of TQM, in practice, environmental management has received little attention in the context of TQM.

References

1   Q. R. Skrabec, Ancient Process Control and its Modern Implications, *Quality Progress*, vol. 23, 1990, 49–52.

2   J. A. O'Keefe, *The Law of Weights and Measures*, Butterworths, Salem, USA, 1978.

3   M. Khan and M. Hashim, A Historical Survey of Quality Standards and Their Development, *Quality Assurance*, vol. 9, 1983, 63–66.

4   L. P. Provost and C. L. Norman, Variations through the Ages, *Quality Progress*, vol. 23, 1990, 39–44.

5   D. A. Hounshell, *From the American System to Mass Production, 1800–1932*, Johns Hopkins University Press, Baltimore, MD, 1984.

6   CMND 3291, *Public Purchasing and Industrial Efficiency*, HMSO, London, 1967.

7   J. A. Slater, Trends in Quality Assurance, *Quality Assurance*, vol. 14, 1988, 90–95.

8   British Standards Institution, BS EN ISO 9001: 1994, *Quality Systems Model for Quality Assurance in Design, Development, Production, Installation and Servicing*, BSI, London, 1994.

9   British Standards Institution, BS 5750: Part 8: 1991, *Guide to Quality Management and Quality System Elements for Services*, BSI, London, 1991.

10 DTI, *The Quality Gurus*, Department of Trade and Industry, London, 1991.

11 British Standards Institution, BS 7850: *Total Quality Management*. BSI, London, 1992–1994.

6

The Systems Approach to Environmental Management

6.1 Parallels Between Environmental and Quality Management

Consider the example of an effluent treatment system receiving wastewater streams from a wide range of batch processes within an industrial complex, and intended to perform to meet the regulator's conditions for discharge of the final effluent to a water body. Simply examining the records of past monitoring of the system, even if all of these proved to have been within the Discharge Consent Condition, may give very limited assurance of the future acceptability of the final effluent quality, for example, because:

- Adequate accuracy of monitoring data cannot be demonstrated.
- Sampling frequency is low in relation to variability of effluent quality.
- Contributing site processes are changing in nature or magnitude.
- The continuing effectiveness of treatment process management cannot be assured.

Similar considerations apply to other areas of environmental performance. Moreover, with respect to *overall* environmental performance, there is a need to ensure that the organization maintains an environmental policy relevant to its changing activities and to the reasonable expectations of its interested parties. It also needs to update periodically the environmental objectives and targets which give practical effect to that policy.

In Chapter 5, the development of the concept of the Quality Management System was traced, and it was shown how such a system seeks to ensure that the quality of a company's products or services meets its quality policy, and the pertinent specifications, and to provide the objective evidence of such quality to company management and customers. Let us therefore now compare a manufacturing process with our effluent treatment system. As Figure 6.1 emphasizes, both take in 'raw' material, and both manipulate that material to produce an output which meets specified requirements.

From the manufacturing viewpoint, future production would not be expected to meet customer needs simply because past production had done so. What is needed is confidence in the system as a whole, for example, that:

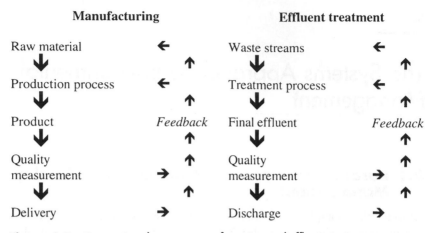

Figure 6.1 Comparison between manufacturing and effluent treatment processes

- Appropriate specifications will be developed and adhered to.
- Raw material will be checked against its specification, and rejected if outside it.
- Suitable production facilities will be used, and plant will be maintained correctly.
- New operators will be trained appropriately.
- Product quality measurement systems will produce adequately accurate data.
- Feedback and corrective action systems will be applied effectively.
- Finished product will be handled and stored correctly.

It is to address this need that the concept of the Quality Management System was developed, as described in Chapter 5, with the purpose of ensuring that the company has in place a management system which embraces:

- A commitment to a documented quality policy.
- Clearly defined responsibilities for all relevant aspects of management.
- A means of ensuring an agreed specification, mutually acceptable to company and customer.
- Documented procedures for procuring raw materials, for the production (or service-provision) processes, for inspection and recording, and for dealing with out-of-specification and non-compliance conditions.

In short, a Quality Management System aims to provide assurance of adherence to policy and specifications through a structured management system, and to enable demonstration of such adherence to third parties through suitable documentation and record-keeping.

Similar considerations apply to a systematic approach to the management of corporate environmental performance: adherence to a suitable environmental policy, the meeting of appropriate environmental objectives (the equivalent of 'specifications' in quality management), and the ability to demonstrate to a wide range of interested parties (the equivalent of 'customers' in quality management) that the policy requirements and objectives are met.

These parallels between effective management of quality and of environmental performance have been recognized by a number of organizations and individuals. For example, by 1990, parts of the chemical industry were applying Quality Management System principles to enhance the effectiveness of environmental management activities at a number of chemical plant. Similarly, one of the authors (D.T.E.H.) was developing a management systems approach to environmental matters in 1990, the fundamental elements of which are shown in Figure 6.2. This approach was first applied by the authors' consultancy within a fast moving consumer goods company, whose Environment Co-ordinator also recognized the applicability of Quality Management System principles to environmental issues.

Recognition of the parallels with quality management reached its natural conclusion when, in early 1991, BSI — responding to a request from the Confederation of British Industry (CBI) — began the process which was to culminate in the publication of the world's first Environmental Management Systems standard, BS 7750: 1992. Later in this chapter, we shall examine that process in some detail, but it is useful first to consider more precisely the potential benefits which can be gained from application of the Environmental Management Systems approach.

6.2 Benefits of a Systems Approach to Environmental Management

In Chapter 4, it was seen how the concept of environmental auditing developed from an examination of environmental performance in relation to legislative and regulatory requirements to an evaluation of '... the performance of the organization, management system and equipment designed to protect the environment ...'.[1,2] This latter definition clearly presupposes the existence of some form of Environmental Management System, but until BS 7750 was developed in 1991, formal initiatives — such as the draft of the then-proposed EC Regulation on Eco-Audit — provided little information on the detailed requirements of such a system.

It is clear from the preceding part of this chapter, however, that without an EMS, 'environmental auditing' cannot be fully effective, and, indeed, typically takes on the character of review rather than audit. Thus, an EMS provides the framework within which a company can manage effectively its environmental

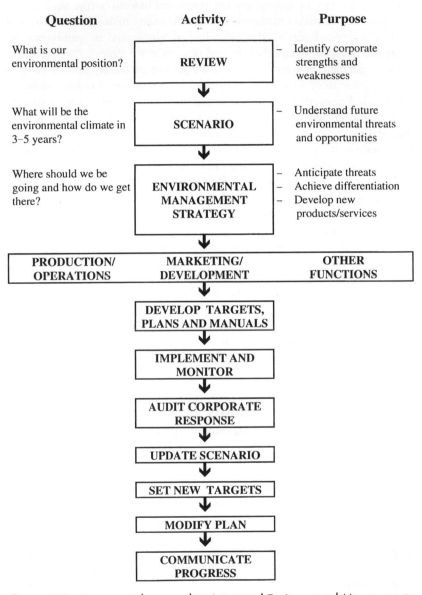

Question	Activity	Purpose
What is our environmental position?	**REVIEW**	– Identify corporate strengths and weaknesses
What will be the environmental climate in 3–5 years?	**SCENARIO**	– Understand future environmental threats and opportunities
Where should we be going and how do we get there?	**ENVIRONMENTAL MANAGEMENT STRATEGY**	– Anticipate threats – Achieve differentiation – Develop new products/services

| **PRODUCTION/ OPERATIONS** | **MARKETING/ DEVELOPMENT** | **OTHER FUNCTIONS** |

DEVELOP TARGETS, PLANS AND MANUALS

IMPLEMENT AND MONITOR

AUDIT CORPORATE RESPONSE

UPDATE SCENARIO

SET NEW TARGETS

MODIFY PLAN

COMMUNICATE PROGRESS

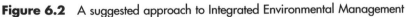

Figure 6.2   A suggested approach to Integrated Environmental Management

performance, in a manner that is pro–active, continuing and systematic. In summary, an EMS:

- Helps to develop a proactive environmental approach.
- Ensures a balanced view across all functions.
- Enables effective, directed environmental goal setting.
- Makes the environmental auditing process optimally effective.

6.3 Development of the British Environmental Management Systems Standard BS 7750

The decision to develop a British Standard on Environmental Management Systems has clearly done much to encourage wide interest in the EMS concept, and it is appropriate, therefore, to devote a part of the current chapter to an account of the history of BS 7750.

As noted previously, the BSI initiative sprang from a growing recognition of the parallels between environmental and quality management, and from a specific request by the CBI for a standard which would assist its members to meet their growing needs for structured environmental management. The objective adopted by BSI in 1991 for the resulting programme of work was to develop a British Standard which would:

- Complement the Quality Systems standard, the then BS 5750 (BS EN ISO 9000) series in the environmental area.
- Target generalists, not environmental specialists.
- Provide a succinct guide to EMS development.
- Apply to all types and sizes of organization.
- Address the environmental aspects of both operations *and* products and services.
- Support current and developing environmental legislation and regulations.
- Facilitate access to environmental information.
- Provide the foundation for a certification process.

Early in 1991, BSI appointed a responsible Technical Committee, with representation from industry, commerce, local and central government, environmental regulatory agencies, consumer and trades union interests, and professional bodies. A formal Draft for Public Comment (DPC) was published in June 1991, and a revised draft in October 1991. The overwhelming majority of respondents expressed satisfaction with the technical content and there was widespread interest in using the proposed standard. Additionally, in August 1991 a new draft of the then-proposed EC Eco-Audit Regulation absorbed much of its text.

Thus, BS 7750 was published in March 1992. Shortly after, a pilot implementation programme was started, involving about 230 implementing organizations. At about the same time, international standards activity on environmental management began, through ISO's Strategic Advisory Group on the Environment (SAGE). (The work of SAGE and its successor, ISO Technical Committee TC 207, are discussed further in Chapter 8.)

The experience gained in the pilot programme led to the publication of a revised version of the standard, BS 7750: 1994, early in the following year. The changes made were relatively minor; they did not alter the fundamental nature of the standard but clarified a number of issues which had arisen in the pilot programme and added certain elements to harmonize with the by-then published EC Eco-Management and Audit Regulation[3] (as the proposed Eco-Audit Regulation had been renamed).

6.4 An Overview of BS 7750 and its Requirements

It is not the purpose of this section to present a full description of the requirements of an Environmental Management System. Such a description is given in Chapter 7, which describes in some detail the essential components of an EMS and how to establish and maintain them. Rather, the intention here is to provide the reader with an introduction to the relevant concepts and system elements, and to do so in such a way as to emphasize their *integration* within the EMS. For, as should by now be clear, the inherent strength of the systems approach is that it provides a structure for combining the individual elements (e.g. policy and objective setting, establishment of control and recording systems, the conduct of audits and reviews) to gain benefits which those same elements cannot in isolation provide.

The fundamentals of the Environmental Management Systems approach are shown in Figure 6.2, which is based on a similar diagram developed by one of us (D.T.E.H.) some years prior to the BSI initiative. The steps shown differ somewhat from those now enshrined in BS 7750 (which will be considered later) because a separate stage of scenario development is identified, reflecting the advice to organizations to examine the likely future circumstances of their operation with respect to environmental considerations, for business planning purposes. This is not emphasized in BS 7750, which deals principally with providing assurance of sound environmental performance rather than with incorporation of environmental considerations into commercial aspects of business planning. Nevertheless, the BS 7750 EMS specification provides a framework within which the commercial aspects of environmental management can readily be incorporated.

The essential elements of an EMS in conformity with the standard are shown in Figure 6.3, which also identifies — for each element — the main requirements. Each of these elements will now be considered briefly, in turn, detailed treatment of each being deferred until Chapter 7.

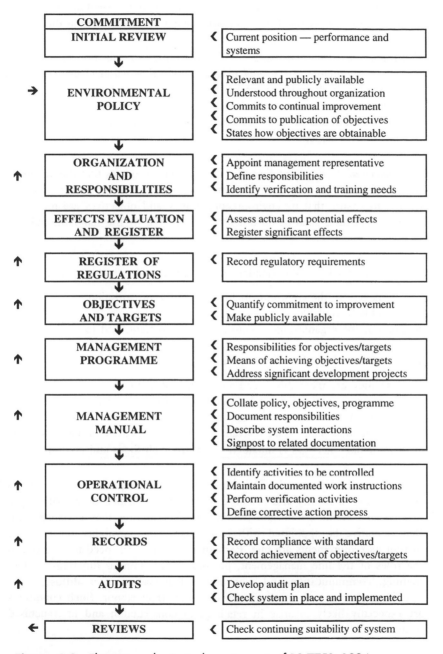

Figure 6.3 Elements and principal requirements of BS 7750: 1994

Commitment The commitment of top management is essential to effective environmental management; the standard states this requirement at the outset.

Preparatory environmental review This preliminary examination of both corporate environmental effects *and* existing environmental management practices provides the foundation for EMS development. It cannot, however, be an assessable element of the standard though it is obviously particularly relevant to organizations in which existing environmental management practices are not well developed.

Environmental Management System The standard requires that the organization shall establish and maintain an Environmental Management System (EMS) to ensure that its environmental policy and objectives are met. The system procedures shall be documented as required by the standard, and implemented effectively.

Environmental policy The standard requires the environmental policy to:

- Be relevant to the environmental effects of the organization.
- Be publicly available.
- Commit the organization to continual improvement, and to publication of objectives.
- State from where the objectives can be obtained.

Because they are inevitably broad statements of principles and 'good intentions', environmental policies risk engendering disbelief or cynicism; it is therefore essential that they focus on major areas of corporate impact. The requirement that policies are relevant and underpinned by publicly available environmental objectives is intended to ensure such focus and credibility.

Organization and personnel The standard sets out requirements relating to responsibility, authority and resource provision, to verification activities, and to internal communication and training. It also requires that a Management Representative be appointed with co-ordinating responsibility for ensuring that all its requirements are met. Particular attention will need to be given to the roles of the line management, personnel and training functions, and to training, communication and motivation, if management is diffuse, or if significant use is made of temporary or subcontract labour. Such conditions are especially likely to arise in retailing, in construction and in franchised operations.

Evaluation and Register of Environmental Effects, and Register of Regulations The standard requires procedures to be in place for examining and assessing the effects of all activities, products and services, and for compiling and maintaining a register of those judged to be 'significant'. It also requires procedures for maintaining a register of pertinent legislation and regulations.

Effects evaluation is seen by implementing organizations as one of the most difficult stages because of the breadth of assessment that may be required. Inevitably, any evaluation of corporate environmental effects is potentially both difficult and contentious. It must balance comprehensive initial coverage against the need to focus upon important effects, and be performed with demonstrable objectivity; it therefore requires knowledge both of the organization *and* of environmental issues.

Environmental objectives and targets   BS 7750 requires the environmental objectives to be:

- Quantified, wherever practicable
- Associated with specific, identified timescales
- Publicly available

The implementing organization may set its own objectives, within the constraint of the commitment to continual improvement in overall environmental performance. This freedom, which is inevitable in a generic management tool, raises concerns that compliance with BS 7750 may be achieved by organizations with poor environmental records. Sector Application Guides may in some cases set minimum performance requirements across a particular sector. However, such cases may be rare because large variations in activities and thus in effects, even within a sector, may preclude agreement of 'fair' performance criteria.

Because objectives are to be publicly available, the ultimate safeguard against unreasonably lax goals will be their scrutiny by interested parties such as the media, environmental interest groups and competitors, together with sound environmental knowledge and due vigilance on the part of assessors when an accredited certification system is implemented (see Chapter 8).

Environmental management programme   Environmental management programmes describe how the objectives are to be met. There is a requirement for separate programmes dealing with projects involving new or modified products, services or processes; this will be of particular concern to sectors in which major developments having potentially significant environmental effects are common (e.g. mining and quarrying, and the chemical, petroleum and energy industries).

Environmental management manual and documentation   The manual is required to draw together key elements of the EMS, and appropriate document control procedures are to be established. Emergency plans are required to address environmental matters. Feedback from the standard development phase revealed fears, among some potential users, that such requirements could lead to unproductive bureaucracy. However, documentation of essential systems and procedures is necessary for effective management and auditing—and for demonstrating environmental probity—and it should be borne in mind that the manual can simply 'signpost', rather than repeat, system documents.

Operational control   Routine operational control of processes and activities will be met in different ways, according to the nature of the activities and the way in which they are carried out. The extent to which working procedures are documented is to depend on the possible consequences of departures from them, and on the experience and qualifications of the staff carrying them out.

Procurement and contracted activities are to be addressed to ensure that suppliers and contractors comply with relevant requirements: a feature which will particularly affect any organization which makes extensive use of subcontracting or which sources raw materials from industries with major impacts. There is also a requirement that effective quality control is maintained over measurement and monitoring activities: an important consideration in view of the unreliability of much historic environmental data.

Environmental management records   The requirement to maintain records again raises concerns about bureaucracy, but they are obviously necessary for effective auditing and assessment of compliance with the requirements both of the standard itself, and of the policy and objectives. There is no requirement to disclose particular information to interested parties (beyond legal and regulatory demands), but pressures to disclose, and demonstrate the validity of, environmental performance data are increasing. There is a requirement to establish a procedure regarding the availability of records to interested parties.

Environmental management audits   As noted in Chapter 4, the term Environmental Audit has come to mean many different things, and BS 7750 uses the term Environmental Management Audits to indicate the requirement for a systems auditing approach in broad conformity with the principles of Quality Systems Auditing, as described in BS 7229 (ISO 10011).[4] It also requires that consideration be given to the frequency of audits, to the expertise required of auditors, and to their training.

Environmental management reviews   These reviews are higher level examinations of the effectiveness of the auditing process, and of the continuing relevance of the environmental policy. Such reviews, together with the periodic revision of objectives, represent the major drivers of continual improvement.

A note on 'establishment and maintenance of procedures'   BS 7750 and other EMS models make considerable use of this phrase, in many contexts. At a superficial level, it can be seen as potentially bureaucratic in its effects. At a deeper level, however, it reflects a fundamentally important feature of the systems approach. That is, that emphasis is placed not just on the *outcomes* of environmental management (e.g. the register of significant effects, the environmental objectives, the monitoring records, the corrective actions) but also on the *mechanisms* by which such outcomes are, and, most importantly, will continue to be, achieved.

6.5 Application of the Standard: General Issues

6.5.1 Practical Links with BS EN ISO 9000 Series

It will by now be quite clear to the reader that Environmental and Quality Management Systems share many common system principles. It should, however, be noted that application of BS 7750 does not demand prior implementation of a Quality System to BS EN ISO 9000, although an organization which has such a system should find it somewhat easier to develop certain elements of an EMS in conformity with the new standard. Figure 6.4 shows the broad system links between the two standards.

It should also be noted, however, that these 'mechanistic' system parallels hide a number of very important differences between quality management and environmental management. The most obvious difference relates to the evaluation and registration of environmental effects, for which there is only a very loose connection with (principally) the contract review element of quality systems. Related to this issue is the fact that the interaction between a supplier and a single customer in quality management is replaced, in environmental management, by the far more complex relationships between the organization and a very wide variety of parties interested in its environmental practices and performance, who may in certain cases have conflicting expectations .

It is also worth noting that clause 4.8 of BS 7750, dealing with operational control, is the generalized equivalent of a large number of clauses in BS EN ISO 9001 which deal with specific aspects of production control. The wide applicability of the environmental management standard, to service as well as manufacturing organizations, necessitates a more general treatment of routine control activities.

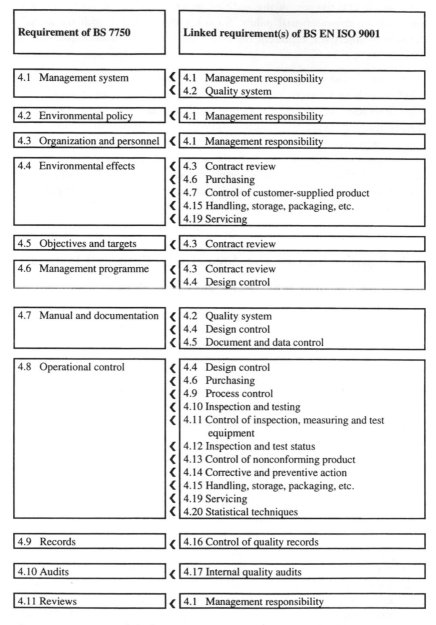

Figure 6.4   System links between BS 7750 and BS EN ISO 9001

Table 6.1 Comparison of major requirements of BS 7750 and of the EMA scheme

Requirement	BS 7750	BS 7750 with certification	EMA scheme
Policy	Yes	Yes	Yes
Initial review	No	No	Yes
Programme	Yes	Yes	Yes
EMS	Yes	Yes	Yes
Audits	Yes	Yes	Yes
Objectives	Yes	Yes	Yes
Environmental statement	No	No	Yes
Independent 'certification' or 'verification' of various system components	No	Yes	Yes
Publication of statement	No	No	Yes

6.5.2 Links with the EU Eco-Management and Audit Regulation

Reference has already been made to the convergence of the Eco–Management and Audit (EMA) scheme (as it has become) towards the systems approach of BS 7750 during their development.

The final form of the EMA scheme and its manner of implementation is shown in Figure 4.1, and a broad comparison of its requirements with those of BS 7750 is set out in Table 6.1. The principal differences are the requirement under EMA to publish an Environmental Statement giving details of environmental performance, and the fact that the preparatory review is an assessable element in the EMA scheme. The relationship between BS 7750 and EMA is considered in greater detail in Chapters 7 and 8.

6.5.3 Sector Application Guides

Some of the working groups of the BS 7750: 1992 pilot programme have developed Sector Application Guides (SAGs) to help explain the requirements of the standard as they apply in their sectors (see Section 7.1). These will not be *mandatory* for its application, but may be helpful both to implementing organizations and to certification bodies. (Certification and accreditation arrangements for BS 7750: 1994 are discussed in detail in Chapter 8.) However, it should be noted that SAGs published to date vary considerably in scope and depth (see, for example, Hillary[5]).

6.5.4 The EMS and corporate strategy

Many authors have emphasized the importance of recognizing and understanding the likely evolution of environmental issues in developing corporate strategy. Figure 6.2, which predates BS 7750 by some years, shows how the practice of environmental scenario generation, as part of normal business planning, combines with what are now elements of BS 7750 to form a broader concept of Integrated Environmental Management. In other words, to obtain the full benefits of the systems approach requires environmental considerations to be integrated with traditional concerns when planning the management and direction of the business, rather than mere 'mechanical' application of the requirements of BS 7750. Scenario generation is considered in greater detail in Section 7.4.

References

1 International Chamber of Commerce, *Environmental Auditing*, ICC Publication No. 468, 1989. Paris.
2 International Chamber of Commerce, *ICC Guide to Effective Environmental Auditing*, ICC Publication No. 483, 1991. Paris.
3 Council Regulation (EEC) No. 1836/93 of 29 June 1993 allowing participation by companies in the industrial sector in a Community eco-management and audit scheme, *Official Journal of the European Communities*, L168/1–18, 10 July 1993.
4 British Standards Institution, BS 7229, *Guide to Quality Systems Auditing*, BSI, London, 1991. (Part 1: Auditing; Part 2: Qualification criteria for auditors; Part 3: Managing an audit programme.)
5 R. Hillary, 'Sector Application Guides: An Overview and Examination of their Current Status', presented at a NEMA seminar, University of Hertfordshire, September 1994.

7

Development and Application of an Environmental Management System

7.1 Planning the Work

It is all too easy, when embarking upon a lengthy and important task (particularly against tight deadlines), to succumb to the urge to jump straight in and get started. The development of an EMS is no exception but in this, as in other activities, time spent planning will usually be more than repaid as work proceeds. The initial planning phase typically involves:

- Defining the overall aims.
- Understanding the constraints.
- Identifying the task elements.
- Setting the overall timetable.
- Determining the resources needed.
- Deciding on the project management approach.
- Establishing progress monitoring systems.

However, the planning itself may not follow this implied path linearly, and other steps may also be involved. Obvious though it may seem it is also important to note that planning is an activity which will be necessary for each individual task element as the work proceeds, and that flexibility is therefore an essential element of the overall plan.

In particular, more detailed planning can be carried out after the Preparatory Review (see Section 7.3) when better and more comprehensive information will be available on existing environmental performance and practices. However, the questionnaire in Appendix 1 provides a simple and rapid means of roughly assessing the extent to which an organization has a formalized environmental management system in place. This is not a substitute for a more thorough review, but if given to a representative range of staff across the organization to complete, can provide a most useful 'snapshot' prior to, and during, EMS development.

7.1.1 Defining the aims

The overall aim, it is assumed, will be the establishment of an EMS — but as a statement of intentions this is inadequate. Consideration should be given to such factors as:

- The EMS model which will be followed (e.g. BS 7750 or a model specific to the organization or sector).
- The intentions regarding certification and registration (e.g. to BS 7750 and/ or EMA, which have some subtly different requirements: see Section 8.2).
- The scope of coverage (e.g. the whole organization, or a particular site or activity).
- The desired deadlines for EMS establishment, certification or registration, etc.
- Intentions regarding environmental performance reporting.
- The desired environmental position, e.g. sector leadership in performance.

Clear statements of aims, particularly regarding the scope of coverage and timetable, avoid later confusion and ensure that all involved have a clear and unambiguous understanding of the purpose of their efforts.

It will also be appropriate at this stage to decide if a combined Health, Safety, and Environment Management System (HSEMS) is to be developed. Whether or not this is the approach to adopt will depend upon the organization and its existing health and safety management practices. While BS 7750 explicitly excludes health and safety from its scope, it also states that it is quite possible to meet its requirements within a joint HSEMS, and the authors have recently worked with the Exploration and Production Forum to produce HSEMS Guidelines for the international oil industry's upstream operations.[1]

A danger to be avoided in setting the aims (and timetable, see below) is a blinkered attitude, looking only at achieving certification or registration to an EMS standard or under EMA, particularly within an unrealistically tight time-table. While such official recognition of the EMS may be important in many companies for marketing or other reasons, it is wise to ensure that the over-riding objective is to build the EMS with the 'grain' of the existing overall management system and organizational culture, and to provide adequate time and resources to do so. This makes the establishment phase easier but, more importantly, it will help ensure that the EMS is readily maintainable and effective in helping deliver good environmental performance and its associated benefits, including enhanced business opportunities.

An EMS which is 'bolted on' to achieve hurried certification, rather than developed as an integral part of the way the organization functions, is unlikely to be really successful in delivering and sustaining good environmental performance. Indeed, organizations already working to BS 5750 (ISO 9000) should be particularly cautious not to fall into this trap. While they will have real

Table 7.1 Characteristics of the organization

1	*Type and ownership* Private or public sector Private company, public limited company, partnership or staff owned Central or local government, department or agency, nationalized industry
2	*Nature of unit* Fully autonomous Single site within wider organization
3	*Nature of work* Activities, products and services, sector Traditional/innovative Sector/market position, success, profitability
4	*Size and operating area* Multinational/national Large, medium, small
5	*Management system, structure and style* Tight/loose structure, documented/oral, BS 5750/ISO 9000 Hierarchical, functional, matrix, centralized/decentralized Authoritarian/delegatory
6	*Staffing characteristics and skills* Demographic characteristics and turnover Expectations, aspirations and motivations Skills and knowledge, understanding of management systems and environmental matters

advantages, in being able simply to extend their existing management systems to meet BS 7750 requirements in a number of areas (e.g. document control), there are many important differences between quality and environmental management systems which they will ignore at their peril.

7.1.2 Understanding the constraints

Obvious constraints include costs — in terms of external assistance and internal resources — but these will need refinement as the work proceeds. At this stage, other constraints to be considered include particularly the inherent nature of the organization, its management system and style, and the skills and knowledge available internally (Table 7.1).

Careful consideration of the nature of the organization, its activities, products and services, its overall management approach, and the capabilities of its staff will help to ensure that EMS development proceeds smoothly. It will also help to ensure that the system, when established, will be consonant with established organizational practices and culture.

7.1.3 Identifying the task elements

The elements of the overall task of establishing an EMS should be, in principle, clear from the EMS model followed. However, they should be examined carefully at the outset and specific responsibilities may be assigned to individuals to undertake entire task elements or parts of them, according to such factors as the nature and size of the organization, the management structure and style, and the individual's knowledge and understanding both of the organization's activities and of the relevant environmental issues.

7.1.4 Setting the overall timetable

Establishing a clear and realistic timetable, with flexibility and allowance for delays is obviously important. If an unrealistic timetable is set, effort may be wasted and enthusiasm for the project diminished. On the other hand, a brisk pace is advantageous in showing those involved that a clear overall goal is to be achieved in a reasonable time, in maintaining enthusiasm by avoiding a 'dragging out' of the EMS establishment phase and in ensuring, so far as is possible, that the system will be set up within a known and established organizational structure. (If major changes in the overall organization and its management structure are foreseen, these should be built into the plan and appropriate allowance made in the timetable.)

While it is true that there is a relationship between the resources allocated and the time taken to establish an EMS, it is not a simple linear one: there will always be some minimum EMS development time which cannot be bettered by 'throwing money at the problem', and the cost penalties of an unrealistically short development period may be considerable.

7.1.5 Determining the resources needed

Only a preliminary assessment of resources will be possible at the outset, but this can be revised, particularly after the Preparatory Review (see Section 7.3). Consideration should be given to internal resource requirements, particularly for undertaking such tasks as the Preparatory Review, Training, the Effects Evaluation and the preparation of EMS Documentation, but also to external assistance if it appears that this will be necessary. External assistance in EMS development may be required for one or more of a number of reasons, including:

- Supplementing limited staff time.
- Furnishing specialized skills and understanding, e.g. for Effects Evaluation and Training.
- Providing an external, objective assessment of practices and requirements.

It should also be borne in mind that capital outlay, e.g. on pollution control equipment, may be necessary or desirable to meet policy commitments or enable objectives and targets to be met. Again, detailed requirements will become clear during the development process — and particularly after the

Preparatory Review — but any identifiable requirements should be noted at the earliest practicable moment, and appropriate provision made.

(Note, however, that in a cost–benefit analysis undertaken as part of the process of gaining top management commitment (see Section 7.2), a distinction should be made between those capital and other costs necessary to establish the EMS, and those which would be incurred in any case in order to comply with new legislation or regulations, for example.)

7.1.6 Deciding on the project management approach

The detailed arrangements will depend greatly upon the size and character of the organization, and upon the timetable for EMS development. For all but the smallest organizations, however, we recommend a Task Group approach, for a number of reasons including:

- Avoiding dependence on a single individual either for progress or for judgements.
- Spreading the workload and gaining specialist expertise.
- Gaining commitment and support from managers and others who will implement the EMS.

The Task Group can be chaired by the Director responsible for environmental matters, or by the Management Representative designate (Section 7.6), who should in any event be a member of the group. The size of the group will depend upon the organization, but should be kept relatively small: for example, by co-opting technical specialists when needed or, in a large organization, by establishing sub-groups to deal with particular activities or sites.

7.1.7 Establishing progress monitoring systems

A procedure should be established for providing regular progress reports to:

- top management
- line managers and other staff involved in the development process
- staff in general

7.1.8 Aids to implementation

Those wishing to develop and implement an EMS (whether in conformity with BS 7750, EMA, ISO/CD 14001 or to their own model) have numerous potential sources of assistance. An implementing organization may obtain information on environmental management matters from Government departments, professional bodies, interest groups, consultancies and other bodies (names, addresses and telephone numbers for a number of which are given in

Appendix 2), as well as from their own trade associations (see below). In addition, conferences, seminars, workshops and training courses on environmental management are numerous and widely advertised.

A number of Sector Application Guides (SAGs) have been prepared following the BS 7750 Pilot Implementation Programme. These have the specific goal of explaining and exemplifying (but not extending) the requirements of the standard in the context of particular industrial or commercial sectors. At the time of writing (October 1994) they are available for the following sectors:

- Waste management
- Electricity transmission and distribution
- Electricity generation
- Transport and distribution services
- Printing and packaging
- Textile and textile products
- Furniture and wood industries
- Healthcare
- Oil refineries
- Food

Further sectors may be covered in due course, and amendments made to current SAGs in the light of experience in their use. For these reasons, we have not listed individual SAGs in the references, but would recommend that intending implementors contact their Trade Associations for further information.

There are a number of PC-based software packages on the market which have been developed to assist the development and maintenance of corporate environmental auditing and/or environmental management systems. These vary quite widely in scope and price (typically £1000 to £5000 for a single-user licence, with much reduced charges for additional users). Those designed specifically for EMS maintenance usually offer database and other facilities to assist such activities as the registration of significant effects and applicable legislation and regulations, the maintenance of records of training, monitoring and suppliers, the programming of audits and the writing of procedures. As with all software, intending users should draw up a specification of their requirements against which to assess different packages, and seek a demonstration of short-listed products before purchase.

7.2 Gaining Corporate Commitment

7.2.1 The importance of commitment

It is common experience that environmental initiatives — and, indeed, initiatives in other areas of corporate activity — require the clear and unequivocal commitment of top management if they are to succeed. Without such commitment, the necessary corporate support (in terms of infrastructure and resources) for sustained effort will not be available; 'bottom-up' environmental initiatives typically wither away quite rapidly.

This point has often been made, but is worth repeating and emphasizing at the outset because:

- By its nature, an EMS is especially demanding of corporate commitment and support.
- A failure to obtain real commitment to its development and maintenance is likely to produce disillusionment and thus damage other, more local, environmental initiatives.

So, for example, an environmental manager or co-ordinator who wishes to introduce an EMS should first consider how to ensure that top management commitment is available before work begins. Initially, this may involve gaining approval for, and commitment to, a preparatory review (see Section 7.3), the results of which will provide a fuller basis for decisions on establishing an EMS.

7.2.2 Who are the top management?

The obvious answer in many companies will be the Board, and specifically the Chairman or Managing Director, or their equivalent. However, even this answer may need further exploration, as the commitment of a higher authority within the larger organization may be required to ensure that the necessary support and resources are available, and both BS 7750 and EMA require that a local (e.g. site-based) environmental policy should have the endorsement of any parent company.

Thus, the question 'Who is top management?' can only be addressed within the context of the specific company or other organization concerned, and care should be taken to ensure that a satisfactory answer is obtained before proceeding.

7.2.3 Gaining top management commitment

If the initiative for an EMS does not itself come from top management, this could simply be because they are unaware of the concept, but are otherwise committed to good environmental performance. In that case, the task of gaining their commitment will be the relatively easy one of making them aware of the benefits of a formal, structured EMS. Informal arrangements are likely to be in place already if the top management commitment to environmental probity is sincere and of long standing.

Alternatively, top management may have yet to recognize the benefits of good environmental performance, or the penalties associated with its absence.

In that case, gaining commitment will involve the rather larger task of convincing them that environmental matters deserve their consideration and time, and an appropriate level of corporate resource. We shall consider how to set about this larger task, and in so doing necessarily address also the simpler issue of preaching the benefits of an EMS to those who are already at least 'environmentally' converted!

Convincing top management of the benefits of sound environmental performance and management may require careful and detailed preparation (see Figure 7.1).

In presenting the case for sound environmental performance and/or an EMS to the decision-makers, use the information gained (Figure 7.1) but be sure to make the case thoroughly but concisely, and clearly demonstrate both the benefits and costs. Be as specific as possible about what is required, and be sure to provide succinct documentation on your case so that decision-makers can make reference to it in their discussions after the formal presentation. This is also of major importance if an intermediary will put your case to the ultimate decision-makers.

Understand the business:

- Public profile and financial position
- Inherent environmental vulnerability
- Business strategy and market position
- Position in supply chain and environmental attitudes and expectations of customers
- Competitor environmental performance
- Costs, monetary and other, of previous incidents and consequences
- Opportunities for environmentally led efficiency improvement

⬇

Understand the key top management decision-makers:

- Business and technical backgrounds
- Responsibilities and current concerns

⬇

Understand the potential benefits and costs:

- Remember that decision-makers will be sceptical of benefits without costs
- Consider the general benefits of good environmental performance (Chapter 1 and Section 7.17) and the potential penalties of poor performance (Chapters 2 and 3 and Section 7.17)
- Consider the specific benefits of an EMS (Chapter 6 and Section 7.17)
- Identify the major benefits in relation to the company and its needs
- Identify the likely costs of EMS development and implementation (Section 7.17)

Figure 7.1 Preparing to gain top management commitment

7.2.4 Maintaining top management commitment

Developing an EMS takes time, and to be effective it must be maintained and developed. It is therefore not enough to obtain top management commitment; it must also be maintained. In part, this will come naturally through continuing involvement of top management in system reviews (Section 7.16). However, it is also essential to ensure that key information is presented to top management at other times, including, for example, summaries of progress towards achievement of environmental objectives and of financial information relating to environmental costs and benefits.

The publication of corporate environmental performance reports (Sections 7.9 and 7.18) represents an excellent mechanism for the public renewal and restatement of top management commitment.

7.3 Conducting a Preparatory Review

7.3.1 Introduction

Once a commitment has been made to establish an Environmental Management System, those charged with its establishment will face the task of deciding exactly what environmental concerns need to be addressed, and what systems will be needed, to keep the organization's environmental effects under control. This may appear to be a daunting task, the risks being that important concerns may not be recognized as such, and will be overlooked, and that over-zealous and hasty effort will be misdirected either towards trivial concerns, or in duplicating pre-existing and adequate management systems. Such risks can be minimized by the conduct of a carefully and logically planned preparatory review.

The review should not, however, be regarded solely as a means of avoiding pitfalls. It provides a means of identifying opportunities; for instance, to reduce costs through waste reduction, to identify local good practices and spread them throughout the organization, and to plan capital expenditure so as to optimize its benefits. The preparatory review should provide information which enables the setting of environmental objectives (see Section 7.11). It is beneficial for the review to examine the whole organization (rather than merely parts of it) so that a global view of its systems and their linkages and communication channels is obtained.

The preparatory review does not appear in the main body of the text of BS 7750, i.e. in the specification, because it does not form an assessable component of the standard. It will be of no interest to assessors operating certification schemes, because it will be performed only once, and thereafter the EMS itself should comprehensively address all concerns and control all effects. This is one of the few significant differences between BS 7750 and the European Union's EMA Regulation. To comply with the regulation, an organization needs to have its preparatory review (or initial review, as the regulation calls it) verified by the external verifier, so care should be taken to document the exercise adequately: see Chapter 8.

The benefit of the preparatory review is in enabling the organization to answer the question 'Where are we now?' (see Figure 6.2). Once answered, the next stage will be to ask 'Where should we be going?'; this will be discussed in Section 7.4.

7.3.2 The information to be gathered

The information which should be gathered by the preparatory review can be divided into two categories: information on outputs and information on systems. Outputs can be described as the consequences of what the organization does. Systems are the ways in which the organization goes about its business, and they may, in practice, be anything but systematic. The reader is advised to read Chapter 7 in its entirety before embarking on a preparatory review, as later sections will amplify the types of outputs and systems which should be examined. There are four key areas which should be covered by a preparatory review. These are discussed in turn below.

Legislative and regulatory requirements

It is a fundamental requirement that any organization should know of all the requirements placed upon it by the regulatory authorities, for unless it knows what these are, it cannot be confident that they are met. It is not uncommon, however, for this information to be poorly documented, dispersed throughout the organization, and known to only a few individuals, not one of whom is aware of all of it. It is easy to understand how such situations have arisen, particularly under the regulatory regimes which operated in the recent past. A discharge consent applying to a factory, for instance, might have been kept in the possession of the person responsible for operating the effluent treatment plant. In the absence of any reason to suspect non-compliance, checks by the regulatory authority would probably have been infrequent. The person responsible for the effluent treatment plant might have kept the paperwork specifying the discharge conditions, and any relevant correspondence with the regulator, in a disordered state or an unspecified place, such that no other person could locate them. In the absence of any reason to suspect a problem, it has often been the case in a situation such as this that no individual within the organization's management has felt it to be their responsibility to ensure this information was readily accessible.

Another example might relate to planning requirements. It is common for planning consents for business or industrial developments to specify conditions intended to protect the environment, and especially to protect near neighbours from nuisance. Such conditions might include maximum permitted noise or lighting levels, for instance, or hours of traffic movement. The organization might then evolve patterns of work which accommodate all such requirements, and after years have passed and staff have changed, the organization's management finds that nobody within it knows what the specified conditions were.

Many more examples could be given. The tracing and collation of such regulatory requirements is a necessary part of a preparatory review (see also Section 7.10).

Evaluation and registration of significant environmental effects

It is important that the organization is aware of, and understands, all the effects which its activities have upon the environment. Without this knowledge and understanding, the organization's management will not be able to make informed decisions about what its priorities should be in setting objectives or in aiming for performance improvement. It will also face the risk of interested parties raising questions which it will find difficult to answer. While the documentation (which is all that is meant by registration) of significant effects is important for future reference (see Section 7.8), there can be advantages in documenting insignificant ones as well. This should not be taken as a recommendation for the production of copious paperwork, but documented evidence of reasoning at this stage may save duplication of effort later on.

Suppose, for instance, that someone in the organization later thinks of some relevant environmental concern, and wonders if the organization should change its practices. Reference to the review documentation might reveal that while the concern is recognized, there are in fact two sides to the argument and that the organization's management decided to continue existing practices until the scientific debate reaches a consensus. Or the review documentation might reveal that the concern in question was recognized, quantified and found to be minor compared to others, so that resources were to be expended on addressing other concerns for the time being. There again the review might reveal that the existing course of action which is being questioned actually produces less detriment to the environment than the alternatives would, and explain how this conclusion was reached. Thus it can be seen that the preparatory review can provide a body of information which will be valuable for reference later on.

Examination of all existing environmental management practices and procedures

Few organizations will find they have no existing EMS in place at all. An absence of prosecutions, complaints and other indications of problems suggests at least some degree of control and management of processes with the potential to pollute. Even if the existing practices and procedures have never been thought of as part of an 'Environmental Management System', they nevertheless constitute a rudimentary one. It is important to understand that the EMS is not an isolated entity; the organization has only one management system, of which the EMS is an integral part. The review should examine the extent to which some system components do exist, but also assess their weaknesses and deficiencies. It should of course also identify the instances where an absence of problems is attributable to good luck rather than good management.

After the preparatory review is completed, and development of the EMS is under way, it will often be found possible to extend existing management systems to encompass environmental management. The identification of such opportunities can be left until later; the review, in order to remain an easily understood and short-term task, should focus on what is needed, rather than how, in detail, to achieve it. This need not prevent the review team from noting and reporting obvious such opportunities which they observe. Examples of such opportunities will be given in later sections of this chapter.

Assessment of feedback from investigation of previous incidents and non-compliance

If there has been a history of mishaps or problems, the preparatory review provides an opportunity for quantifying the problem, finding its root cause (or at least identifying a need for further study to find it) and remedying it. Even if management are aware of a problem, they may not be aware of its magnitude, or its importance relative to other concerns. Records of investigations into such past incidents may provide useful information, and the preparatory review should ascertain the fate of recommendations made as a result of such investigations. Were the recommendations followed? If not, why not? And if so, were they successful in alleviating the problem?

It is important throughout the review to consider not only the normal situation but abnormal and emergency ones as well. In this context, abnormal situations can be considered to be any which are not encountered very frequently, for instance:

- Start up and shut down of plant which normally operates without interruption for long periods of time.
- Occasional maintenance activities.
- Manufacture of goods to a different specification or formulation from those normally used.
- Provision of services different to those usually provided.
- Unusual, but foreseeable, weather conditions.
- Loss of a usual waste disposal route or mechanism.

Some examples of emergency situations which might be foreseen are:

- Fire
- Spillage/leakage of material
- Vandalism
- Traffic accident
- Flood

7.3.3 How to conduct the review

The review team

In all but very small organizations, it is likely that more than one individual will be needed to conduct the preparatory review. This does not mean that extensive resources are required; expertise in a certain field may be essential, but the individual providing it may well be able to do so in a very few hours. It is not efficient to have non-specialists spending days researching subjects with which they are not familiar; it might be more cost-effective to consult a specialist in the first place.

While the exact mix of knowledge required of the review team will depend on the nature of the organization, it is always the case that the leader of the team needs good general knowledge in two areas: the activities of the organization, and environmental issues in general. This knowledge will enable the leader to assemble a team of individuals with the right mix of experience and knowledge to conduct an effective preparatory review.

This experience and knowledge should enable the information gathered to be assessed critically. Much of this information will be supplied by non-specialists who, while meaning well, may not always know the answers to the questions they are asked. For instance, if a respondent says that a manufacturing plant is not subject to control of atmospheric emissions, could the team be confident that this is really the case?

Methodology

As can be seen from the discussions above, the methodology for conducting the preparatory review should enable the drawing together of existing information dispersed throughout the organization. A need to seek further information from sources outside the organization will often become apparent during the course of the review, but whether this is done as part of the review itself, or left to subsequent studies recommended in the review report, will be a matter for judgement on the part of the review team. In practice, budgetary or time constraints may be deciding factors. The review should not be a lengthy process; it will usually be possible to complete it in 6–10 weeks, from identifying the team members to issuing the report. The temptation to persist until perfect knowledge has been attained should be resisted; if information is not readily available, this indicates where and how the EMS needs to be developed, which is what should be emphasized in the review report. Likewise, if questionnaires are not returned or key personnel cannot find time to be interviewed, this may indicate problems of resourcing or commitment (see Section 7.2).

The detailed methodology of a preparatory review will depend on the nature and activities of the organization, but will usually include some combination of questionnaires, interviews and site inspections. Often all three will be appropriate, and a typical approach is illustrated in Figure 7.2. The methodology should be designed in detail during a review planning stage, which should also be used to compile checklists of all the issues to be addressed. Such checklists are vital, and need to be compiled with reference to the organization's activities, in conjunction with knowledge about environmental concerns and the organization's likely contribution to them.

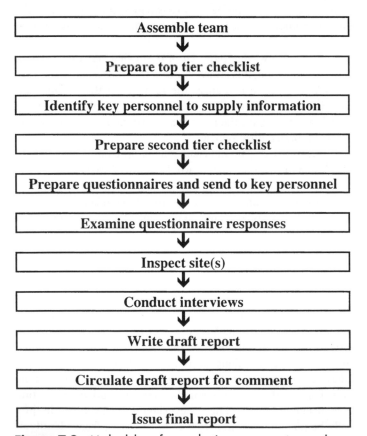

Figure 7.2 Methodology for conducting a preparatory review

The information to be gathered

Checklists can be developed in stages, each addressing different levels of detail. While high level (or first tier) checklists may be useful for the construction of questionnaires, more detailed, low level (second or third tier) checklists are useful for identifying the more detailed information to be sought from interviews. Some examples of the typical contents of checklists are listed in Table 7.2. These are in no way exhaustive, and a specific preparatory review checklist should be drawn up taking into account both the nature and activities of the organization and the requirements of any relevant EMS standard or draft standard (e.g. BS 7750, EMA or ISO/CD 14001). In doing so, the further examples of checklists in, for example, references 2–8 may also be helpful.

The preparatory review report

It should be borne in mind that the report will be aimed at the most senior management, that is busy people with many other concerns. As discussed earlier, though, it is a good idea to document much of the information collected, especially on environmental effects. These two aims can be reconciled by the production of a report of whatever length may later be useful, which contains a stand-alone executive summary. This should include recommendations, but specification of detail of the EMS needed will probably not be appropriate. Recommendations of the nature of: 'A system should be established to. . .' or 'The effectiveness of the effluent treatment plant should be investigated for. . .' are required at this stage. The objective is to highlight strengths, weaknesses, opportunities and threats, together with recommendations for developing the EMS.

7.3.4 Future reviews

After the EMS has been established, it is the role of senior management to review the EMS periodically to ensure its continuing suitability in the light of changing circumstances (see Section 7.16). All such reviews should refer back to the previous review, whether this was the preparatory review or a later one, so that progress can be measured and duplication of earlier work avoided.

7.4 Developing a Scenario

7.4.1 The need for a strategy

Having answered the question 'Where are we now?' (Section 7.3) the organization's management is then in a position to ask itself: 'Where should we be going?' This will necessitate thinking about the direction the organization

Table 7.2 Examples of information to be sought from a preparatory review. Under each main (top tier) heading, the questions (second tier) in the left column relate primarily to *outputs*, while those in the right column relate primarily to *systems*

Current legislative and regulatory requirements

Are any discharge consents in force? Are any planning conditions in force? Are any atmospheric emissions standards in force?	Are the requirements documented, up-to-date, accessible to anyone in the organization who might need them?

Expected changes in legislation and regulations

Are there any proposed bans on chemicals used in product formulations? Are there any proposed changes to emission limits?	Is there a system for finding out about such proposals? Is correspondence with regulators filed in an orderly way?

Areas where environmental performance could be improved

Are there areas which are known barely to comply with requirements? Are there areas which are known to fail to comply with regulatory requirements? Could resource consumption be reduced? Is the site ugly or untidy in appearance?	Is compliance measured? Are measurement systems adequate? Has anybody examined the possibilities for resource minimization? Is anybody responsible for site appearance?

Environmental probity of suppliers

Are raw materials purchased, whose gathering is environmentally damaging? Are manufactured materials purchased, whose manufacture is environmentally damaging?	Is the feasibility of substituting other materials known? Is the environmental probity of suppliers considered in purchasing decisions?

Pollution abatement measures

Are measures adequate to meet present requirements? Are measures adequate to meet future requirements, in the light of expected changes in activities, production, etc.? How efficient and cost effective are existing measures, compared with alternatives?	Are there systems for assessing the continuing suitability of such measures? Does the organization collect information about the alternatives?

Environmental aspects of emergency planning

What would be the fate of fire-fighting water, if there was a fire on site? What would be the fate of any hazardous substances released in a traffic accident? Is the site secure against vandalism, which might result in release of hazardous substances?	Are the emergency services informed of any special response required of them? Do those responsible for emergency planning consider the environment?

Table 7.2 (cont)

External communications and their follow-up

What environmental complaints and enquiries have been received during, say, the last three years?	Are there procedures for switchboard staff to follow if a neighbour telephones to complain?
Does the organization know what environmental pressure groups think of its activities?	Are there procedures to follow up such calls? Are there procedures for seeking the views of relevant interested parties?
Would potential investors (such as a bank) regard the site as an asset, or a liability?	

Nature conservation

Are there vulnerable or rare species or habitats in the vicinity of the site?	Do mechanisms exist to collect such information? Do mechanisms exist to act upon the information gained?
Are any valuable habitats provided by the site itself?	
What are the opportunities to provide facilities or expertise for local conservation groups?	

Fuel and energy consumption

What pollutant emissions are associated with energy and fuel use, both on-site and off-site?	By what means are environmental effects considered when energy sources are chosen?
Are staff aware of the importance of energy conservation?	Have any energy efficiency/staff awareness campaigns been conducted?

Adequacy of resources

Are adequate manpower, skills and equipment available for environmental programmes?	By what means are resource requirements identified and met?

Internal communications

Are staff aware of the environmental policy?	What mechanisms exist to promote staff awareness of environmental policy and roles?
Are staff aware of the importance of their own contribution to environmental performance?	Are environmental issues addressed in induction programmes?

might take in the future and, if it is a commercial organization, the position it wishes to occupy in the market-place relative to its competitors.

The decisions to be made will be those necessary for the achievement of the purpose of the organization. Every organization has a purpose; for a company, it is to provide a return to the shareholders. For non-profit making organizations, the purposes are more diverse: for example, the purpose of an educational establishment is to provide education; of a charity, to provide some benefit to the disadvantaged, and so on. This purpose will not, of course, be pursued without constraints. Many will be imposed by law, but the organization will choose to work within others: it will decide how it will behave towards its work-force, customers, competitors and all the other groups or individuals with whom it interacts. This framework of constraints has been called an 'ethos'.[9] This implies that the framework of constraints is determined by the values of the directors, shareholders or whoever holds, and chooses to exercise, power.

While this may be so, as companies' behaviour increasingly comes under public scrutiny it may not always be easy to dissociate the desire to behave according to certain values with the need to be *seen*, by interested parties, to be doing so; the ethos and the purpose begin to overlap. The trend towards corporate advertising indicates the perceived value of a positive company image. This 'ethos' or set of self-imposed constraints now, in the 1990s, often addresses intentions to protect the environment, as well as a whole range of others such as the working conditions provided for employees, and contributions to the local community. The distinction between those of an organization's objectives which relate to its purpose and its ethos is discussed in detail in Argenti.[9]

All organizations need a strategy, and this may simply be described as the means by which the organization will achieve its purpose, within the constraints of its ethos. This will be first and foremost a business strategy, but environmental considerations play an increasingly important role. For instance, in the 1990s many manufacturing companies need to plan major capital investments to replace old, polluting plants because they will shortly be incapable of complying with regulations. The determination of business strategy is a major theme of management texts and is beyond the scope of this one.

Most organizations do develop strategies to ensure their continuing survival, growth and success. This is particularly true of businesses, but most other bodies, from political parties to charities and churches, do so too. Those that do not develop strategies, or do so badly, sooner or later fail.

7.4.2 'Scene-setting': the role of a scenario

A major theme of management texts is the need to look to the future and to predict the conditions under which the organization will be operating. This is as vital to environmental management as it is to any other area of management. The vision of future circumstances can be described as a scenario.

The behaviour of organizations is often described in terms borrowed from biology. Like a species which manages to survive despite predators and competitors, the successful organization must be able to:[10]

- Sense information
- Interpret information
- Create appropriate responses

The following discussion focuses on the profitability of businesses, but many of the concepts could be readily adapted to the needs of non-profit-making organizations.

Businesses need to be constantly evaluating their future profitability, and comparing this with the profitability they might achieve if they changed from their present course of action, either by seeking new or different products or markets, or making existing products in different ways, different locations and so on. In this respect, future environmental pressures become just some of the many factors which will influence the attractiveness (in terms of profitability and level of risk) of the various options available.

The other factors include, for example, technological developments in the company's R&D laboratories. There may also be changes in supplies of inputs: the supply of capital, affected by changes in interest rates; the availability of a suitable work-force, affected by changes in population or education; the supply of components, affected by changes in technology; and the availability of raw materials, affected by political upheaval in the countries where they are sourced. These may sound like the concerns of large organizations, but in practice even the one-person business monitors many of these, if in some case indirectly, and over shorter time-scales, depending on its nature.

It is vital that environmental issues and developments are integrated into the mechanisms which the organization deploys to collect and evaluate information of the type exemplified above. The determination of strategy, of course, will be made at board level, and provides a compelling reason for the need for commitment to sound environmental management from the highest level of the organization (see Section 7.2). The remainder of this section is concerned with the development of environmental scenarios in particular.

A comparison with Quality Management can be made here. The sector of the market-place, in terms of quality of product, which the business is to occupy, is clearly a decision for the highest level of management and, appropriately, BS 5750 calls for a quality policy to be seen to have support from this level in the organization. Similarly, only the highest level of management will have the broad perspective needed to evaluate environmental issues in conjunction with all the other factors influencing the future of the organization. This implies a need for a high level input to such activities as the setting and maintaining of environmental objectives and targets (Section 7.11) as well as the obvious example of establishing a policy (Section 7.5).

The breadth of the scenario should range from issues which have not attracted external concern as yet, but which the organization has reason to believe will attract attention in the future, to those that have already given rise to legislation soon to come into force. The need to develop this scenario is illustrated by developments over the last few years, which have amply illustrated the pace at which environmental concerns change; Chapter 2 illustrates this point in detail.

7.4.3 Causes of change in the environmental scenario

Changes in environmental concern are driven by changing circumstances, such as:

- Changes in technology
- Environmental damage becoming tangible
- Improved understanding of environmental science

Useful lessons may be learned from considering the following examples which illustrate the ways in which the future scenario may differ from the present, and the type of circumstances which an organization should prepare for.

Changes in technology

Many examples might be given of changes in technology alleviating concerns, rendering their cause obsolete, and giving rise to new ones. The smogs which frequently occurred in winter in UK cities up until the 1960s were caused almost entirely by the smoke and sulphur dioxide emissions from domestic and industrial coal burning. The elimination of this type of winter smog was brought about by several influences. Changing patterns of fuel use had caused smoke concentrations in London to fall gradually from the 1920s, and The Clean Air Act of 1956 gave local authorities powers to declare 'smoke free zones'. This Act ensured that the change to less polluting fuels continued, with a consequent sharp reduction in sulphur dioxide concentrations.[11] However, the discovery and exploitation of natural gas in the North Sea made it easy to bring about great improvements in urban sulphur dioxide and smoke pollution, as city dwellers happily adopted gas-fired central heating.

Environmental damage becomes tangible

Gradual environmental degradation may go unnoticed until it reaches an advanced stage. Declining fish stocks in a river, for instance, are not likely to be noticed by the non-fishing public, but the river's eventual filthy appearance might attract attention. Declining populations of species which are becoming rare often go unnoticed for a long time, but once numbers become dangerously low, publicity campaigns to save the species are likely to get a sympathetic hearing. The history of whales and the whaling industry provides a good example.

Improved understanding of environmental science

Many examples could be given of 'developments' in technology turning out to have such damaging, but unforeseen, side-effects that they have had to be abandoned. For instance, polychlorinated biphenyls (PCBs) began to be used on a commercial scale in the 1930s. Their low electrical conductivity combined with low flammability and high heat resistance made them useful components of a variety of products, but especially electrical transformers. They are, however, toxic and persistent, and they accumulate in food chains. The extent of the danger they pose is such that in 1976 the European Community banned their use in manufacturing.

Chlorofluorocarbons (CFCs) provide a similar example. Their development in 1931 and their apparently inert properties led to their widespread use, principally as refrigerants, as solvents in the electronics industry, aerosol propellants and in insulating foams. Their causation of depletion of the stratospheric ozone layer was predicted as far back as 1974,[12] and by 1978 they were being banned from certain applications in the USA. Eventually the Montreal Protocol was signed and — spurred on by measurements showing the damage proceeding at an accelerating rate — EU Member States have since agreed to phase out production of these compounds even more quickly than required by the Protocol.

7.4.4 Drawing up the scenario

In compiling the scenario, the organization should consider the views and positions of various groups. These range from its own business strategists to legislators, and the information to be sought from some of them is suggested below. Of course there may not be a need to consult them all directly; information gleaned from their publications, or from third parties such as the specialist press or personal contacts, may be adequate.

The information to be sought, compiled and evaluated is extensive and diverse. It has been claimed that organizations appear to act on very small portions of the total available information,[13] and if this is so, the relatively small amount of information used must be carefully selected. In any organization, the capacity to assemble, store and utilize information is finite, and so to be optimally effective, the effort expended on drawing up the scenario should be carefully planned and follow a structured approach.

The organization is advised to consider not only the scientific evidence for future events, but also the *perceptions* of the interested parties. Tempting as it may be to ignore perceptions which are clearly unfounded or misguided, this is unwise. While pandering to misperceptions is never to be encouraged — not least because to do so could result in changed courses of action which *increase* environmental damage — it is in the organization's commercial interests to be aware of them and to formulate a strategy for responding to them. Failure to do so is to risk being caught out by consumer pressure or changes in legislation. The sources of information which may be used in developing the scenario include the following.

The organization's existing plans

The scenario must have some pre-defined boundaries if it is not to be an open-ended exercise, so irrelevant issues should be excluded. The boundaries can be defined with reference to the organization's existing strategy for such matters as:

- Expansion
- Rationalization
- Acquisition
- Diversification
- Specialization
- Relocation
- Marketing strategy

Of course the potential will exist for these plans to be revised in the light of the scenario; this constitutes one of the greatest benefits in drawing up the scenario, in its usefulness as an aid in planning. But some existing plans will be more firm, or more constrained, than others and thus may be used to indicate the boundaries of the scenario. Boundaries apply not only to scope but also to time-scale; the choice of time period to be examined is discussed at the end of this section.

Environmental scientists and technologists

It will be relatively easy for a large organization, especially one with its own scientists, to keep in touch with advances in understanding of environmental processes, by the usual means of communication between scientists: scientific journals, conferences, etc. Some industries will be supplied with information by their trade associations or research organizations, and some will seek advice from external advisors.

Some organizations — and they need not be large — will themselves be shaping the technologies of the future. Others will obtain information from their suppliers, their regulators, their counterparts overseas, their own in-house trials, etc.

Immediate neighbours

The contribution of neighbours to the future scenario might be assessed along the following lines:

- Are the neighbours concerned?
- What are they concerned about?
- Are their concerns justified?
- Have their concerns been addressed?

- Are the neighbours likely to enlist support from the local authority, a pressure group, the local press, their Member of Parliament?
- If they do, what might be the outcome?

Customers

The contribution of customers to the scenario might be assessed along the following lines:

- What have our customers already asked of us?
- What are the customers, or future customers, learning about?
- What pressures are our competitors under from *their* customers?
- If the customer is not the consumer or end-user, can we foresee what demands the consumer might make?
- How could we improve environmental performance to attract customers from our competitors?

Investors

The contribution of investors to the scenario might be assessed along the following lines:

- What signals are the shareholders giving about their concerns?
- If our shareholders aren't giving any, what about our competitors' shareholders? (Note that shareholder initiatives have put environmental proposals to the vote at the AGMs of over 40 US companies.[14])
- Is our bank asking about environmental performance as a condition of funding?
- What questions are *other* banks asking, if not ours?
- If we were asked such questions, as a condition of funding, how would we fare?
- What insurance would we like against environmental liabilities?
- Are we likely to be granted it?
- If not, what measures could we take to change this?

Legislators

In this respect the activity of developing the scenario begins to overlap with the task of keeping abreast of legislative and regulatory requirements (see Section 7.10), which may or may not be fully established in the organization which is just embarking on setting up its Environmental Management System.

If the scenario is being developed as part of the review (see Section 7.16) of an existing EMS, the register of legislative and regulatory requirements required by BS 7750 will of course already exist and may well include legislation known to be coming into effect soon. It will make sense for many organizations to attempt to follow future developments in legislation as part of the activities described in Section 7.10. For an organization which has only just conducted its initial review, however, information about future legislation and regulations can be sought from such sources as:

- Specialist publications
- Trade associations
- Government white papers
- Reports of Select Committees and other bodies reporting to Government
- Government's responses to the reports of Select Committees
- External advisors

7.4.5 How far to look?

One last question remains to be answered, which is 'For what time period should the scenario be conducted?' This can only be left to the judgement of the individuals developing the scenario, and will be determined at least partly by business considerations such as the lifetime of existing plant and the lead time for developing new products or services. As far as possible, environmental scenario development should cover a time-scale commensurate with that used for business development strategy. The individuals responsible for developing the scenario must judge whether their existing sources of information are adequate, or new ones should be sought; and they must judge their reliability. The dangers of trying to look too far ahead are illustrated by the examples given above under 'Changes in technology' and 'Improved understanding of environmental science' (page 118), and also in Chapter 2. The only certainty in these respects is that the future will hold surprises.

Some aspects of scenario development require judgements where independence and impartiality are beneficial; a real example can be given. Late in 1991, the authors took part in a briefing to some representatives of a company whose products included aerosol cans of household products. Our briefing included the suggestion that, in the face of growing concern about emissions of volatile organic compounds (VOCs), environmental pressure groups might try to encourage consumers to avoid buying aerosols containing VOC propellants. This suggestion was dismissed by a member of the audience, yet just three months later (in early 1992) it was reported[15] that consumer groups in Germany had launched just such a campaign.

Some advice can be given on realistic time-scales for anticipating future legislation. So much legislation designed to protect the environment now derives from the EU, that the time between its initial proposal and its entering into force in the UK typically takes several years. Thus the next, say, three years can be expected to hold few major surprises; it would be wise, and not unrealistic, to try to look further ahead. At the time of writing (1995) some emission standards brought into being under the 1990 Environmental Protection Act are not due to be enforced until 1999;[16] likewise proposals for some EU legislation now being discussed are not expected to affect some industries directly until 10 years after the proposed Directive comes into force.

7.5 Establishing a Policy

7.5.1 The proliferation of environmental policy statements and their purpose

Many organizations responded to the upsurge in environmental concern in the late 1980s by producing environmental policy statements. This trend was encouraged by The Royal Commission on Environmental Pollution which published its 12th report in 1988, stating:

> '... companies have established policies specifically designed to reduce or curtail the impacts which their operations have on the environment. We wish to encourage the preparation of such environmentally sensitive policies .... We consider that all industrial enterprises should have a written environmental policy and that this should be well publicised.'[17]

More recent encouragement of the production of corporate environmental policy statements has come from the CBI (Confederation of British Industry) which advises that:

> 'Any company aiming to bring about positive environmental improvements should start by establishing a realistic policy to minimise the environmental impacts of its operations and an effective management system for achieving that policy.'[18]

The importance of a management system in conjunction with the policy is thus clearly recognized by the CBI, and the establishment of such a system will be discussed in detail in later sections.

Some of the earliest environmental policy statements were mere statements of intent to obey the law (of which more will be said later) but most now make more far-reaching commitments. The value of such statements, in isolation, can be judged from the results of some research conducted by Dewe Rogerson Limited.[19] In 1992 they questioned a large number of city fund managers, analysts and financial journalists. Only about half the fund managers and analysts, and two-thirds of the financial journalists, believed that an established environmental policy is a sign of a company with a sound long-term environmental strategy. The implication is that while many of those questioned have realized that an environmental policy is important, they also realize that it alone is no guarantee of sound environmental management.

The purpose of having an environmental policy statement is two-fold:

1 It provides a policy definition for those within the company, i.e. it tells them what is their common purpose with regard to environmental matters.
2 It provides a definition of principles, priorities and intentions to those outside the company.

In either respect it defines the organization's 'ethos', referred to in Section 7.4. Of course, the majority of policy statements are intended for distribution to the public, and our own experience shows that a growing number of organizations are being asked (usually by customers) for such statements. The rest of this section will be concerned with the construction of sound and meaningful policy statements which both provide a clear focus for the organization itself, and give interested parties useful information about its principles and intentions with respect to environmental issues.

7.5.2 The contents of environmental policy statements

Scope statement

It is clearly important that the statement makes its scope clear to the reader, in terms (for example) of the parts of an organization which it covers; indeed, this is a requirement of BS 7750 and of EMA. Thus, for example, it may need to indicate that it covers only a particular site or area of operations, or that it includes all corporate operations, including those of wholly owned subsidiaries. BS 7750 and EMA also require that the policy statement of an entity within a larger company or group should have the endorsement of its parent organization.

Intent to comply with legislation: why state this?

As expressed above, some early environmental policies were little more than statements of an intention to obey applicable environmental legislation and regulations, and many more recent policies still include this, though usually with additional commitments. It is surprising that environmental legislation, rather than any other type, is singled out in this way; companies do not, for example, normally issue statements saying they intend to comply with financial or employment law. Moreover, many areas of environmental impacts are unregulated, but provide organizations with numerous opportunities to set and achieve objectives (and, often, reduce costs); energy efficiency and minimization of resource consumption are obvious examples.

Bald statements of intention to comply with the law suggest that this might be regarded as optional, or a novelty, and we do not recommend that they be included as such in policy statements. We are not implying that a simple commitment to legal compliance alone is other than an honourable approach, albeit one which may preclude compliance with BS 7750 and EMA (unless the company's activities fall under Part A of the Prescribed Processes and Substances Regulations made under the Environmental Protection Act 1990, in which case the changing nature of BATNEEC could satisfy the requirement for continual improvement). Rather, we are suggesting that organizations taking that approach should consider carefully whether or not it is necessary and appropriate to issue an environmental policy statement simply to say so.

In any event, a commitment to legal compliance may be needed in the policy statement, not least, for some companies, because the EMA scheme requires participants to make one! The best approach then is to make such a statement within the context of a wider and/or deeper commitment, for example, by combining it with a pledge to exceed minimum legal requirements where it is practicable to do so.

Another opportunity to refer to legislation and regulations arises when an organization has operations in several countries, whose environmental legislation differs in stringency. It is increasingly common for policies to commit multinational companies to work uniformly, in *all* their countries of operation, to the legal standards of the most stringent, some examples being:

> 'Bayer's subsidiaries throughout the world are obliged to apply the same standards of environmental protection and safety as Bayer AG.'

> 'ICI will require all its new plants to be built to standards that will meet the regulations it can reasonably anticipate in the most environmentally demanding country in which it operates that process. This will normally require the use of the best environmental practice within the industry.'

Again, we are not suggesting that operation to the most stringent national standard is necessarily and always the only honourable option for a multinational to take, although these and many other such companies have chosen it. Complex moral and ethical (as well as business) considerations are involved, raising, for example, questions of rights of national self-determination, and balances of benefit to employees and the wider environment.

This one example also illustrates very clearly the more general point that environmental policy statements, though they may appear obvious and even facile to the casual reader, do enshrine the environmental ethos of the organization and therefore require the most careful consideration in their development, or revision.

How much detail?

Ideally, a policy statement should be brief, such that it can be contained in just one or two pages, or in a small pamphlet. This makes for easy dissemination to the public, and also increases the likelihood of the statement being read, and understood. It is important that the policy statement be meaningful to the layperson, so technical or specialized language should be avoided.

Refer to objectives

Given that an intention simply to obey the law is insufficient to justify a policy statement, the organization must necessarily provide indications of what more is to be achieved; for example, how much better than the legal minimum is the environmental performance to be, and what is to be done regarding matters that are unregulated. Statements of exactly how much is to be achieved, and by when, are called objectives (see Section 7.11), and BS 7750 and EMA require that such objectives (quantified wherever practicable) be made publicly available.

This is to be recommended in any event, even if an organization is not seeking registration under either scheme, because policy statements tend inevitably to be broad statements of principles and intent, the credibility of which needs to be underpinned by more detailed commitments. Making such commitments public enables interested parties to compare the practical intentions of different organizations, and thus provides a safeguard against policy statements being used to disguise a lack of serious effort to secure good performance and improvement.

It may be possible to include the objectives in the policy statement itself, an example being provided by ICI:

'ICI will reduce wastes by 50 per cent by 1995. It will pay special attention to those which are hazardous.'

More commonly, however, quantified objectives are not included in policy statements, possibly often for brevity and readability; although the ICI example above is both brief and readable.

Typically, the policy will contain broader statements of principle and intent, such as the following:

'The Glaxo Group of companies is firmly committed to the protection of the environment. It is the policy of the Group that environmental regulations laid down by governments and public authorities are treated as minimum standards, to be improved upon wherever practicable.'

'Where Mobil becomes aware of a hazard, representing a risk not covered by existing laws or regulations, Mobil, where appropriate, will develop its own environmental standards and practices to provide for adequate protection of public health and the environment.'

SmithKline Beecham: 'Facilities will be designed, constructed, operated and maintained to achieve the goals and mandates of both the appropriate laws and regulations in this area and Corporate Environmental Standards.'

Although these policy statements do not define the precise standards to be adopted, it is clear that each of the companies concerned intends to go beyond statutory minimum requirements. Publicly available objectives would, however, be beneficial in supplementing such policy statements; as noted above, they are a requirement of BS 7750, which also demands that the policy statement make clear to its readers how those objectives may be obtained.

The following are two examples of environmental commitments being made within clearly stated constraints:

The Shanks & McEwan Group PLC aims to '. . . conserve resources by maximizing the recovery of energy and materials from waste when economically viable.'

SmithKline Beecham will '. . . endeavour to design the packaging of its products so as to protect its customers while minimizing the resources required and maximizing the ability of the packaging to be recycled.'

Although care needs to be taken not to vitiate commitments by needless or thoughtless qualification, it will obviously be necessary on many issues to set bounds on pledges, for sound and valid reasons. Careful use of language can help to make clear the reasoning behind the qualification, just as its careless use can give a false impression of equivocation or evasion.

Externally driven commitments

Those developing or revising policy statements should give detailed considera-tion to any commitments which the organization may have made by virtue of its membership of (for example) a trade association or stated commitment to principles published by some other industry environmental grouping. Examples include the Responsible Care Programme of the Chemical Industries Association (CIA), the Environmental Forum of the Confederation of British Industry (CBI), the Valdez Principles, and the Business Charter for Sustainable Development published by the International Chamber of Commerce (ICC).

Relevance

Many environmental policies are written in such general terms that they could be adopted by almost any company or organization. There can be benefit, however, if policy statements are clearly tailored to the activities in which the organization is involved, because this illustrates that the organization has given careful thought to the environmental issues which it needs to address, and that it intends to address the important ones. Indeed, BS 7750 specifically requires that the policy statement be relevant to the organization's activities, products and services, and their effects on the environment.

Thus, for example, a retail organization may choose to describe its policy on purchasing and the way it works with its suppliers. A manufacturer of household cleaning materials may wish to emphasize how it selects the substances used in its formulations.

For an organization in the very early stages of developing an EMS, it may be that the most important issues have not yet been identified (they will not always be as seemingly obvious as the examples given, and the apparently obvious ones may well turn out not to be the most important ones). Yet a policy may still be required; for in a sense one needs a policy (as implicitly acknowledged by the CBI advice quoted above) to address environmental management before embarking on more detailed work. In this case a generalized policy statement may be all that can be produced, but of course this, like all policy statements, should be re-examined for continuing suitability as part of the management review (see Section 7.16) of the EMS, or, ideally, even earlier following the environmental effects assessment (see Section 7.8). Examples of elements of policy statements which are clearly relevant to the activities of the organizations concerned are:

> The Shanks & McEwan Group plc aims to '... improve the landscape by healing the scars left by former mineral workings and industrial dereliction using waste materials creatively to restore the land'.

> '... BT will ... protect visual amenity by the careful siting of buildings, structures and deployment of operational plant in the local environment and respect wild life habitats ...'

> 'WRc's business is directed towards improvement in the wider environment, and this work is carried out to the highest professional standards.'

This last example is an acknowledgement that potentially the greatest environmental impacts of WRc, a company engaged in environmental research and consultancy, are through the quality of the advice it gives to its clients.

Continual improvement

Organizations wishing to seek certification to BS 7750 will need to include, in their policy statements, a commitment to continual improvement of environmental performance. The extent of this is for the individual organization to decide, and it need not be quantified in the policy itself, but it should be quantified in the objectives, where practicable. The publication of the chosen areas, and of the extent of improvement, is important to give credibility to the commitment to improvement. Examples of some commitments to continual improvement are given below:

> 'BT is committed to minimizing the impact of its operations on the environment by means of a programme of continuous improvement.'

('Continual' was preferred to 'continuous' in BS 7750 because it more closely connotes the reality that improvement will often be stepwise over short time periods, rather than truly continuous, but the distinction is a minor one.)

> SmithKline Beecham will '... strive continually to improve the efficiency of its operations so as to minimize both the use of materials and the generation of waste'.

(It should be noted, however, that this latter commitment, being only to '*strive* continually', might be thought not to meet the requirement of BS 7750 exactly: see also the comments on precise wording below.)

Commitment from the top

Obviously for the policy to have any chance of being implemented it must have the backing of the most senior management of the organization. One way of making this commitment visible is by associating the name of one of the organization's directors with the policy, e.g. by having it clearly signed by the chairman and/or managing director.

Dissemination of the policy

The policy statement will usually be made public; but it is equally important that the policy be not merely known of, but understood, throughout the organization, and that every relevant individual should understand his or her role in enabling its effective implementation. This will be discussed further in Section 7.7 on education and training.

Language

Finally, a brief policy statement necessarily contains few words, so they should be chosen with care. As was noted earlier in respect of qualifying statements, the choice of language can carry important messages to the reader, as well as fundamental differences of meaning. Consider, for example, the following variations on the same general concept of reducing impacts:

- 'The organization will aim to reduce ...'
- 'The organization will endeavour to reduce ...'
- 'The organization will strive to reduce ...'

- 'The organization is committed to reducing ...'
- 'The organization will reduce ...'.

They show a gradation of commitment; the first two sound rather weak, whereas the last could not be more determined. The interested party may perceive, rightly or wrongly, a great deal from the language used. The policy should not impress by committing the organization to achieve the impossible; conversely, it provides an opportunity to advertise genuine initiatives.

7.5.3 Compliance of environmental policy statements with BS 7750 requirements

We recently examined environmental policy statements produced by 10 (mostly large) UK and multinational companies in relation to some of the requirements of BS 7750: 1994; the results are given in Table 7.3. This shows that they commonly fail to address the requirements in respect of:

1 A commitment to make objectives publicly available.
2 Indicating where such objectives may be obtained.

The second of these requirements was introduced in the 1994 revision, but the first was included in the original BS 7750: 1992.

Some of the companies involved do in fact make their objectives public, but do not give the relevant information in the policy statement, so the failure was sometimes a technical one. However, because policy statements require top management approval, they cannot always be changed quickly, even if amendments are minor. It follows that companies with existing statements intending to seek BS 7750 or EMA registration should re-examine them at an early stage, and not assume that they will necessarily meet the requirements.

Table 7.3 Compliance of policies with BS 7750

Requirement	Policy									
	A	B	C	D	E	F	G	H	I	J
Clear relevance to activities	✔	✔	✔	✘	✔	✔	✔	✔	✔	✘
Commits to continual improvement	✔	✔	✔	✔	✘	✔	✘	✔	✔	✘
Commits to publishing objectives	✘	✘	○	✘	○	✔	✘	○	○	✘
States where they will be available	✘	✘	○	✘	○	✘	○	○	○	✘

Key: ✔ clear and explicit, ○ implicit, ✘ not included.

7.5.4 Example of an environmental policy statement

As has been remarked earlier, each organization should develop its own statement to meet its own particular situation, so any example can do no more than give a 'flavour' of the genre. However, the example in Figure 7.3 of a policy statement which might be formulated by a company manufacturing consumer

---

$\mathcal{MM}$ **Mythological Manufacturing Ltd**

Enviromental Policy Statement

Mythological Manufacturing Ltd manufactures a wide range of consumer durables at a number of sites in the United Kingdom. This policy statement applies to all our UK operations and sites, and is endorsed by our parent company, Mythological Industries plc.

We are committed to conducting our activities with due regard for environmental protection, and to improve continually our environmental performance.

Recognizing our particular responsibilities as makers of durable goods widely used in the home, we will continually seek new ways to reduce the environmental effects of our products while in use and at the end of their useful lives, as well as in manufacture.

In particular, we will:

* Promote energy efficiency and recycling by good product design.
* Provide appropriate environmental information to users of our products.
* Provide high standards of servicing, to maintain the efficiency of our products in use.
* Meet or, wherever practicable, exceed the requirements of all relevant legislation and regulations, and set our own demanding standards where none exist.
* Reduce, wherever practicable, emissions and wastes from manufacturing operations.
* Work with our suppliers to improve environmental performance.
* Provide appropriate environmental training to our staff, and encourage them to apply good environmental practice, both at work and at home.

Sound environmental management principles and practices will be applied to meet these commitments, and to achieve demanding and publicly available environmental performance objectives. We will set those objectives annually; wherever practicable, they will be quantitative, and we will monitor our progress towards meeting them.

Our Annual Reports will contain an environmental performance review, to provide a true and fair picture of that progress, and of our wider environmental performance.

Copies of our environmental objectives and performance reviews may be obtained by writing to: The Environmental Manager, Mythological Manufacturing Ltd, Styxside House, The First Circle, Hades, HE11 4AL, who would also welcome any observations on the environmental aspects of our activities.

Lou Cifer   *I.M.A.de Ville*

Chairman   Chief Executive

Mythological Manufacturing Ltd

1 March 1993

Figure 7.3 Example of an environmental policy statement

durables may prove of interest to those about to embark on the task for their own company. They would also be well advised to obtain, and read carefully, a cross-section of the many company policy statements which are already publicly available.

7.6 Organizing and Assigning Responsibilities

7.6.1 Introduction

The success of an EMS depends ultimately on the commitment of top management to providing adequate resources, and to creating an organization and culture in which people can work effectively to promote and achieve good environmental performance.

Everybody in an organization can contribute something to the achievement of environmental excellence, but to do so they need leadership and motivation, within an overall structure which ensures that environmentally critical activities are soundly managed and co-ordinated. The EMS cannot function without the clear identification of roles and responsibilities, and allocation of necessary authorities and resources.

Each organization has its own unique structure, management system and corporate culture; effective environmental management must operate with, rather than against, the grain of existing arrangements and practices. Thus, each organization must establish an appropriate EMS structure of its own, and neither this book nor any EMS standard can prescribe the detailed approach which it should adopt. However, certain fundamental principles can be identified, applicable to all types of organization, which are essential to EMS effectiveness.

7.6.2 Organizing: the core environmental management team

Director responsible for environmental matters

Though it is not a requirement of BS 7750 or the EMA scheme, many organizations choose to assign responsibility for oversight of environmental matters to a board member (or other senior manager, if the organization is not controlled by a board of directors). This has the benefit that an identified individual has the specific task of ensuring that the environment receives appropriate attention within the highest management circle. He or she is able to raise environmental issues at an early stage of planning, to facilitate the handling of urgent matters with necessary dispatch, and to provide a known channel of communication on environmental matters between the wider organization and the board.

While the practice has advantages, it should not — in fact or appearance — detract from the involvement in environmental matters of the chairman, managing director or chief executive, and other directors as appropriate.

Top management

The most senior management of the organization (typically the board of directors) have general responsibilitites for developing, reviewing, and maintaining conditions conducive to complying with, the environmental policy. They have overall responsibility for ensuring that appropriate resources are allocated for the effective operation of the EMS and, in particular, for:

- Facilities, plant and equipment necessary to meet, and to verify compliance with, legislative and regulatory requirements, policy commitments and objectives.
- Personnel, equipment and organizational infrastructure to respond to, and mitigate the effects of, emergencies.
- The time of management, specialists and other staff for EMS audits and reviews.
- Sound management of environmental aspects of new developments.

It should be borne in mind that 'fine words butter no parsnips': staff and other interested parties will see a readiness to allocate necessary and justified resources for environmental matters as indicative of true corporate commitment to environmental policy and objectives.

Management representative

The management representative is charged with:

- Overseeing EMS development and implementation.
- *Co-ordinating* environmental management across the organization.
- Monitoring environmental developments in general.
- Ensuring that the EMS is maintained and updated accordingly.

A key element in this list is the concept of *co-ordination*; the role of the management representative is to work in conjunction with managers and specialists and not to usurp the functions of, act as a substitute for, or assume the responsibilities of, line managers in respect of environmental matters. The person appointed should:

- Provide a personal focus for, and be a champion of, the EMS.
- Facilitate the collation and distribution of information.
- Provide a channel of communication on general environmental matters.
- Help ensure consistency of approach and avoid duplication of effort.
- Act as the primary EMS guide, coach and mentor.

To fulfil these roles effectively and efficiently, the management representative needs to be a senior manager or specialist sitting on, or with ready and direct access to, the board or other top management group, and to be seen to have their backing and support. He or she should have no significant conflict of interest from other responsibilities; it will be possible in many cases for the representative to undertake combined health and safety *and* environmental co-ordination roles, but there is no necessity to arrange matters in this way.

The representative will need to have, or be able quickly to acquire, a good understanding of all the activities of the organization, and of the systems approach to environmental management. In large organizations, and in those with many complex and significant environmental effects, it may be considered desirable or essential to appoint a scientist or technologist with a substantial background in environmental matters, but in many organizations broad familiarity with, and interest in, such matters will be sufficient.

For a role involving co-ordination rather than direct control, and requiring close contact with a potentially wide range of managers, specialists and other staff, good interpersonal skills are likely to be at least as important as technical ones: the representative will need to be an effective communicator, a diplomatic but resourceful co-ordinator, and an inspiring coach and mentor.

Environmental management team

Many organizations will wish to establish a team of some kind to co-ordinate the development of the EMS, and, possibly, to steer its subsequent implementation and maintenance. Such an approach can bring numerous benefits; for example, by providing a means to share the work, to help gain broader management commitment, and to facilitate access to specialist expertise. The team could be — but does not have to be — chaired by the top manager or director responsible for environmental matters, thus ensuring close contact between the board and the EMS itself.

Adoption of a team approach is in no way inconsistent with the appointment of a management representative: he or she could, for example, chair the group, or act as its 'technical secretary'. Of course, whatever arrangement is adopted, effective communication between the representative and the team is essential.

As with the role of the management representative, a combined health and safety and environmental management team could be employed. Care should be taken, however, to avoid making the team too large, particularly in the EMS development phase.

7.6.3 Line management responsibilities

While the management representative will co-ordinate environmental management activities, primary and direct responsibility for EMS implementation lies with the line managers of the relevant functional units, which may include:

- Corporate planning

- Marketing
- Research and development
- Product and process design
- Operations
- Production
- Distribution
- Sales
- Finance
- Site engineering services
- Personnel
- Estates

Line managers should be responsible for developing, implementing and maintaining the EMS elements relevant to the activities of their groups. Typically, they will need to be involved in such matters as:

- Developing and documenting local EMS organization.
- Identifying environment-critical activities and documenting relevant responsibilities.
- Developing and maintaining effective, two-way communication.
- Identifying and satisfying training needs.
- Documenting procedures and work instructions.
- Helping to set objectives and targets.
- Developing and managing improvement programmes.
- Devising and implementing monitoring systems.
- Managing corrective action.

They may also be involved in other activities, which are likely, however, to be performed on a broader basis than the individual functional unit, for example:

- Identifying and evaluating environmental effects.
- Recording relevant legislative and regulatory requirements.

Finally, depending on the nature and size of the organization, and the manner in which it organizes EMS auditing, they may participate in audits of areas outside their responsibility. (They may also organize and/or participate in self-audits of their own areas: see Section 7.15.)

In addition to being responsible for the control of their local direct environmental effects, individual managers will need to establish the means to control indirect effects arising from the work of their units, which may often be more important than the direct ones. Examples include:

- A design department addressing effects arising throughout the product life cycle.
- An R&D department doing the same, albeit at a broader level.

- A finance department addressing the need for accounting systems to assign environmental costs to those units which incur them (e.g. waste disposal).
- All departments addressing the effects of contractors operating under their control, unless central, corporate control systems are in place for contracted activities.

Some departments and individuals, by virtue of their particular responsibilities, may be involved on a corporate basis with the implementation of specific elements of the EMS itself, for example:

- The personnel department, in concert with line managers, developing and implementing environmental communication and training programmes, and keeping training records.
- The legal department maintaining the register of legislative and regulatory requirements.
- The corporate audit department organizing and implementing the EMS auditing programme.
- The purchasing department, in respect of environmental aspects of suppliers and contracted-out activities.
- An environmental specialist giving advice to line managers on specific problems.
- The board maintaining the environmental policy and reviewing the EMS.

7.6.4 Defining, documenting and communicating key responsibilities

Who are key personnel?

BS 7750 refers (in clause 4.3.1) to '. . . key personnel who manage, perform and verify work affecting the environment . . .', and goes on to give a list of specific characteristics, namely that such people:

- Provide resources and staff.
- Initiate action to secure policy compliance.
- Identify and record problems.
- Initiate, recommend or provide solutions.
- Verify that solutions are implemented.
- Exert control until problems are corrected.
- Act in emergencies.

However, all human activities 'affect the environment' to some degree, so it is necessary to qualify this requirement in some way. It is logical to consider the phrase 'affecting the environment' in terms of the environmental effects register, which lists 'significant' effects (see Section 7.8). Thus, key personnel can be considered as those managers and others who address, in terms of the above list of characteristics, 'environment-critical' activities, where the latter include all activities which bring about, or could bring about if control was lost, significant environmental effects, or a breach of environmental policy.

In assessing who are the key people during EMS development, it is therefore prudent not only to consider what individuals' environmental responsibilities are known or believed to be, but also to ask them directly: they may carry out environmentally critical tasks which are not formally recorded within existing systems.

In the EMS 'cycle' of BS 7750, organizing and identifying responsibilities precedes effects assessment. Thus if key personnel are those managing and controlling environment-critical activities which relate to significant effects, should not effects evaluation precede assignment of responsibilities? Two points may be made in response:

1   In developing an EMS, it is recommended that a Preparatory Review be undertaken, which involves an evaluation of effects as a precursor to setting up the EMS structure.
2   The cycle chronology is not rigid; in an established EMS, if a new significant effect is identified, the organization step is revisited and new responsibilities assigned if necessary.

Organizational structure and allocation of responsibilities

This should reflect the role and responsibility of line management in implementing and maintaining relevant aspects of the EMS, and will need to ensure that the organization:

● Identifies those responsible for key, environment-critical activities, eliminating gaps and overlaps.
● Defines their responsibilities in respect of such activities.
● Provides them with the necessary authority and resources.
● Describes their interrelations with other key EMS personnel.
● Documents, and communicates as necessary, the above information.

Meeting the first four of these requirements is illustrated in Table 7.4. Documentation and communication of the required information is done through the Environmental Management manual, job descriptions, procedures and work instructions (see Section 7.13). Organizational diagrams can of course be helpful in summarizing responsibilities and identifying reporting chains and liaison activities, and it is convenient to refer to positions rather than to individuals, to avoid the need to change documentation with every staff change.

Table 7.4   Definition, documentation and communication of key responsibilities

Identifying those responsible for key activities:

The Waste Disposal Supervisor (WDS) is responsible for solid waste storage and disposal.

Defining their responsibilities for such activities:

The WDS is responsible, in accordance with authorized procedures and work instructions, for maintaining the waste storage area, supervising its staff, receiving waste consignments from production units, storing wastes in designated areas according to their classifications, arranging collection by approved waste disposal contractors, and maintaining specified records of all waste transfers to and from the waste storage area.

Providing necessary authority and resources:

The WDS is authorized to reject consignments if they are not labelled or packaged in accordance with authorized procedures, or if he/she considers them otherwise unsafe to handle or store. Provision of adequate resources to maintain the waste storage area is the responsibility of the Site Services Manager (SSM), acting in consultation with the WDS.

Describing interrelations with other key staff:

The WDS reports to the SSM, receives quarterly listings of authorized waste disposal contractors from the Contracts Manager, and sends consignment rejection notes to the SSM and the relevant Production Unit Manager.

7.7 Undertaking Education and Training

7.7.1 Introduction

An EMS provides a framework within which environmental issues can be handled effectively, but the tasks required ultimately devolve upon people at all levels of the organization. To carry out their environmental management duties efficiently they need to be equipped with the necessary skills, understanding and experience, and may require training of various kinds. EMS models therefore lay considerable emphasis upon both training and internal communication.

The fundamental approach to specific training to ensure the competencies of key, environmentally critical tasks is shown in Figure 7.4; in addition, general awareness training is likely to be required for all levels of staff.

7.7.2 Competencies of personnel

The company should maintain procedures for identifying the competencies required to conduct environmentally critical tasks, and for ensuring that personnel selection ensures that those assigned to undertake them have such competencies: by virtue of their education, training and/or experience. These procedures should apply to initial recruitment and to the selection of staff to carry out new activities, or use new technologies; they should also ensure that the continuing competence of relevant staff to perform critical tasks is assessed

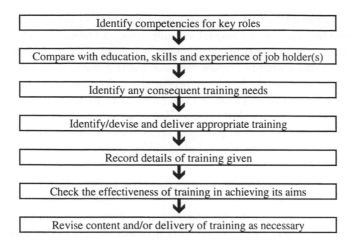

Figure 7.4 Addressing competencies and training needs for key staff performing environmentally critical tasks

at appropriate intervals. Environmentally critical roles and tasks should be included in job descriptions, and performance appraisals should assess:

- Performance of environmentally critical tasks against agreed objectives.
- Regular updating of environmentally relevant job targets.
- Needs for personal development and training for changing activities and technologies.

7.7.3 Training

The company should maintain procedures for identifying training needs, and for providing appropriate training—both job-specific and general environmental—for all personnel. Training may be provided through formal courses and/or through structured development in the work-place, and particular attention should be paid to both induction and refresher courses. The extent and nature of training should be sufficient to ensure achievement of the company's policy and objectives, and should meet or exceed that required by legislation and regulations. Appropriate records of training should be maintained, and systems developed to monitor the effectiveness of programmes and introduce improvements where necessary (see below).

There are, of course, many different types of environmental management and technical training available, from a wide range of providers. General or tailored courses dealing specifically with environmental management systems are now commonly advertised by educational establishments, specialized training providers and environmental consultancies. Additionally, 'DIY' course packs are also becoming available, allowing in-house trainers to provide tailored courses without having to prepare the basic training materials themselves. One such series of packages has been prepared by the Institution of Chemical Engineers. This includes a slide and computer-based package on environmental mangement systems[20] (with the production of which one of us (D.T.E.H.) was closely involved), as well as packages on environmental awareness, environmental legislation and specific technical subjects.

Job-specific training

This training will need to be undertaken as necessary to ensure that any identified competency gaps are filled. It may include training to ensure that:

- Operators and specialists have the necessary skills and knowledge to undertake particular technical tasks.
- Managers understand the EMS, have the necessary knowledge to play their part in it, and appreciate the criteria by which its effectiveness will be judged.
- Managers and other staff have the skills and knowledge necessary to undertake specialized EMS-related tasks, including:
  - the role of the management representative under BS 7750, EMA and ISO/CD 14001;
  - effects evaluation;
  - audits;
  - management reviews.
- New staff, and existing staff assigned to new tasks, equipment and procedures, have the necessary understanding to perform their intended roles effectively.

In contemplating who in the organization needs training, consideration should be given to the roles played by individual managers and specialists in the implementation of the EMS, and by operators in the conduct of environmentally critical activities. It should also be noted that interpersonal, as well as technical, skills may be needed for some jobs: the example of the management representative has already been remarked in this respect — and training programmes should be designed or selected accordingly.

General training and awareness programmes

These are needed to ensure that all staff at all levels are aware of:

- Importance of compliance with the environmental policy and objectives, and their roles and responsibilities in achieving it.

- Environmental risks and hazards of their work activities, and the controls and mitigation measures that have been established.
- Potential consequences of departure from agreed operating procedures.
- The potential environmental benefits of improved performance.
- Mechanisms for suggesting, to management, improvements in the procedures which they and others operate.

7.7.4 Training records

A full record of all environmentally related training, internal and external, should be maintained for each individual, so that the skill base available, and any gaps in training, can be readily identified. Responsibility for record maintenance should be defined, and records should cover:

- Trainee's name and location
- Date and duration of each training course
- Scope and nature of the training
- Provider(s) of the course
- Trainee feedback
- Results of subsequent checks of training effectiveness

7.7.5 Internal communications

Special consideration should be given to internal communications, so that the staff feel a sense of 'ownership' of, and personal responsibility for, the EMS. This requires them to have a good understanding of the system and its benefits, and an understanding of their potential contribution to its success. Effective internal communication should be two-way, and may be achieved by such measures as:

- Active encouragement of employees' suggestions through:
  - newsletters;
  - suggestion boxes;
  - competitions.
- Encouragement of staff participation in internal and external environmental initiatives.
- Awareness programmes and campaigns directed towards specific environmental issues.
- Clear descriptions of staff roles in meeting company goals.
- Progress reports on corporate and local achievements.

Recognition of good environmental performance — for example, when objectives and targets are achieved — is also very important for motivating staff towards a proper regard for environmental concerns and for the success of the EMS.

Effective communication requires careful consideration of the message to be transmitted — or the information to be sought — and to the most appropriate medium for doing so. The need to communicate in an appropriate language and style needs to be borne constantly in mind, particularly when transmitting technical information to non-specialists. This is especially important in relation to emergencies, when clarity of arrangements is essential. Internal communication and its importance is further discussed in Section 7.9.

7.7.6 Contractors

Many organizations rely on contractors to perform a number of activities (e.g. plant construction and maintenance). Unless specific steps are taken, the actual and potential environmental effects of these activities may be overlooked, or considered outside of the control of the organization. Indeed, environmental incidents have not infrequently resulted from contractor activities, not least because contractors' staff are inherently less likely to be familiar with site-specific hazards than are the company's own employees.

For these reasons it is particularly important to ensure that the EMS of a company addresses the activities of its contractors and subcontractors. BS 7750 requires that an implementing organization should maintain procedures to ensure that its contractors are made aware of (subclause 4.3.5) and comply with (subclause 4.8.2) relevant EMS requirements and provisions, and gives greater prominence to (but does not fundamentally alter) this requirement in its 1994 revision.

The key to successful environmental management of contracted activities is effective *communication* with the contracting company, and particular attention needs to be paid to such matters as:

- Consideration of environmental factors (e.g. EMS implementation, environmental training and environmental performance) when selecting contractors.
- Effective communication of relevant elements and requirements of the company's EMS.
- Agreement of the environmental performance criteria to be met by the contractor, and on methods of monitoring.
- Establishment of clear communication between company and contractor staff, at all levels, and for sharing relevant information which may affect the environmental performance of either party. (Suitable tools for ensuring continuing communication of environmental awareness to contractor's staff may include brochures, videos and meetings.)
- Use of Permit to Work systems and clear procedures for the management of change.

- Understanding of emergency plans, and of procedures for incident reporting and follow-up.
- Arrangements for providing continuing feedback and guidance to contractors, and for audit and review of their activities, if appropriate.

7.8 Evaluating the Environmental Effects of Corporate Activities, Products and Services

7.8.1 The purpose of effects evaluation

Identification and evaluation of environmental 'effects' (BS 7750, EMA) or 'impacts' (ISO/CD 14001), hereafter called 'evaluation of effects', forms part of both the Preparatory Review and the routine operation of an established EMS. In both situations, it is of fundamental importance in identifying and providing information on the organization's significant interactions with the environment. Such information is needed both for maintaining effective day-to-day management and control of environmental impacts, and for setting sound environmental objectives and targets.

BS 7750, EMA and ISO/CD 14001 provide generic EMS specifications, and do not specify detailed performance standards to be achieved. Indeed, for the diverse range of organizations to which these initiatives apply, it is simply not feasible for them to do so. None is a conventional environmental regulation, and all leave organizations to set their own performance objectives — based on an understanding of the effects of their activities upon the environment. Effects evaluation — which provides such an understanding — is therefore especially important in *objective-setting* systems such as BS 7750 and EMA, in which the scrutiny by interested parties of publicly available objectives (and, in the case of EMA, of outcomes) provides the basis of credibility.

7.8.2 The scope of evaluation

BS 7750 defines an environmental effect as 'Any direct or indirect impingement of the activities, products and services of the organization upon the environment, whether adverse or beneficial'. It requires that the organization identify and evaluate its effects, and list those it judges to be 'significant' in a Register. The scope of evaluation includes:

- Direct and indirect effects
- Past, current and planned activities, products and services
- Normal, abnormal and emergency situations

and covers the following types of effect:

- Controlled and uncontrolled emissions to atmosphere
- Controlled and uncontrolled discharges to water

- Solid and other wastes
- Contamination of land
- Use of land, water, fuels and energy, and other natural resources
- Noise, odour, dust, vibration and visual impact
- Effects on specific parts of the environment, including ecosystems

Indirect effects are effects that are realized through the agency of an intermediary (*The Concise Oxford Dictionary* defines direct as 'without an intermediary'). It should be noted that they are not inherently less important than direct effects, though their evaluation may present greater difficulties. The principal activities giving rise to indirect effects are:

- Product use and disposal
- Purchasing
- Development of specifications
- Contracting-out
- Investment
- Providing advice

Debate has also surrounded the extent to which BS 7750 requires consideration of the effects of past activities and products, and indirect effects arising from purchasing, contracting, and product use and disposal. With respect to the effects of past activities and products, the standard:

- Refers to consideration of *known or suspected* consequences.
- States that consequences of past activities should be considered, giving the example of liability for former products.
- Specifies no temporal limit, as some consequences, e.g. site contamination, could persist for long periods, and still be remediable. (Of course, evaluation makes sense only if action can still be taken; for example, consideration of product disposal makes sense only if significant numbers of it are still in existence.)

With respect to indirect effects arising from purchasing, from contracting, and from product use and disposal, BS 7750:

- States that the environmental probity of suppliers should be considered.
- Recognizes that it will not always be possible to compile a detailed register of suppliers, but states that it should often be possible to compare alternative suppliers in respect of their most important environmental effects.
- States that if a supplier is part of the same group of companies, it should demonstrate that it observes the policy requirements of the organization.
- Does not require detailed Life Cycle Assessment of products/services, unless to meet policy commitments, but requires effects from all phases of the life cycle to be considered, using available evidence.

- Requires that consideration be given to all those effects which the organization can control, and all those over which it could reasonably be expected to
have influence.

7.8.3 The evaluation process and the judgement of 'significance'

It is important that effort and resources are not dissipated in addressing trivial
effects, but directed towards truly important ones, which BS 7750 calls the
'significant effects'.

This concept of 'significance' has been much discussed, and it has been
frequently suggested that BS 7750 should give more specific guidance on the
meaning to be attached to it. However, this is simply not practicable in a
generic standard, which can only advise that subjective judgements will be
necessary, and that the evaluation system should be self-consistent. Specific
guidance, or even the results of such deliberations, may, however, be given in
Sector Application Guides, described in Section 7.1.

The remainder of this section discusses ways of determining significance.
Some of the fundamental issues to be taken into account include:

- The breadth of the evaluation, which means that a structured approach is
required.
- The fact that all activities have effects, so that a continuous process of effect
identification and evaluation is necessary. In other words, one cannot simply
list *all* effects and then evaluate their significance: some degree of evaluation
is necessary in the initial identification step.
- The identification and evaluation process involves a fundamental conflict
between on the one hand ensuring that important effects are not overlooked,
and on the other that most attention is paid to potentially significant effects.

In evaluating potential effects, BS 7750 requires that communications and
complaints from Interested Parties be considered. However, information will
also need to be gathered from a wide range of sources, such as:

- Government departments
- Regulatory agencies
- Trade associations
- Consultancies
- Research organizations
- Local residents
- Conservation bodies
- Environmental interest groups
- Environmental journals
- Specialist press

Table 7.5   Checklist to help identify environmental effects

Air	Water
Global warming	Oxygen demand
Ozone layer	Hydrocarbon spills
Acid emissions	Eutrophication
Ground level ozone	Hazardous substances
Hazardous gases/fumes	Hazardous organisms
Smoke	Acidification
Radioactivity/radiation	Thermal discharges
	Radioactivity
Land	Foaming, colour, litter
Hazardous waste	Taste
Radioactive waste	Water usage
Non-hazardous waste	Ecosystem disturbance
Site contamination	
Disturbance	*Nuisance*
Soil erosion	Visual
	Dust
Resource usage	Odour
Minerals/raw materials	Noise vibration
Energy	
Fuels	
Stock exploitation	

The detail in which the various effects are examined will depend on such factors as:

- The likely environmental significance of the effect in question.
- Any regulatory requirements relating to it.
- The extent of concern of interested parties.
- The nature and extent of existing information on the effect.

Figure 7.5 shows a conceptual matrix of effects versus stage of product or service life cycle (familiar from Life Cycle Assessment) which provides a possible structure for the *identification* of effects. An alternative approach is illustrated in Figure 7.6, based on a breakdown of the activities of an organization and based on material in The Electricity Association Guide.[21] Table 7.5 shows a high-level checklist to aid the development of such matrices. These can, of course, be expanded as necessary, e.g. 'hazardous substances' in water can be divided according to class of substance, or down to individual compounds.

It is not essential to use this approach, and in many cases it may be appropriate and convenient to look at resource consumption, emissions and waste arisings across an entire site or facility. However, care must be taken to ensure that such a site-based approach does not exclude examination, where appropriate, of indirect effects, for example, arising from product use and disposal.

	Stage of life cycle				
Effects	**Raw material (RM)**	**Production (P)**	**Distribution (D)**	**Use (U)**	**Disposal/ recycling (D/R)**
On air					
On water					
On land					
Resources					
Nuisances					

Figure 7.5 Conceptual matrix for effects identification: a possible approach

Factors to consider in evaluating the significance of individual effects include:

- Potential risks and consequences for the environment
- National and International environmental standards: actual and prospective
- Relevant market-based instruments: actual and prospective
- Industry sector Codes of Practice
- Interested parties' concerns, views and perceptions
- Contributions of others to the same effect
- Strength of scientific evidence for the effect
- Other effects of the organization

The practicalities and costs of reducing a given effect should *not* be included, as such factors could prejudice the evaluation process; they can validly be addressed when consideration is given to the setting of objectives (see Section 7.11).

With regard to the judgement of significance, effects which are subject to regulatory control are automatically 'significant'; even though the regulatory control prevents environmental damage, the effect it addresses is considered significant because a failure to comply with the regulatory requirement could lead to such damage. Thus, evaluation of regulated effects poses essentially no problem: the organization may simply accept that made by the regulator, unless its policy makes commitments which require a further evaluation to be made.

	Effects				
Activities	**On air**	**On water**	**On land**	**Resources**	**Nuisances**
Driving vehicles					
Vehicle maintenance					
Operating machinery					
Installing and maintaining switchgear and transformers					
Laying and maintaining underground cable					
Erecting and maintaining overhead cable					
Tree cutting					
Gardening and grounds maintenance					
Weed control					
Building operations and maintenance					
Painting					
Civil works					
Catering					
Office work					
Meter reading					
Billing customers					
Meeting customers					

Figure 7.6 Conceptual matrix for effects identification: an alternative approach

(Of course, the organization may decide that it wishes to anticipate likely changes in legislation, and for that reason also may conduct its own evaluation of a regulated effect.)

Evaluating effects which are not regulated, but which appear to be potentially significant, poses the real difficulty, not least because there is no universal metric for comparing widely differing effects (for example, the discharge of a hazardous substance to a watercourse with an increase in energy use, or with a loss of habitat). Generic EMS models, designed to have wide applicability, cannot provide detailed guidance on this matter although Sector Application Guides may provide some useful assistance.

Such evaluation will always be to a degree subjective, but can at least be made as consistent as possible by establishing and documenting a framework and rules, and using an informed group rather than a single individual (however expert in environmental matters he or she may be) for the final evaluation of significance. The use of a group allows a broader view to be taken, avoiding personal biases, and helps maintain consistency of judgements despite changes of staff and responsibilities. It is also important to recognize that an evaluation may lead not to an immediate assessment of significance, but rather to an interim objective to gather more data or information.

The question is often asked: 'Is quantification of effects necessary in the evaluation process?' Several points can be made in reply:

- It is wasteful of effort to seek detailed data if the effect is likely to be judged insignificant.
- Some quantification may, however, be needed to reach that judgement.
- Quantification will in any event usually be required for setting objectives.
- Quantification is likely to prove increasingly necessary as performance improves, such that decisions on the relative significance of residual effects become less easy to make.

A number of approaches are available for the detailed process of judging whether or not an effect is significant. In dealing with potential environmental hazards, extensions of the HAZOP and HAZAN approaches commonly applied in safety management may be used (see, for example, Kletz[22]), and several participants in the BS 7750 pilot programme employed a variant of the risk assessment techniques known as Failure Modes and Effects Analysis (FMEA): see Figure 7.7 and Table 7.6.

Of course, application of this approach does not obviate the need to decide what threshold C_f value to use to reflect 'significance'. This can be selected by having the evaluation group 'brainstorm' against a range of familiar effects for which C_f values have been assigned, to obtain a consensus regarding 'significance' from which the threshold C_f value can be derived.

A more fundamental problem is the limited applicability of the approach to such issues as resource consumption or contribution to a regional or global effect, e.g. global warming. In these cases, the value of F tends to a maximum (continuous effect) and that of L to unity (no control loss involved); thus, the

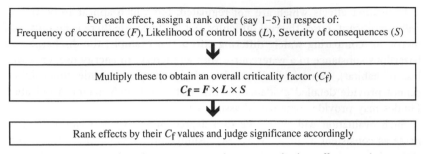

Figure 7.7 A simple risk assessment technique applied to effects evaluation (I)

Table 7.6 A simple risk assessment technique applied to effects evaluation (II)

Frequency of occurrence (F)
1 = very rare, e.g. infrequent production campaign, to
5 = continuous, e.g. a treated effluent discharge

Likelihood of control loss (L)
1 = extremely unlikely, e.g. complete failure of a robust process control element, to
5 = highly likely, e.g. a small spillage of widely used solvent

Severity of consequences (S)
1 = very limited, localized impact, e.g. local dust problem, to
5 = extensive and severe damage, e.g. toxic spillage to a large watercourse

judgement of significance hinges on the value assigned to Severity of Consequences (S).

Such issues require a different approach. One possibility is to make an assessment of the relative usage or contribution of the organization compared with that of others (an approach used by British Telecommunications plc —BT — in their reporting of environmental performance). A possible mechanism is shown in Figure 7.8. Note, however, that the necessary data may be difficult to obtain, and that absolute usage or consumption, and the inherent nature of the effect itself, will also need to be considered.

Tables 7.7 and 7.8 show some example calculations using this method. Data on such matters as the national consumption of resources, the national production of carbon dioxide, the magnitude of the economy (GDP) and the size of the national work-force can be obtained from various Government and other compilations of statistics (see, for example, Hyde[23]). Such publications contain some data disaggregated by industrial sector, but more detailed or appropriate data may also be available through trade associations and similar bodies.

For carbon dioxide production, as Table 7.8 shows, various assumptions have to be made concerning the conversion of fuel to the gas. In the example given the primary source is heating oil, but more complex considerations would apply in a case where electricity consumption was the dominant source.

Corporate contribution or consumption	C_c
Equivalent 'total' figure (e.g. total for sector or UK)	C_t
Relative contribution or consumption	$C_r = C_c / C_t$

⬇

Corporate production or other size measure (e.g. production total, turnover, work-force size)	P_c
Equivalent 'total' figure (e.g. sector production, Gross Domestic Product, GDP, sector/national work-force)	P_t
Relative size of production/organization	$P_r = P_c / P_t$

⬇

| Obtain significance factor | $S = C_r / P_r$ |

⬇

$S > 10$	Almost certainly significant
$S = 10$ to 1	Probably significant
$S = 1$ to 0.1	Probably not significant
$S < 0.1$	Almost certainly insignificant

⬇

Consider absolute magnitude of usage or contribution as well as S-value, in making final decision on significance

Figure 7.8 A possible approach to assessing significance of contributions to regional or global effects, or consumption of resources

Table 7.7 Example of assessing significance of electricity consumption

A manufacturing company with a turnover of £45 m pa has an annual electricity consumption of 310 GWh:

Corporate electricity consumption	$C_c = 310$ GWh
UK industrial consumption	$C_t = 273\,000$ GWh
Relative consumption	$C_r = C_c/C_t = \mathbf{0.0011}$
Corporate turnover	$P_c = £45$ m
UK Gross Domestic Product (GDP)	$P_t = £543\,000$ m
Relative size of organization	$P_r = P_c/P_t = \mathbf{0.000083}$
Significance factor	$S = C_r/P_r = \mathbf{13}$
	Almost certainly significant

7.8.4 The wider context of effects evaluation: the example of BEO Assessment

Environmental effects evaluation in its broader sense is not, of course, unique to implementation of a formal EMS. It is also, as implied above, a part of Life

Table 7.8   Example of assessing significance of CO_2 production

A company with 530 employees calculates its annual carbon dioxide production (principally from heating) to be 1470 tonnes:

Corporate production	$C_c = 1470$ tonnes
UK industrial/commercial production	$C_t = 158$ m tonnes
Relative contribution or consumption	$C_r = C_c/C_t = \mathbf{0.0000093}$
Corporate work-force	$P_c = 530$
UK work-force	$P_t = 25$ m
Relative size of organization	$P_r = P_c/P_t = \mathbf{0.000021}$
Significance factor	$S = C_r/P_r = \mathbf{0.44}$
	probably not significant

Table 7.9   Basis of proposed approach to assessing BPEO

Consider releases to air, water and land (via air).

Examine also:
- Short Term Site Specific Effects
- Global Warming Potential
- Photochemical Ozone Creation Potential
- Waste Arisings
- Other Relevant Environmental Factors.

Having thus addressed the Best Environmental Option (BEO), consider also costs to determine what is the Best Practicable Environmental Option (BPEO).

Cycle Assessment (LCA), and also of Integrated Pollution Control (IPC) and Environmental Impact Assessment (EIA) for new projects. Its methodology is therefore the subject of a convergence of interests, and it is instructive to consider here the approach proposed by HMIP[24] for identifying, under Integrated Pollution Control (IPC), the Best Practicable Environmental Option (BPEO, see Chapter 3), because it:

- Is a clear example of this convergence of interests in effects evaluation.
- Will define 'Continual Improvement' in relevant sectors.
- Will be part of the basis of Effects Evaluation in affected companies.
- May be more widely helpful as an approach to Effects Evaluation.

The proposed approach is outlined in Table 7.9. Assessment of Best Environmental Option is based on consideration of releases to air, water and land (via air) in relation to an Environmental Quality Standard (EQS) — or an HMIP Environmental Assessment Level (EAL) where no EQS is available — coupled with examination of a range of other issues. Cost factors are then taken into account to determine the Best *Practicable* Environmental Option (BPEO), a further step which need not concern us here.

The Predicted Environmental Concentrations (plant contribution plus ambient level) for releases to air, water and to land (via air) are compared with the

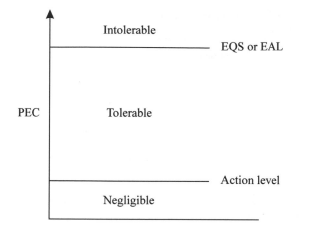

Figure 7.9 Consideration of releases to air, water and land (via air)

Table 7.10 Consideration of releases to air, water and land (via air)

The Environmental Quotient for the substance is given by:

$$EQ_{substance} = \text{Plant contribution} / \text{EQS or EAL}$$

The Environmental Quotient for the medium is given by:

$$EQ_{medium} = \sum_{\text{Substances}} EQ_{substance}$$

The Integrated Environmental Index for the process is given by:

$$IEI_{process} = \sum_{\text{media}} EQ_{medium}$$

relevant EQS or EAL values as shown in Figure 7.9. Any which exceed the standard or limit are declared intolerable, and the relevant process rejected. Those which fall between the EQS or EAL and a lower Action Level (AL, typically one-tenth to one-hundredth of the EQS or EAL) are considered tolerable but significant: the same terminology as in BS 7750. Those falling below the AL are deemed to be negligible or insignificant.

For candidate process options which do not result in any PEC exceeding the EQS or EAL, Environmental Quotients — for individual substances and for the different media — and an overall Integrated Environmental Index (IEI) — for the process option — can be computed as shown in Table 7.10.

The other specific issues to be considered (in addition to Short Term Site Specific Effects and Other Relevant Environmental Factors) are the Global Warming Potential (GWP), Photochemical Ozone Creation Potential (POCP) and Waste Arisings. These are addressed as shown in Tables 7.11 and 7.12.

Table 7.11 Consideration of Global Warming Potential, Photochemical Ozone Creation Potential and Waste Hazard Score

$$GWP_{total} = \sum_{Substances} \left(GWP_{substance} \times Mass_{substance, per\ annum}\right)$$

$$POCP_{total} = \sum_{Substances} \left(POCP_{substance} \times Mass_{substance, per\ annum}\right)$$

$$WHS = \sum_{Substances} \left(UHS_{substance} \times \log_{10} Mass_{substance, per\ annum}\right)$$

WHS: Waste Hazard Score, UHS: Unit Hazard Score for individual substance (see Table 7.12).

Table 7.12 Derivation of Unit Hazard Scores

UHS values are to be derived from considering:

Aquatic exposure
Solubility, adsorption, degradation, bioaccumulation
Aquatic toxicity, direct mammalian effects, mammalian reproductive or mutagenic effects

Air exposure
Volatility, degradation
Direct mammalian effects, mammalian reproductive or mutagenic effects

Table 7.13 Selection of BEO (based on HMIP example[24])

Characteristic	Base case*	Process option			
		Option 1	Option 2	Option 3	Option 4
Integrated Environmental Index (IEI)	5	3	2	0.6	0.5
Total Global Warming Potential (GWP_{total})	20	17	15	10	12
Total Photochemical Ozone Creation Potential ($POCP_{total}$)	1000	500	500	50	300
Waste Hazard Score (WHS)	4500	3250	3000	500	2000
Rank Order for BEO	5	4	3	1	2

* For example, existing process.

The values of the Integrated Environmental Index (IEI), total Global Warming Potential (GWP_{total}), total Photochemical Ozone Creation Potential ($POCP_{total}$) and Waste Hazard Score (WHS) having been calculated for each candidate process option which does not result in EQS or EAL exceedance, the BEO can be considered as shown in Table 7.13.

In discussing this example, HMIP states that examination of the IEI values leads to Option 4 being first considered as BEO, but that subsequent examination of the other three factors leads to Option 3 being finally selected as BEO.

Several observations may be made about the overall approach proposed by HMIP:

1 Combined assessment (through the IEI value) of releases to air, water and land (via air) is sound only if the underlying EQS and EAL values for the different media (see Figure 7.9 and Table 7.10) have comparable bases.
2 In the HMIP example (see Table 7.13), a difference of 0.1 units between the IEI values of Options 3 and 4 is offset by more favourable values of all other factors; what would the decision be if:
    (a) The IEI difference had been greater?
    (b) The other factors had not been uniformly more favourable?
3 The values of the IEI, the GWP_{total}, the $POCP_{total}$ and the WHS are not directly comparable (they have no units) and range over 3–4 orders of magnitude. This makes their joint consideration difficult, and it would seem preferable to normalize them (e.g. to 0–1), give each a weight and compute an overall score. It might be objected that the weighting factors would be subjective; however, *any* judgement would involve subjective weighting of the characteristics and a more explicit statement of 'preferred' weightings would seem more conducive to consistent judgements. A 'Delphi' approach, such as has been used in Life Cycle Assessment of detergents,[25] might be used to derive an agreed weighting set.

It is concluded that the proposed approach to BEO Assessment has interest in the wider context of effects evaluation in EMS implementation. It is not suggested that all organizations implementing (say) BS 7750 or EMA will need or want to apply the evaluation scheme, but it (or parts of it) may have relevance beyond the application of IPC, and because HMIP will derive and tabulate the relevant data (e.g. EAL and UHS values).

7.8.5 Format of the effects register

There is no prescribed format for the register in either BS 7750 or the EMA Regulation, but it needs to contain summary details only of significant effects. Under both these EMS models, there will be some overlap with the register of legislative, regulatory and other policy requirements, but this can be minimized by cross reference. Examples of entries in an effects register are shown in Table 7.14.

7.8.6 Summary of effects evaluation

The establishment and maintenance of a system to identify, and evaluate the significance of, corporate environmental effects, both direct and indirect, is one of the most demanding activities in environmental management, because of the breadth of assessment which is necessary, and its potentially difficult and

Table 7.14 Examples of entries on a Register of Significant Environmental Effects

Mythological Industries: Hades Site Register of Significant Environmental Effects   MI/HAD/EFF   V2.0 14/5/92

Item	Nature of effect	Status	Source	Area(s) affected	Objectives and programme
5.3	Air–VOC emission	Significant – developing concern – competitor product changes	Use of butane in 'Killospray' product	Local–regional	Investigation of alternative product delivery systems underway
6.2	Water – oxygen demand – zinc – colour	Regulated MI/HAD/LEG/6-2	Effluent treatment plant	Local–River Styx	30 per cent BOD reduction by end 12/94. Elimination of zinc by end 04/96. MI/HAD/PRG/3-2
8.1	Resource use–transport fuel	Significant – comparison with UK national usage	Distribution fleet Company cars	Local–global	Cut fuel use (per employee) by 5 per cent by end 06/93. MI/HAD/PRG/6-2
9.2	Dust	Possibly significant – complaints, but may be from deliveries to Cerberus Veterinary Products	? Main Unloading Bay, Hades Avenue	Local–Hades Avenue	Investigation underway with Cerberus Veterinary Products plc

contentious nature. Thus, such an evaluation system must strive to balance comprehensive initial coverage with the need to focus upon important effects. Moreover, the procedures adopted need to be clearly defensible, despite the absence of a universally accepted method for comparing the various possible effects, for example, across different environmental media.

It is all too easy to become overwhelmed by the potential magnitude and difficulties of the task; to counteract this, one must recognize the subjective nature of many of the judgements involved, and realize that structured and (if necessary) quantified approaches to the task are available. Moreover, without a soundly based effects evaluation, there can be no confidence that defensible corporate objectives will be set, or that day-to-day management will secure effective control of corporate impacts; in this respect, the process is simply a facet of good business management.

7.9 Communicating with Interested Parties

7.9.1 Introduction

As noted in Section 7.8, it is important to consider the views of interested parties, and information which they may supply, when identifying and evaluating environmental effects. It is for this reason that BS 7750 includes the subject of communication with interested parties under the general heading of environmental effects. In this section, we consider communication with interested parties, both in relation to effects evaluation and in its wider context.

7.9.2 Interested parties

As environmental concern has grown (see Chapter 2), so has the number of groups and individuals with an interest in the environmental probity of organizations. The range of interested parties is shown in Table 7.15.

The relative importance of each group will vary according to the nature and circumstances of the organization, and therefore with time. Some examples are shown in Table 7.16. The authors have sometimes been asked if the interested parties which the organization has identified should be documented, but this implies a somewhat artificial distinction between those which are 'on' or 'off' the organization's list. Most of the examples shown in Table 7.15 will be of relevance to most organizations. Obviously not all organizations have shareholders (they might instead have subscribing members, for instance) but all are subject to some form of regulation, even if only the requirement not to cause a statutory nuisance. It is only the *relatively important* interested parties which can be singled out at any one time, but it should be remembered that even those who are quiet and *apparently* contented may still have opinions of the organization which are not what the organization would wish them to be.

Table 7.15 The interested parties

Regulators	*Work-place/community*
HMIP	Employees
NRA	Trade unions
MAFF	Neighbours
HSE	Local authority
Local authority	
Opinion shapers	*Market-place*
Pressure groups	Customers (trade)
Media	Customers (consumers)
General public	Competitors
Lenders	*Insurers*
Banks	
Investors	
Shareholders	

Table 7.16 Relative importance of different interested parties

Circumstances	Important interested party
Manufacturer of consumer products whose rivals are engaged in 'green advertising'.	Consumers
Manufacturer of products sold to retailers who scrutinize the environmental probity of suppliers.	Customers
Manufacturer whose raw materials are the subject of a campaign by a pressure group.	Pressure group
Operator of a service whose waste disposal practices are the cause of local annoyance.	Neighbours, media, local councillors
Organization wanting planning permission for development or expansion.	Neighbours, media, local councillors
Organization heavily dependent on loan capital.	Banks

7.9.3 Communications with external interested parties

Communications with interested parties can be one- or two-way. Some interested parties will actively let the organization know its views (a dissatisfied regulator, complaining neighbour), others will be more passive and wait to be asked what they think. Young people, for instance, may be idealistic and not wish to seek employment with organizations which they perceive as having a poor environmental record, but they will not themselves let the organization know why it is not attracting the best recruits. There are numerous reasons why it is beneficial to be aware of interested parties' views:

- A company may be losing sales to competitors, without understanding why.
- An application for regulatory authorization may, when placed on the public register, meet public opposition.

- An application for new or extended planning permission might meet opposition.
- A pollution incident may be first noticed by a concerned neighbour.
- A pressure group may be successful in its aims to change consumer behaviour or legislation.

While all of the above examples may be viewed as negative or threatening situations, they can conversely be viewed as opportunities. The company which actively informs its consumers of its achievements may stay ahead of its competitors. The organization that is known to have a sound record of environmental protection is likely to be successful in its wishes to expand, in attracting new employees, and so on.

There are obvious links between the views of the interested parties and the development of the future scenario, described in Section 7.4. One of the better-known pressure groups has recently, or is currently, conducting the following campaigns:

- Against the import of tropical timber from ecologically unsustainable sources
- Challenging planning applications for quarrying activities
- Making formal objections to Integrated Pollution Control applications
- Encouraging returnable or refillable packaging
- For reduced lead levels in drinking water
- Against the use of products containing peat
- Against the use of certain pesticides
- For reduced uses of nitrogen fertilizers

Many of the 'wishes' on this list have met with some success, and whether or not this was due to the pressure group's actions is not the issue; the fact is that a monitoring of its campaigns would have provided *some* indication of likely future trends.

This is not to advocate passive acceptance of campaigns which are poorly founded, misguided or worse. Hostility may sometimes be encouraged by individuals such as a disaffected, unsuccessful job applicant, or an eccentric, but these are unlikely, single-handed, to carry much influence without evidence. The merely ignorant, however, are likely to be fearful and suspicious of circumstances that they do not understand. In such cases, the benefits of being informed of interested parties' opinions lies in the opportunity to correct misperceptions. Too often the industrialist's cry is 'It's impossible to talk with these people' but non-communication is in nobody's interest. If a minority group really cannot be reasoned with, a counter-measure might be to steal their audience, and educate them.

Before considering the means by which this might be done, consideration should be given to avoiding some pitfalls and winning the audience's confidence. For example:

1 Avoid issuing blanket reassurances. The audience cannot be expected simply to trust the organization; why should they? Its behaviour may have always been exemplary, but that of others has not, as the audience well knows. It may not be fair for one organization to be seen as representative of an entire sector with a poor reputation, but nevertheless, only the organization can put this right.
2 Don't blind the audience with science. Many of them, especially older people, may have had little scientific education.
3 Don't patronize. Complex scientific issues or technologies can usually be presented in terms which lay people can understand. Seek help with this if necessary.
4 Tell the truth.
5 Don't moan or complain (about the state of the economy, unjust legislation, etc.); be positive.

All of the above may seem obvious, but putting it into practice will be new for many companies. A representative of the European chemicals industry recently said, 'Our industry is an economic giant, but it is a dwarf in matters of communication'.[26] As stated above, communication can be one- or two-way, and one-way can mean the organization telling the interested parties its views, or listening to theirs. Some possible communication mechanisms are suggested below in Table 7.17, which indicates the broad suitability of different methods of receiving, and transmitting, messages from, and to, different groups. (Mechanisms of environmental reporting in particular are considered in more detail in Section 7.18.)

7.9.4 Communications with internal interested parties

Internal interested parties obviously include employees, but may include others such as contractors and the representatives of trades unions. The reasons for ensuring good internal communications are rather different from those for external communications; the successful operation of the Environmental Management System depends upon them, for success can only be assured when all employees understand their roles and feel motivated to participate fully (see also Section 7.7).

Obviously, the explanation and supervision of specific tasks is the responsibility of line management. The commitment of senior management, however, and the importance of the EMS for the whole organization, may be better presented by the most senior managers themselves. This may be easy to do directly in a small organization. In larger organizations, a presentation by the management could be video-recorded, and subsequently seen by all employees. There will be value, though, in following up such demonstrations of commitment with further information. Regular reports to employees (by company

Table 7.17 Some possible communication mechanisms

Telling

Special report or environmental section in annual report.
Newsletter delivered to plant neighbours.
Advertisements in national or local press, according to message and audience.
Press releases for major announcements.

Listening

Establishing procedures to ensure that telephone callers speak to the right person, and that their comments are recorded and followed up.
Using existing customer 'complaint' procedures (probably established initially to deal with quality issues).
Scanning the literature of pressure groups.
Using opinion polls and market surveys, whether commissioned by the organization, a body representing the sector, or others reported by the media.
Reading letters in local and national press, observing the content of TV/radio news and documentaries.
Reading consumer publications.

Telling and listening

Establishing local liaison committees, on which regulators, neighbours and others meet the organization's representatives on a regular basis.
Corresponding with interested parties, proactively, or in response to issues raised by them.
Arranging site visits, e.g. for school students, employees' families, neighbours.
Sending speakers to occasions as varied as the local school and international conferences.
Discussing environmental matters at AGMs.

newsletter, special notice-board, or any other appropriate mechanism), particularly those which highlight progress made in the form of targets achieved or savings made, will encourage and renew motivation.

Communications with employees should be two-way, with employees encouraged to report problems and also to be innovative and make positive suggestions. Pre-existing employee suggestion schemes could be used for the latter.

Remember the importance of non-verbal communication. Unspoken messages, conveyed by the availability of resources, size of budgets or apparent priorities of management (do productivity bonuses provide incentives to maintain output in the face of a potential environmental incident, for instance?) will carry more weight than any number of fine words.

7.10 Keeping Abreast of Legal and Regulatory Requirements

7.10.1 The purpose of registering legal and regulatory requirements

As indicated in Chapter 3, environmental legislation is evolving at such a pace that the task of keeping track of it may seem daunting indeed, especially to the busy environmental manager who is not a specialist in this field and who

Table 7.18 Examples of entries on a register of legislative, regulatory and other policy requirements

Mythological Industries: Hades Site Register of Legislative, Regulatory and Other Policy Requirements		MI/HAD/LEG V2.0 8/5/92	
Item	Law, Regulation or Policy Requirement	Area(s) affected	Relevant procedure(s)
4.1	Environmental Protection Act 1990	Site-wide waste handling/disposal and the Duty of Care	MI/HAD/11 MI/HAD/12
6.2	Water Resources Act 1991 Discharge Consent No: Issued by: NRA Hades Region	Discharge to River Styx	MI/HAD/19
6.3	Water Industry Act 1991; Competition and Services (Utilities) Act 1992, s43(2). Discharge Consent No: Issued by: Styx Water plc	Discharge to sewer at Lethe Road	MI/HAD/20
8.2	Mythological Industries Environmental Policy Statement: Commitment not to use brimstone in any product range	Product formulation	MI/HAD/33

perhaps has many other business responsibilities. Of course, most organizations will not need to keep track of *all* of it, but even small ones with simple activities may need to maintain awareness of numerous issues and emerging proposals. In this respect the task begins to overlap with that of updating the scenario, described in Section 7.4.

BS 7750 requires (subclause 4.4.3) a '... register of legislative, regulatory and other policy requirements'. Some readers have feared that this necessitates a comprehensive collection of Acts and Regulations. Such a collection, perhaps held by the legal department of a large organization, may or may not form a useful starting point, but alone it is insufficient.

It should be understood that the purpose of the 'register' is a demonstration that the requirements which *apply at the site(s)* are understood by those who are responsible for ensuring that they are met (Table 7.18). It is insufficient for the company's solicitor to know that the company is bound by the Environmental Protection Act 1990; it is the management's understanding of the consequent authorization that matters.

Note that BS 7750 requires not a register of legislation itself, but of *requirements*; it is the practical implications in terms of day-to-day activities which need to be demonstrably understood. The purpose of the EMS is to facilitate compliance with these requirements, and it is important to keep this end in sight.

7.10.2 The procedures needed

In recent years there has been a proliferation of sources of information (hard copy and computerized) which may be helpful in keeping abreast of legislation and regulations. These range from publications which are devoted specifically to this purpose, to publications which primarily serve a specific group of readers (e.g. a learned society, industrial sector) and now include coverage of those environmental matters which are of particular concern to their readers. It is unlikely to be necessary for the organization to scrutinize all the potentially useful publications; identification of the few most relevant ones will keep the volume of required reading to a manageable size.

The next task is to identify who needs to receive this information. The Management Representative is an obvious example, but perhaps he or she could be relieved of part of the work by delegating the task of sifting out the relevant information to, for example, the library or legal department of a larger organization. Others may include those with responsibilities for:

- Business development
- External communications
- Waste handling and disposal
- Research and development

Not all of these will need to scan all information, and some preliminary sifting of the sources for the relevant and useful could be conducted on behalf of each of them. The procedures needed to ensure circulation of the information are likely to be fairly simple, based on distribution lists signed by the receivers.

Some sources of information, the less formal ones, are less amenable to such control. A discussion heard at a conference, for instance, or information gleaned from informal conversations with anyone outside of the organization — activities which might be described as 'keeping one's ear to the ground' — cannot themselves be bound by rigid procedures. However, if all concerned are made aware of who needs to receive such information, and mechanisms are in place to record and disseminate it, the Management Representative can be confident that no current requirements are being overlooked, and that the scenario will be as complete as it can be.

Having circulated information about requirements to the relevant people, it is also necessary to have procedures for its storage and ready retrieval. This could be done using computer software or hard copy, whichever the organization finds more convenient. A certain amount of paperwork will in any case be necessary, as authorizations from regulators will usually be received in this form. The requirements may all be documented in one place, or in a number of files or offices. Organizations which have an Environmental Management manual may choose to list the requirements in it; for others they will be too numerous or lengthy for this, but the manual might usefully tell the reader where to find them. It is important that the information is readily accessible to all who need it within the organization.

The 'register' will of course be continually evolving, and procedures will be needed to ensure that it is updated comprehensively and promptly. This is one of the most important aspects of document control (see Section 7.13); confusion of out-of-date requirements with current ones could be disastrous for the organization!

Although the above discussion has concentrated on legislative and regulatory requirements, the organization may choose to abide by others; those of its trade association, for instance, or those which it simply chooses to set itself, perhaps forming part of its policy and objectives. An example of the requirements of a trade association is the voluntary reporting under the Chemical Industries Association's (CIA) 'Responsible Care' initiative.

7.10.3 Sources of information

As stated above, it is important that each organization identifies those sources of information which are the most relevant to its own particular circumstances. However, there are a number of commercially available publications which compile legislation and provide their subscribers with regular updates. These publications may provide a useful starting point for some organizations in the task of keeping abreast of legislative and regulatory requirements. Some examples are given in Table 7.19.

Books are relatively inexpensive, but can of course quickly become dated in a fast-changing area of law. Subscription to a regularly updated loose-leaf binder service is more expensive, but largely overcomes the problem of being up-to-date, at least with regard to current and imminent laws and regulations. Computerized systems are more expensive still, but offer certain advantages of access, for those who need it, and can give the complete text of laws and regulations in computer-searchable form.

Keeping abreast of current and imminent laws and regulations is one matter; being aware of embryonic and developing legislation is more difficult, and may require, among other steps, both close contact with trade associations and regular scrutiny of environmental newsletters.

It should also be noted that the Department of the Environment (DoE), Her Majesty's Inspectorate of Pollution (HMIP), the National Rivers Authority (NRA) and other regulatory agencies hold, sponsor or participate in conferences and workshops on emerging regulatory issues. At the time of writing (mid-1995), such issues include the plans for the Environment Agency, the assessment of Best Practicable Environmental Option (BPEO) and the application of Toxicity-Based Consent (TBC) conditions to effluent discharges.

Table 7.19 Examples of information sources on legislation and regulations

Format	Title	Reference
Books	*Yearbook of International Environmental Law*	27
	European Community Environment Legislation	28
	Regulating the European Environment	29
	NSCA Pollution Handbook	30
	Tolley's Environmental Handbook: A Management Guide	31
	Environmental Law	32
	Corporate Environmental Responsibility: Law and Practice	33
	The Environmental Protection Act 1990	34
	Waste Management Law. A Practical Handbook	35
	Wisdom's Law of Watercourses	36
	Water Law. A Practical Guide to the Water Act 1989	37
	The Law of the National Rivers Authority	38
Booklets	Various law firms' occasional reviews, e.g.	
	Clifford Chance: *Environmental Law Guide*	39
	Denton Hall: *A Guide to Environmental Registers*	40
Loose-leaf systems	*Barbour's Health, Safety and Environmental Index*	41
	Croner's Environmental Management	42
	Croner's Waste Management	43
	Garner's Environmental Law	44
	Encyclopedia of Environmental Health Law and Practice	45
	Manual of Environmental Policy; the EC and Britain	46
	European Environment Law for Industry	47
Computer-based systems	Enflex Info (ERM)	48
	Silver Platter	49
Newsletters and journals	*Environment Business*	50
	The ENDS Report	51
	Environment Information Bulletin	52
	Environmental Law Monthly	53
	European Environmental Law Review	54
	Environmental Law Reports	55
	Environmental Law Brief	56
	Various law firm's environmental law newsletters, e.g.	
	Simmons and Simmons' *Environmental Law Newsletter*	
	Nabarro Nathanson's *Environment Law Matters*	

Finally, it should be noted that there exists a United Kingdom Environmental Law association (UKELA), details of which are given in the list of useful addresses in Appendix 2.

7.11 Setting Objectives and Targets

7.11.1 The purpose of objectives and targets

BS 7750 defines environmental objectives as 'The broad goals, arising from the environmental policy and effects evaluation, that an organization sets itself to achieve, and which are quantified wherever practicable'. It defines environ-

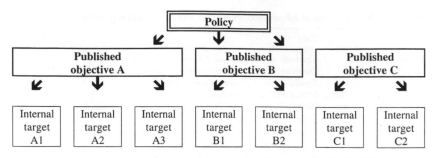

Figure 7.10 Hierarchy of policy, objectives and targets (to BS 7750)

mental targets as 'Detailed performance requirements, quantified wherever practicable, applicable to the organization or parts thereof, that arise from the environmental objectives and that need to be set and met in order to achieve those objectives'. Thus, policy, objectives and targets form a hierarchy as shown in Figure 7.10.

Objectives and targets define the rate of continual improvement which the organization intends to make in its environmental performance, and thus they are essential to underpin the policy. It is not good enough for the organization's top management to state hopefully that the organization and everyone in it will strive to do better; how much better, and the rate of progress, need to be pre-defined.

The authors are sometimes asked for clarification of the difference between objectives and targets; the difference is one of level and degree of detail, and the requirement under BS 7750 that objectives be made publicly available. It is possible that in a small or simple organization, the distinction will be unnecessary.

7.11.2 Choosing objectives and targets

A prerequisite for choosing objectives and targets is an evaluation of environmental effects. A guiding principle in choosing objectives and targets is that these should address significant environmental effects, although BS 7750 does not require that *all* such effects are targeted simultaneously.

In deciding which of the significant effects to address, economic and business considerations will be important. If one particular effect can only be lessened by means of a substantial capital investment in new plant, it may be necessary to concentrate efforts on other effects, especially if unilateral, but expensive, action would put a company at a competitive disadvantage. In these circumstances, objectives set in conjunction with waste minimization or energy efficiency projects with short- or medium-term payback times may be more appropriate. This course of action is permissible; BS 7750 does not call for all significant effects to be addressed simultaneously, neither does it specify how many areas of improvement should be identified and pursued. The standard does, however, recommend that objectives be '. . . demanding, quantitative and achievable'.

Setting objectives and targets which address less significant effects may also be considered, because effective action can often be inexpensive, and helpful in involving — and demonstrating environmental commitment to — a wide range of staff not otherwise closely involved in the EMS. Large-scale schemes for environmental improvement, such as planning modifications to plant, may involve few members of staff and leave the remainder feeling that the EMS is of no concern to them.

To take a common example, many organizations sell canned drinks in their staff restaurants, and it makes sense for these aluminium cans to be collected for recycling. The benefits of recycling aluminium are clear, and while the energy savings and waste volume they represent may be trivial compared with other activities of the organization, it would be unwise to neglect such a simple, cost-free way to benefit the environment. Employees who are in the habit of using can banks provided near their homes may question the commitment of an organization which does not provide similar facilities at work.

An organization committed to making only small, or slow, improvements, may do so because it is already far ahead of its competitors and has reached a point where diminishing returns will be received on further investments. Conversely, an organization committed to making great or rapid improvements may find these relatively easy, because it is starting from a baseline of poor environmental performance and has not yet taken measures already taken by its competitors. Publication of objectives, provided they are stated in an appropriate way, should allow interested parties to understand these different positions.

The above discussion implies that the costs of various courses of action are known to the organization before it chooses its objectives and targets. There is little point in impressing the interested parties by setting a grandiose objective, such as reducing emissions by 50 per cent, if it turns out that a reduction of 49 per cent, can be achieved at a minimal cost, or even providing savings, while the last 1 per cent is prohibitively expensive. It is better to cost all the options and choose those that make the most business sense. Indeed, many organizations which boast of their environmental achievements admit that their actions are primarily driven by economic pressures; see, for example, the October 1993 issue of ENDS. This carried a report of a project undertaken by 11 firms, which between them identified over 500 waste minimization measures, almost all of which had payback times of less than 3 years.

In identifying possible objectives and targets, it is important to consult widely within the organization. Objectives and targets imposed unilaterally by line management stand less chance of being met than those which have

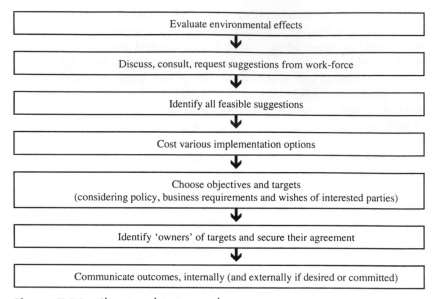

Figure 7.11   Choosing objectives and targets

been agreed by all concerned. Valuable suggestions of ways in which improvements may be made may come from those with the most detailed involvement in the organization's day-to-day activities, and who may show enthusiasm to strive to meet targets more demanding than senior management might have thought to impose. The sequence of events involved in choosing objectives and targets is illustrated in Figure 7.11.

7.11.3 Expressing objectives and targets

Care should be taken in the way that objectives are expressed. In order to allow for increased output (most organizations will hope to expand their activities, however these are quantified) objectives should ideally be expressed on a 'per unit output' basis. This not only prevents the organization being trapped by some self-imposed limit, it also allows interested parties the fairest means of comparing and understanding the organization's position. Exceptions to this principle are objectives of the 'phase-out' variety, such as 'cease using chlorinated fluorocarbons within 2 years', or 'stop disposing of waste to land fill by the end of next year'. These still meet the requirement that the objective should be quantified (the reduction being 100 per cent in each case) and have a defined time-scale. Some examples of objectives and targets are shown in Tables 7.20 and 7.21.

Table 7.20   Example of setting objectives

Cerberus Veterinary Products plc uses an electrically powered production process.
This results in high emissions of pollutants to water.
An alternative process, eliminating emissions and using 60 per cent less electricity, is available but represents a major capital investment.
The company suspects that the new process will be declared BATNEEC in a few years.

The company decides to install the new equipment and have it operational in 3 years' time. It sets environmental objectives to:

1   Reduce electricity consumption per unit production by 60 per cent over the next 3 years.
2   Eliminate emissions to water in 3 years' time.

Table 7.21   Example of setting objectives and targets

Mythological Industries cannot readily reduce its transport requirements.
It examines the scope for replacing some vehicles with smaller ones.
By this means it estimates a cut in fuel use, and hence CO_2 emissions, of 5 per cent over the next 2 years.

It commissions a firm of energy consultants to advise on fuel use to heat its buildings.
As a result, it considers investments which have a payback time of 2 years or less.
These are expected to reduce the consumption of heating oil, and hence CO_2 emissions, by 20 per cent (after allowing for fluctuations in seasonal temperature).

The company decides to make the necessary changes and investments, and sets environmental objectives and targets as follows:

1   Objective A: Reduce CO_2 production (per employee) by 15 per cent over the next 2 years.
2   Target A1: Cut vehicular fuel consumption (per employee) by 5 per cent over next 2 years.
3   Target A2: Cut heating oil consumption (per employee) by 20 per cent over next 2 years.

As the publication of objectives becomes commonplace, it is likely that certain aspects of expressing environmental performance (e.g. units, methods of normalization to production levels or facility size) will become the norm within particular industrial sectors. Sector Application Guides (see Section 7.1) may, in some cases, identify or suggest any such agreed or common conventions.

It should be remembered that, to comply with BS 7750, the objectives must be publicly available, so — as with policy statements — they should be expressed in terms which avoid technical jargon as far as possible. A mechanism for publishing the objectives must be chosen and explained in the policy statement. For example, the objectives could be published with the policy itself, in an annual report or a separate annual environmental report, or they could be obtained by application to a public relations department.

7.12 Devising a Programme to Meet Objectives

7.12.1 The purpose of the programme

BS 7750 describes an environmental programme quite simply as 'A description of the means of achieving environmental objectives and targets'. It was explained in Section 7.11 that the extent and rate of improvement in environmental performance need to be pre-defined, and likewise the means of achieving this improvement need to be planned; they should not be left to chance. In this respect environmental management is no different from the management of change in any other aspect of the business. For each environmental objective or target, there should be a corresponding programme showing:

- What will be done
- How it will be done
- When it will be done
- Who will be responsible

In BS 7750, particular emphasis is given to programmes relating to new developments, products, services or processes, where the modification introduces significantly different environmental effects. The emphasis is justified, because new projects often provide opportunities to phase out or abandon old materials, techniques and practices and to begin using new, less environmentally damaging ones. This will obviously be the case where, for example, the new development is driven by pressure from regulators, or a customer has requested a product with improved environmental performance, but almost any new project will provide some such opportunities.

As it is frequently the case with new developments that unforeseen circumstances arise or unexpected findings are encountered, care must be taken to ensure that these do not result in the environmental objectives being overridden. The system should contain mechanisms for, in the words of BS 7750, '... dealing with changes and modifications as projects proceed . . .'. Figure 7.12 illustrates how environmental objectives, along with other goals, should always be considered during the design of a new product.

It is possible that during development, conflicts between the various criteria become apparent, for instance, between cost and any other attribute, or between safety and environmental performance. An example is the use of hydrocarbons as refrigerants. As chlorofluorocarbons (CFCs) are phased out, some manufacturers are marketing refrigerators with hydrocarbons as refrigerants. The hydrocarbons do not damage stratospheric ozone, as the CFCs do, but they are flammable, and fears have been raised about the risk of explosion, should they leak into a confined space. Such examples are a powerful argument for the close integration of health, safety and environmental management.

For those new developments requiring Environmental Impact Assessments (EIAs) as part of the planning process (see Chapter 3), the EIA provides a

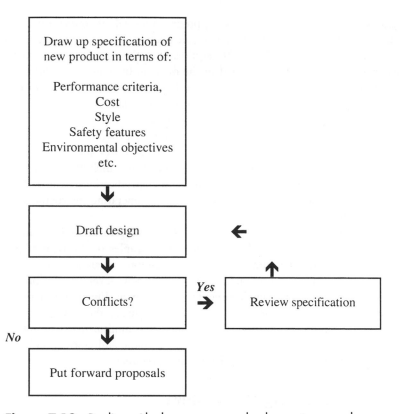

Figure 7.12 Dealing with changes as new developments proceed

mechanism for considering alternative means to achieving a given objective, and this can be regarded as the first stage in drawing up an environmental programme.

The degree of complexity of environmental programmes will vary enormously, as will the number of people involved in them. A staff awareness campaign, for example, may well be addressed at everyone, but be achieved by very simple means. In contrast, the programme for replacing a major plant will be complex, but implemented by few individuals. The following examples illustrate such variations.

7.12.2 Examples of environmental programmes

In Section 7.11 some examples of objectives and targets were given (Tables 7.20 and 7.21). These will be used as the basis for examples of environmental programmes in this section. In practice, programmes will of course need to be documented. The environmental manual (see Section 7.13) provides an appropriate place for this, and BS 7750 requires that the overall environmental management programme be included in the manual. In some cases, individual programmes may, as they develop, become large and complex pieces of documentation (e.g. for the construction of a major new plant) such that inclusion in the manual would not be practical or desirable.

Thus, for example, Figure 7.13 shows a summary programme which could conveniently be included in the environmental manual. For such a project the *overall* documentation would be voluminous and would include, for example, the relevant budgetary information, permissions, specifications, tender documents, contractual paperwork, technical drawings, operating instructions and commissioning data.

The programmes illustrated in Figures 7.14 and 7.15 are related to the targets described in Table 7.21. They provide examples of the type of programmes which might be found in many organizations, in all sectors.

The final example of a programme shows how new developments provide opportunities for improved environmental performance. Illustrated in Figure 7.16, it might belong to the company which produced the example policy statement in Figure 7.3. That policy included a commitment to promoting recycling by good product design, and the programme addresses an objective to produce a product with improved recycling potential.

7.13 Documenting the System

One of the most common areas of concern voiced about implementing an EMS is that of documentation; fears arise about bureaucracy, diversion of resources, and the creation of a 'paper' rather than a 'practical' system of environmental management. Such fears are sometimes linked to the speaker's own experiences, or to reported problems, in implementing a quality system to BS 5750/ISO 9000.

Concern of this degree cannot be lightly dismissed, if only because its frequency suggests that either the role of documentation in a quality system has been misunderstood or because there have been instances when that role has been exaggerated at the expense of other, no less important, requirements.

Equally, however, it would be quite wrong to respond by playing down the true importance of *appropriate* system documentation, which is essential to the EMS concept.

In addressing this concern, therefore, one must point to the important role of documentation in managing any complex set of activities, but also to the fact that no sensible proponent of the EMS approach would recommend the unthinking proliferation of written documentation. Indeed, it should be noted that BS 7750, in Clause 4.8.2 on Control, states that written procedures

Cerberus Veterinary Products plc

Title: Programme for refurbishment of Hades Plant with 'Lo-Power' Technology
Document number: CDF/EMS/Prog/03
Project file: CDF/QMS/Proj/17
Purpose: Achievement of EMS Objective CDF/EMS/Obj3
Project co-ordinator: Engineering Manager

Action required	Responsibility	Completion
Develop budget costing	Engineering Manager	31/01/96
Approve budget	Board	29/02/96
Seek outline planning permission	Environment Co-ordinator	29/02/96
Draw up specification, including emission limits	Engineering Manager	30/04/96
Secure regulator's approval	Environment Co-ordinator	30/05/96
Seek tenders from contractors	Purchasing Manager	31/08/96
Apply for planning permission	Environment Co-ordinator	31/08/96
Evaluate tenders	Engineering Manager	30/09/96
Award contract	Purchasing Manager	31/10/96
Start construction — supervise contractors	Project Engineer	28/02/97
Complete construction — supervise contractors	Project Engineer	28/02/98
Commissioning	Project Engineer	31/05/98
Start production	Production Manager	30/06/98
De-commission old plant	Project Engineer	31/09/98
Dismantle and dispose old plant	Site Services Manager	31/10/98

Document Revision Record

Date	Revision	Description	Issue	Check	Approval
07/12/95	1.0	Use	*PBR*	*JH*	*LOJ*
18/11/95	0.0	Comment	*PBR*	-	-
			Eng Man	Prod Man	Man Dir

CDF/EMS/Prog/03/v1.0/071295   **Page 1 of 1**

Figure 7.13 Summary programme to achieve environmental objective of reducing electricity consumption and eliminating aqueous emissions

or work instructions '. . . shall be prepared for situations where the absence of such instructions could result in infringement of the environmental policy' (and similar wording, taken from a draft of the standard, is also found in the EMA Regulation).

Mythological Industries plc

Title: Programme to reduce fuel consumption by Hades Site vehicles

Document number: MI/Had/EMS/Prog/12 (see also File MI/Proj/27)
Aim: Achievement of target to reduce vehicular fuel consumption, per employee,
     by 5 per cent by March 1997 (Target No MI/Had/EMS/Targ3/1)

Action	Responsibility	Completion date
Overall project management	*Fleet Manager*	-
Review fuel consumption data when replacing vehicles	Fleet Manager	On-going
Review booking procedures to ensure vehicles used appropriately	Fleet Manager	Sep 1995
Seek external advice on optimization of fuel consumption	Fleet Manager	Sep 1995
Brief all drivers on economical driving techniques	Fleet Manager	Nov 1995
Revise inspection and maintenance procedures	Garage Supervisor	Nov 1995
Train garage staff in modified procedures	Garage Supervisor	Jan 1996
Commence modified programme of inspection and maintenance	Garage Supervisor	Jan 1996

Revision status

Date	Revision	Description	Issued by	Checked by	Approved by
03/07/95	1.0	For use	*PJB*	*BER*	*DJT*
21/06/95	0.0	For comment	*PJB*	-	-
			Fleet Man	Env Man	Site Man

MI/Had/EMS/Prog/12/v1.0/030795   **Page** 1 **of** 1

Figure 7.14 Programme to achieve reduced vehicular fuel consumption

It is emphasized, therefore, that the preparation of written procedures and instructions is essential only when two conditions are met:

1 The activity is critical to fulfil the policy, or achieve objectives which flow from it.
2 The absence of written instruction could result in infringement.

Mythological Industries plc

Title: Programme to reduce heating oil consumption

Document number: MI/Had/EMS/Prog/3-2 (see also File MI/Proj/29)
Aim: Achievement of target to reduce consumption of heating oil, per employee, by
20 per cent by March 1997 (Target No MI/Had/EMS/Targ/3-2)

Action	Responsibility	Completion date
Overall project management	*Site Services Manager*	-
Conduct staff awareness campaign: posters, stickers, article in staff magazine	Environmental Co-ordinator	Sep 1995
Devise and implement a detailed recording system for fuel use	Site Services Manager	Oct 1995
Upgrade insulation, as recs. 4, 5 and 6 of consultant's report (MI/Had/EMS/Rep17)	Site Services Manager	Dec 1995
Install thermostatic radiator valves, as rec. 7 of consultant's report	Site Services Manager	Dec 1995
Install improved boiler controls, as rec. 8 of consultant's report	Site Services Manager	Dec 1995
Prepare report to Finance Director on costs and benefits of improvements	Environmental Co-ordinator	Jan 1997

Revision status

Date	Revision	Description	Issued by	Checked by	Approved by
21/08/95	1.0	For use	*GNW*	*ðεR*	*DJT*
11/08/95	0.0	For comment	*GNW*	-	-
			S Ser Man	Env Man	Site Man

MI/Had/EMS/Prog/12/v1.0/210895   **Page** 1 **of** 1

Figure 7.15 Programme to achieve reduction in heating oil consumption

Similarly, with regard to written records, dealt with in Section 7.14, one must again stress the importance of *appropriate* records of performance to the effective functioning and credibility of an objective-based system.

Finally, it is emphasized that there is no need to duplicate, within the EMS, documentation which has already been produced within the existing management system (e.g. for quality, or for health and safety, management). It is

---

$\mathcal{MM}$ **Mythological Manufacturing Ltd**

Title: Programme to improve recyclability of 'Hells-A-Freezin' portable air
     conditioner range

Document Number: MM/Had/EMS/Prog/2-4 (see also File MM/Proj/13)
Aim: Achievement of target to re-design the 'Hells-A-Freezin' range so that 90 per cent
(by weight) of the housing can be recycled, by July 1996 (Target No.
     MM/Had/EMS/Targ/2-4)

Action	Responsibility	Completion
Overall project management	*Research Manager, HAF*	-
Review properties of current and novel housing materials	Head, Materials Research Group	Dec 1995
Monitor developments in recycling technology and practice	Head, Materials Research Group	Commence Dec 1995, on-going
Shortlist most promising materials	Head, Materials Research Group	Jan 1996
Approach suppliers to ascertain barriers to recycling	Purchasing Manager	Feb 1995
Design housings made from recyclable material(s)	HAF Design Engineer	June 1996
Present designs to Marketing Manager	Research Manager, HAF	July 1996

Revision status

Date	Revision	Description	Issued by	Checked by	Approved by
01/08/95	1.0	For use	*HJY*	*DAJ*	*JS*
15/07/95	0.0	For comment	*HJY*	-	-
			Research Mgr, HAF	Head, MRG	Director R&D

MM/Had/EMS/Prog/12/v1.0/010995   **Page** 1 **of** 1

Figure 7.16 Programme to achieve improved recyclability of consumer durable
product

uld they leak into a confined space. Such examples are a powerful argument for
the close integration of health, safety and environmental management.

Table 7.22 Key questions answered by EMS documentation

Question	Examples	
What	... objective is to be achieved?	... measurements are to be taken?
Why	... is a procedure to be followed?	... is a record required?
Who	... is responsible for an action?	... is to be consulted in uncertainty?
How	... is a task to be performed?	... are changes to be made?
When	... are measurements to be taken?	... is action required?
Where	... is information to be found?	... is emergency equipment kept?

Taken together, these principles do not obviate the need for careful consideration of the need for written documentation in specific circumstances; they should, however, help to allay concerns that EMS implementation demands needless production of paperwork.

7.13.1 The Purpose of EMS documentation

EMS documentation is intended to provide information to the organization's staff on environment-critical activities and functions, to help ensure that:

- Goals are clear
- Responsibilities are clear
- The correct way to carry out activities is clear
- Undesired outcomes (e.g. waste, exceedance of release limits, incidents and accidents) are avoided
- Excessive reliance on specific individuals is avoided
- New staff can be efficiently trained
- Records are kept to show that what has been planned is being achieved (or correction made)

It may also provide evidence to interested parties (e.g. regulators, certifying bodies) that such activities and functions are being effectively controlled. Thus, all system documents deal with some or all of the key questions in Table 7.22. Similarly, the purpose of documentation *control* is to ensure that:

- Correct documents are available to those who need them, when they need them.
- Wasted time — through re-invention or in seeking existing information — is avoided.
- Documents are updated to cope with change, in the organization and its surroundings.

7.13.2 Elements of EMS documentation

Figure 7.17 shows the typical components of EMS documentation, and the relationships between them as envisaged by BS 7750. Leaving aside the Registers, which have been discussed in previous sections, and the Records, to be discussed in Section 7.14, the principal (internal) documents are the Environmental Management Manual, the Procedures and the Work Instructions.

7.13.3 Environmental Management Manual

This is a requirement of BS 7750, but is *not* intended as a compendium of all environmentally relevant documents within the organization. Rather, it is a summary and 'signposting' document, providing an overview of the EMS and a basis for co-ordination and control of environmental management activities across the organization. Containing as it does the policy, objectives and targets, and programme, and addressing the other issues shown in Figure 7.17, it describes:

- Principles and general intentions
- Key elements of organization and responsibility
- The general functioning of the EMS within the overall management system
- Specific performance goals
- Plans to achieve them

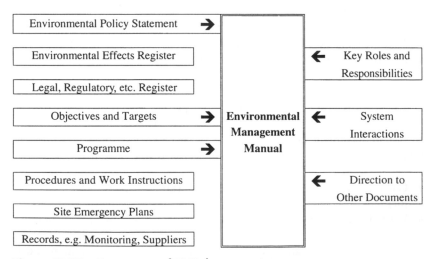

Figure 7.17 Components of EMS documentation

BS 7750 does *not* require that the Manual contain all the EMS Procedures, which would make it a cumbersome document in larger organizations. However, a list of relevant Procedures may usefully be appended to it.

7.13.4 Procedures and Work Instructions

Although BS 7750 refers to both these types of document, it provides no definitions to distinguish them and it is not essential to do so if it is not helpful (or, indeed, to use either term if existing terminology is different). In common practice, however, Procedures provide instructions for particular *areas* of activity. The individual *tasks* within such areas are addressed (when necessary) by written Work Instructions.

As noted previously, BS 7750 requires that written Procedures and Work Instructions be prepared for 'environment-critical' activities and tasks (whether undertaken by staff or contractors), where their absence could result in infringement of the policy. The first issue, therefore, is how to decide if written instruction is required to address a particular activity or task which is considered to be 'critical'. There is no simple answer, as each situation must be considered separately, but factors such as the following will need to be considered:

- The nature of the activity or task.
- The nature of its criticality, including its importance to meeting legal and policy requirements and achieving goals, and the environmental risks associated with it.
- The education, training and/or experience of the staff involved (see Section 7.7).
- The degree of supervision under which they will work.
- The frequency with which they will perform the activity or task.
- The continuity of staffing.
- The extent to which written material is an effective form of instruction (compared with, say, oral instruction with refresher training).

In cases of doubt, it is better to err on the side of caution and produce written documentation. Note also that, even if written material is not itself the best way to instruct the operators, it may be needed as a basis for the development of training programmes.

Once it has been decided that a written Procedure or Work Instruction is required, its production should be carefully planned and executed. Stebbing, in his text on quality assurance,[57] identifies the steps of Procedure production (which apply equally to Work Instructions). These steps, somewhat modified, are shown in Figure 7.18.

Step	Actions
Review current practice ↓	Discuss with operators; review existing documents
Analyse current practice ↓	To determine if satisfactory, or if amendment needed
Develop draft procedure ↓	To format; What? Why? Who? How? When? Where?
Release draft for comment ↓	To staff involved, including operators, for comment
Review comments and revise ↓	Incorporate applicable changes
Issue for acceptance ↓	To all staff involved
Obtain approval ↓	By responsible person and management
Issue for use ↓	To those who need it
Implement ↓	Including training to familiarize operators
Monitor and review	After period, audit implementation and effectiveness

Figure 7.18 Preparing procedures. (After Stebbing[57] with modifications.)

For details on writing Procedures and Work Instructions, the reader is referred to Stebbing,[57] but we here emphasize the following points to bear in mind:

- Involve those who carry out the activities and tasks in the production.
- Ensure that instructions are accurate, realistic, contain clear criteria to be met (when required), and are adequately flexible.
- Be precise and avoid ambiguity: as Stebbing[57] points out, a good test is to check if instructions can be turned simply into questions (e.g. 'The Environmental Manager is responsible for . . .' — 'Who is responsible for . . .?').
- Seek clarity and ease of use by:
  - describing the principal stages of the activity or task in logical sequence
  - using simple rather than complex words and expressions
  - avoiding the passive voice ('Calibrate the meter by . . .' rather than 'The meter is calibrated by . . .')
  - punctuating effectively, avoiding long sentences and paragraphs
  - maintaining consistency of format and style within and between documents.

Mythological Industries plc

Title

PROCEDURE FOR UPDATING THE REGISTER OF SIGNIFICANT
ENVIRONMENTAL EFFECTS FOR THE HADES SITE

Document number

MI/Had/EMS/Pro/027

Revision status

03/05/94	1.0	For Use	ЬЄR	DJT	PL
12/04/94	0.0	For Comment	ЬЄR	-	-
			Env Man	Site Man	Man Dir
Date	**Revision**	**Description**	**Issued by**	**Checked by**	**Approved by**

MI/Had/EMS/Pro/027/v1.0/030594   **Page** 1 **of** 6

Figure 7.19 Example of a procedure (Continued on pages 182–186)

Many books are available giving advice on good writing; the authors find Gowers' *Plain Words*[58] particularly useful. It should also be noted that modern word processing software may provide facilities for calculating and interpreting indices of readability, which can be used to check that writing is suitable for its intended readership.

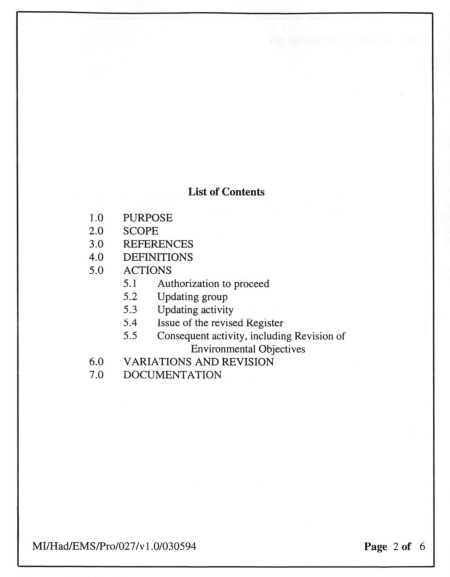

List of Contents

1.0	PURPOSE
2.0	SCOPE
3.0	REFERENCES
4.0	DEFINITIONS
5.0	ACTIONS

    5.1   Authorization to proceed
    5.2   Updating group
    5.3   Updating activity
    5.4   Issue of the revised Register
    5.5   Consequent activity, including Revision of
                Environmental Objectives

6.0	VARIATIONS AND REVISION
7.0	DOCUMENTATION

MI/Had/EMS/Pro/027/v1.0/030594   **Page** 2 **of** 6

Figure 7.19 (cont.)

An example of a procedure is given in Figure 7.19; as befits an instruction for carrying out a complex, high–level EMS activity, namely the updating of the Register of Environmental Effects, it is intended to allow reasonable flexibility of approach, within a clear statement of overall requirements and responsibilities. Further discussion and examples of procedures are given in Section 7.14 on Operational control.

1.0   PURPOSE

1.1   To describe the process for updating the Register of Significant
Environmental Effects for the Hades Site of Mythological Industries plc, as a basis
for setting objectives and maintaining effective control of relevant activities.

2.0   SCOPE

2.1   This procedure shall apply to the updating of the Register of Significant
Environmental Effects for the Hades Site, with respect to all activities and
products managed from, or produced at, that site. It therefore applies to all
Departments at the Hades Site.

3.0   REFERENCES

3.1   Hades Site Register of Significant Environmental Effects, MI/HAD/EFF.
3.2   British Standard BS 7750:1994 Environmental Management Systems.
3.3   D.T.E. Hunt and C.A. Johnson, *Environmental Management Systems*,
McGraw-Hill, London, 1995.
3.4   Procedure for Filing of Hades Site EMS Documents, MI/Had/EMS/Pro07.
3.5   Procedure for Issue of Hades Site EMS Documents, MI/Had/EMS/Pro08.
3.6   Procedure for Revision of Hades Site Environmental Objectives, EMS/031.
3.7   Procedure for Maintenance of Hades Site EMS Documents, MI/Had/EMS/Pro09.

4.0   DEFINITIONS

4.1   For the purposes of this Procedure, the definitions in BS 7750: 1994 apply.
4.2   The term 'Register' in this Procedure shall refer to the Hades Site Register of
Siginficant Eviromental Effects.
4.3   Updating Group — A group of Site staff convened to update the Register — see
5.2.1 below. The term 'Group' in this Procedure shall refer to this Updating
Group.

5.0   ACTIONS

5.1   Authorization to proceed

5.1.1   The Hades Site Manager, in consultation with the Environment Manager,
shall determine the need to update the Register.

MI/Had/EMS/Pro/027/v1.0/030594   **Page** 3 **of** 6

Figure 7.19 (cont.)

7.13.5 Emergency plans

The emphasis of an effective EMS should be on the prevention of avoidable
deleterious environmental effects. Thus, the process of effects evaluation is
required to identify potential, as well as actual, effects of significance (see
Section 7.8). This identification will entail an evaluation of risk. (The term
'risk' is commonly used with two meanings:

5.1.2   The Hades Site Manager may decide to update at any time, as circumstances require. However, at the beginning of each calendar year the Environment Manager shall formally consider the need for updating .

5.1.3   The Environment Manager shall make recommendations on updating the Register to the Hades Site Manager, in writing, by 1 February each year.

5.1.4   The Hades Site Manager shall notify the following, in writing, of any decision to update: the Environment Manager, all other Departmental Managers, the Site Services Manager and the Chairman of the Site Environmental Forum.

5.1.5   Once a decision has been taken to update the Register, the Hades Site Manager and the Environment Manager shall agree a timetable for updating. This shall provide for the issue of a revised Register not later than four calendar months after notification to update.

5.1.6   The Environment Manager shall be responsible for managing the updating. The Environmental Department shall provide secretarial and primary technical support for the updating process.

5.2   Updating Group

5.2.1   The Environment Manager shall convene a Group of Hades Site staff to carry out the updating, and shall chair its meetings. The Group shall consist of: the Environment Manager, the Marketing Manager, the R&D Manager, the Operations Manager, the Site Services Manager, and the Chairman of the Site Environmental Forum.

5.2.2   The Environment Manager shall obtain such other assistance as the Group considers necessary, liaising with relevant line management as appropriate. Any difficulties in providing such assistance, which cannot be resolved by the Environment Manager and Departmental Managers, shall be referred to the Hades Site Manager for resolution.

MI/Had/EMS/Pro/027/v1.0/030594   **Page** 4 **of** 6

Figure 7.19 (cont.)

1   Risk = Probability of Occurrence
2   Risk = Probability of Occurrence × Severity of Consequences

Here, we use the term in the second sense.)

Various technical approaches are available for risk evaluation (see Section 7.8) but, however the task is done, identification of potentially significant environmental risks will be followed by an assessment of the control mechanisms needed to prevent them, or more accurately minimize, within practical

5.3   Updating activity

5.3.1   The Group shall review the current Register, considering:
- any changes in activities and products since the last update,
- changes in performance since the last update, including achievement of, or
        progress towards, environmental objectives and targets,
- changes or potential changes to relevant legislation, regulations,
        Market-Based Instruments and industry sector Codes of Practice,
- the views of interested parties, including any communications received,
- changes in scientific evidence concerning effects and contributions thereto,
- such other factors as the Group may consider relevant.

5.3.2   The Group shall identify and examine the environmental effects of all activities
managed from, and all products produced at, the Hades Site. It shall
determine which effects are "significant", and produce a draft revised Register.
The scope of the examination shall follow the requirements of Reference 3.2 (in
particular, those in its Clause 4.4.2).

5.3.3   The Group shall decide the methods for identifying effects and evaluating
their significance, as appropriate to the activities, products and types of effect.
The methodologies may include, but shall not be restricted to, those described
in Section 7-8 of Reference 3.3.

5.3.4   The members of the Group (as defined in 5.2.1 above) shall each have one
vote in any ballot taken, including those addressing decisions on the
significance of environmental effects. If there is a tie, the Chairman's casting
vote shall decide.

5.3.5   The Environmental Department shall, from the work of the Group, prepare the
draft revised Register to the required format (see Reference 3.1). The Group
shall check and agree the draft. The Environment Manager shall then submit
it to the Hades Site Manager for approval to issue for use.

5.3.6   The Environmental Department shall file the Minutes and working papers of the
Group, according to Reference 3.4.

MI/Had/EMS/Pro/027/v1.0/030594   **Page** 5 **of** 6

Figure 7.19 (cont.)

constraints, the likelihood of their realization. This will in turn be followed by
development or refinement of the necessary organizational structures and
responsibilities, procedures, training and monitoring arrangements.

One should not act, however, on the principle that such anticipation can be
wholly effective in ensuring that emergencies and incidents with environmental
consequences will never arise. Indeed, it is a fundamental principle of sound
risk management that the resources deployed in prevention are commensurate
with the risk, and that complete assurance of prevention is impossible.

5.4   Issue of the revised Register

5.4.1   The Environmental Department shall issue the revised Register, according to Reference 3.5.

5.5   Consequent activity, including Revision of Environmental Objectives

5.5.1   The Environment Manager shall, within one calendar month of the issue of the revised Register, initiate revision of the Hades Site Environmental Objectives, according to Reference 3.6.

5.5.2   The Environment Manager shall also consider any other changes necessary in the light of the revised Register. He/she shall make written recommendations to the Hades Site Manager within two calendar months of the issue of the revised Register.

6.0   VARIATIONS AND REVISION

6.1   The written authorization of the Hades Site Manager is required for any variation to this Procedure. He/she shall consider variation only in response to a written request from the Environment Manager giving the reasons for the variation requested.

6.2   The Environmental Department shall file Requests for, and authorizations of, variations, according to Reference 3.4.

6.3   The Environment Manager is responsible for maintaining this Procedure, according to Reference 3.7. He/she shall review its requirements and operation, and advise the Hades Site Manager, in writing, if there is a need to change it. This shall be done within two calendar months of a revised Register being issued.

7.0   DOCUMENTATION

         None

MI/Had/EMS/Pro/027/v1.0/030594   **Page** 6 **of** 6

Figure 7.19 (conc.)

It is therefore important that planning for emergencies and incidents addresses, where appropriate, their environmental consequences. Note that this does not require the preparation of *separate* emergency plans to deal with environmental matters, which would tend to detract from the clarity and unity of purpose essential to deal with such situations. Rather, it is a requirement of BS 7750 that site emergency plans *include* relevant environmental information and associated instructions, addressing such issues as:

- Possible environmental consequences of likely emergencies.
- Control of such consequences, and amelioration of their effects, including:
  - Responsibilities, authorities and management procedures
  - Procedures for conducting control and remediation work
  - Procedures for communication with external agencies, e.g. regulatory bodies, and sources of information/assistance
  - Procedures for communication with neighbours, the public and the media.
- Responsibilities and procedures for follow-up investigation and action.

It is also a requirement of the standard that mechanisms and procedures for dealing with the environmental aspects of emergency situations be tested, wherever practicable, by appropriate means. What these means are will depend on the particular situation and its risks, but they may range from simple checks of the components of the emergency response arrangements through to full-scale simulations involving the active participation of outside organizations, such as regulatory agencies and emergency services.

Given the wide range of possible environmental emergencies which can arise in organizations of different kinds, it is impossible to offer more specific advice here. However, we would simply draw attention to two points:

1 Emergencies may have *both* health and safety *and* broader environmental consequences (e.g. a fire in a chemical storage area), or they may have only the latter (e.g. spillage of a large quantity of milk into a watercourse).
2 Health and safety matters are more likely to have been fully addressed in many site emergency plans.

It follows, therefore, that existing site emergency plans, though they should be considered in environmental effects assessment, may not address all relevant emergencies from an environmental standpoint.

7.13.6 The principles of document control

Possessing written instructions is of little value if, for example, it is not clear to what they apply, they are not checked and agreed before use, they are not available to those who need them, or they are not updated when their subject matter changes. Similar considerations apply to other types of EMS documentation.

Control systems are therefore needed to ensure that documents are:

- Identifiable: to the subject they address, and with regard to their currency
- Authorized before issue
- Reviewed and revised as necessary
- Available, in current version, to those who need them

BS 7750 specifically requires that appropriate documentation control procedures are established and maintained; in this respect, its requirements are essentially identical to those of BS 5750/ISO 9000.

Indeed, wherever practicable, the same document control procedures and document formats should be applied to all subsystems of the overall management system. This makes control and use of documents easier, facilitates cross-referencing and thereby avoids duplication, and minimizes the risk of ambiguity in document identification. It also emphasizes the unity of the overall system.

Unfortunately, different control systems may have arisen within an organization for different management subsystems. Immediate remediation of this may be impractical, but should be set as a longer-term goal. Therefore, when setting up an EMS in such circumstances, it is sensible to consider what the organization plans to do to harmonize existing subsystems, and proceed accordingly.

The remainder of Section 7.13 briefly describes the elements of document control; more detailed discussion of document control practices may be found in Chapter 11 of the text on quality assurance by Stebbing.[57]

7.13.7 Document identification

Assuming that an integrated document control system is in use, an EMS document identification system might contain the following:

```
           MI  /  Had  /  EMS /  Pro  /  027  /  v1.0  /  030594

Company    __|          |       |        |        |        |
Site        _____|            |        |        |        |
Subsystem   _____|             |        |        |
Document type  _____|         |        |        |
Serial number  _____|            |        |
Revision status  _____|        |
Date  _____|
```

Wherever possible, descriptive letters (EMS, Pro) are used in preference to numbers. There is no necessity to distinguish major and minor revisions ('v1.0'), but the practice is becoming well known from its use in software identification, and may be helpful.

7.13.8 Document authorization and review

EMS documentation, including policy, objectives, management programme, procedures and work instructions, should be authorized before issue, and periodically reviewed by an appropriate person, to ensure continuing relevance and accuracy.

Responsibility for review may usefully be noted in the document itself ('The Environment Manager is responsible for maintaining this Procedure . . . '), and will be determined by the nature of the content. Thus, for example, the Policy statement needs to be reviewed by the chairman or chief executive, and procedures and work instructions by a designated member of staff within the relevant area of activity or function. Similarly, responsibility for authorization to issue documents can be assigned appropriately.

7.13.9 Document distribution

It is important (and a requirement of BS 7750) that current — and only current — versions of relevant documents are available, where they are needed, to those who need them to perform operations essential to the effective functioning of the EMS. Moreover, as Stebbing[57] notes, there is no purpose, and very real risk of confusion, in distributing documents more widely than is necessary, merely because copying technology allows it. In particular, needlessly wide distribution makes it more difficult to ensure that only current versions of documents are extant and used.

Procedures should therefore be established to control the distribution of EMS documents, both within and outside the organization. A matrix of document identifier versus staff positions and external recipients, simple to hold on a computer spreadsheet or database, makes this task straightforward.[57] It may also be sensible to assign responsibility to a nominated person or persons to adjudicate on the availability of identified types of document, should the need arise.

Updating documents can be achieved by issuing amended pages only, with suitable instructions for their incorporation, or by issuing the entire revised document. The latter approach is simpler and more secure, but obviously wasteful in the case of large documents subject to frequent minor changes. In either case, BS 7750 requires that procedures be in place to ensure that superseded documentation is withdrawn from points of use. This can be achieved by requiring return of the relevant pages/documents to the issuing point, or of a signed declaration of destruction from the recipient.

To enable documents to be made available to those not on an established distribution list (e.g. to external assessors), uncontrolled copies may be released, provided that:

- Such release is appropriately authorized.
- The status of such copies is made clear (e.g. they are stamped 'Uncontrolled').
- The copies carry a notification that they may not be the latest version.
- Recipients are advised that they will not be notified of later amendments.

7.14 Securing Operational Control, Monitoring and Recording

7.14.1 Introduction

Once the policy, objectives and targets, and programme have been drawn up and documented, environmental management can be built into relevant day-to-day operations to ensure that they are properly planned, and that they, and the associated environmental effects, are under control. Control involves planning the conduct of functions, activities and processes, performing them as planned, monitoring the outcome to check if it is satisfactory, and taking corrective action if it is not (Figure 7.20). Depending on the individual situation, monitoring data may be retained only so long as is required to effect control through the feedback loop, or may be recorded to provide a record of the outcome. Because they are intimately linked in the cycles of Figure 7.20, operational control, monitoring and recording are discussed together in this section.

Variations on this essentially four-stage cycle are found in numerous texts: see, for example, Health and Safety Executive[59] and Oil Industry Exploration and Production Forum.[60] The common theme is that action is never taken without being planned, and without arrangements being in place for monitoring its effectiveness. If the action does prove to be effective it can be repeated without modification, but subject to continued monitoring. If at any stage the action proves ineffective, it must be corrected so that it becomes effective, and the cycle continued. (Correction consists of two types of action: modification of the plan, if it has proved to be inadequate to deal with an unforeseen condition, or correction of the implementation of the planned arrangements, if this has been faulty.)

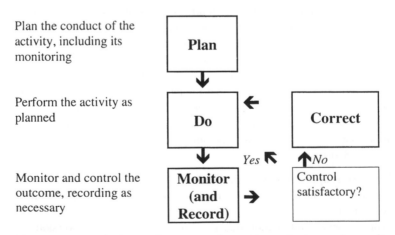

Figure 7.20 The basis of operational control, monitoring and recording

7.14.2 What needs to be controlled?

The purpose of operational control is to maintain the environmental performance of the organization within predetermined limits. The activities over which control may need to be exerted may be diverse and widely spread throughout the organization. BS 7750 states that it is necessary to identify functions, activities and processes which affect, or could affect, the environment significantly (which we shall call 'environment-critical activities'), and then ensure that they are carried out under controlled conditions.

The first step in identifying the environment-critical activities is to consider the organization's:

1 Policy
2 Register of legislative, regulatory and other policy requirements
3 Register of significant environmental effects
4 Objectives and targets

It might be argued that only the second and fourth of these need to be considered, but significant environmental effects may need to be controlled, without being the subject of legislative or regulatory requirements, or of a specific objective at a given time. Thus, while the need for operational control to achieve quantified objectives may be obvious, control needs stemming from policy requirements may be far-reaching. It is prudent, therefore, to check the policy and the register of significant environmental effects, as well as the register of legislative, regulatory and other policy requirements and the current objectives and targets, when determining the need for control activities. (Indeed, the potentially far-reaching nature of control requirements arising from policy commitments provides a compelling reason for care in preparing policy statements (see Section 7.5) and emphasizes the importance of a sound and comprehensive environmental effects evaluation (see Section 7.8).)

The kinds of functions, activities and processes which may need to be controlled are inevitably numerous but may include, among others:

- Design of products/services
- Purchasing
- Materials handling
- Contracted work
- Production/service provision
- Pollution abatement
- Disposal of waste and discharge of releases
- Emergency handling
- Administration
- Maintenance
- Investment

Care should be taken to identify not only the activities and effects of the organization which *inevitably* happen, and need to be controlled, but also those which *might* happen if things go wrong. An obvious example is the containment of fire-fighting water on a site where toxic materials are used or stored, which should be addressed by operational control elements in the site emergency plan (see Section 7.13).

7.14.3 What degree of control is needed?

It is important that the necessary *extent* of control — the 'performance criteria' — be clearly understood by all who are involved in maintaining that control. This means that the performance criteria should be carefully determined, communicated appropriately, and documented in the relevant procedures and work instructions. Some criteria will be set by regulators (e.g. 'The pH of the effluent discharged must be between 6 and 11' or 'All waste generated on site must be dealt with according to Duty of Care procedures'). Others will stem from general policy commitments beyond legal compliance, or be defined by corporate objectives and targets. For example, a policy commitment to be 'a good neighbour' might translate, in practice, to a stipulation that all deliveries are to be made to a particular site entrance, to avoid heavy traffic on village or suburban streets, and/or at particular times, to avoid noise or other nuisance.

7.14.4 Types of control mechanism

The mechanisms by which control is exerted can vary greatly, according to the nature of the activities under control. Technical means might be used to control, for example, emissions to air, water or land, where the means might be filtration, scrubbing or other abatement equipment to control emissions to atmosphere, or an effluent treatment plant to control emissions to surface water or sewer.

In many cases, control will be exerted not by the deployment of specialized equipment, but by adherence to specific procedures. The disposal of waste provides such an example, where procedures will be needed to ensure that wastes are segregated, stored and dispatched correctly. Of course, procedures will be necessary to ensure effective operation and maintenance of pollution control equipment as well.

7.14.5 Developing control arrangements and procedures

It is important that the development of control arrangements and procedures takes into account existing practices, operational requirements and the views of those who are responsible for both the management and the conduct of the relevant work. The benefits of consulting those doing the work to be controlled can hardly be overemphasized. Apart from the importance of their feeling involved, control arrangements and procedures which do not actually function effectively, or which are needlessly cumbersome or onerous, may be completely disregarded, and will certainly bring the EMS into disrepute.

It is a common concern of those considering the implementation of an EMS that written procedures and instructions will be emphasized disproportionately, and that the importance of such factors as good oral instruction, competent staff and sound training will be neglected. In fact, BS 7750 (as an example of an EMS model) specifically states that documented procedures and instructions need to be developed '. . . for situations in which the absence of such instructions could result in infringement of the environmental policy'. This — taken with the standard's emphasis on training — clearly provides for a flexible approach to achieving control, by an appropriate mixture of methods, and helps ensure that EMS principles and concepts can be applied in organizations of all types and cultures.

A sequence of steps for developing written procedures and work instructions is given in Section 7.13: see, in particular, Figure 7.18 and the text on Procedures and Work Instructions. Many of the steps described are also applicable to the development of control arrangements which are not encapsulated in written instructions, but which are the basis of other means of achieving control, such as training.

7.14.6 Examples of Control Procedures and Work Instructions

As noted previously, the range of activities for which procedures may be required is obviously very wide. Nevertheless, some examples will be given, which address fairly common activities. The first, shown in Figure 7.21, illustrates a work instruction for an aspect of procurement control. (Procurement is an activity for which environmental and quality management may be closely integrated using a single supplier database.) Note the clear designation of responsibilities, and the use of a flowchart to aid understanding of the procedure. This not only assists those involved to understand their tasks, but also helps an internal auditor (or, if external certification is sought, an external assessor) to follow the working of the procedure.

The second example, shown in Figure 7.22, shows an instruction dealing with the segregation of waste arising on a manufacturing site. This takes the form of a notice posted on the wall in the production area, immediately visible to all who work there, illustrating the fact that written procedures and instructions are not documents to be prepared and then filed away, but essential elements of day-to-day control.

The third example (Figure 7.23) is a procedure for the disposal of waste from the same site. (The examples given in Figures 7.22 and 7.23 form part of

---

Heaven in Hell Furnishings plc

Title

WORK INSTRUCTION FOR ENVIRONMENTAL SCREENING OF SUPPLIERS

Document number

HIHF//EMS/Pro/WI23

Revision status

Date	Revision	Description	Issued	Checked	Approved
05/06/94	1.0	For use	*BJB*	*VFW*	*JL*
15/05/94	0.0	For comment	*BJB*	-	-
			Purchasing Manager	Env. Manager	Purchasing Director

HIHF/EMS/Pro/WI23/v1.0/050694   **Page** 1 **of** 5

Figure 7.21 Example of a work instruction to control procurement. (Continued on pages 195–198).

the same system as Table 7.4, where the responsibilities of the Waste Disposal Supervisor are described.) Notice that this includes an example of verification and corrective action, in its reference to examining the contents of receptacles to check the segregation of waste, and rejecting, for proper sorting, any which have been incorrectly segregated. Such measures should be built into procedures wherever appropriate; see also the discussion below on Corrective action.

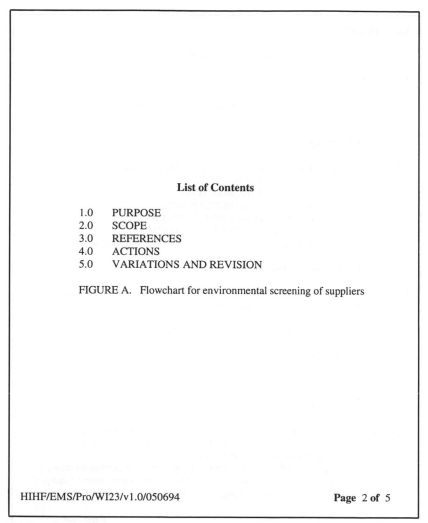

List of Contents

1.0 PURPOSE
2.0 SCOPE
3.0 REFERENCES
4.0 ACTIONS
5.0 VARIATIONS AND REVISION

FIGURE A. Flowchart for environmental screening of suppliers

HIHF/EMS/Pro/WI23/v1.0/050694   **Page** 2 **of** 5

Figure 7.21 (cont.)

7.14.7 Monitoring implementation

The effectiveness of controls may be vitiated by one or both of the following:

- If users do not understand why the procedure must be followed.
- If users find easier (but less environmentally acceptable) ways of doing things, and believe them to be adequate.

Thus, a perfect paper system does not guarantee effective operational control, and it is the responsibility of line management to ensure that work really is

---

1.0   PURPOSE

1.1   To check the environmental probity of suppliers to BS 7750, Clause 4.8 (3.1).

2.0   SCOPE

2.1   This instruction describes the checking of supplier environmental probity by the Environmental and Purchasing Departments.

3.0   REFERENCES

3.1   British Standard BS 7750:1994 Environmental Management Systems.
3.2   Supplier Questionnaire (HIHF/QMS/NSQ)
3.3   New Supplier Procedure (HIHF/QMS/PRO/14)
3.4   Supplier Environmental Criteria (HIHF/EMS/SEC)
3.5   Supplier Environmental Evaluation (HIHF/EMS/FOR/12)
3.6   EMS Record Filing Procedure (HIHF/EMS/PRO/07)
3.7   Supplier Environmental Audit Programme (HIHF/EMS/PROG/05)

4.0   ACTIONS (see also attached flowchart)

4.1   The Purchasing Manager shall send to any potential supplier the New Supplier Questionnaire (3.2), in accordance with the New Supplier Procedure (3.3).

4.2   The Purchasing Manager shall copy the returned questionnaire (or further information or supplier response, or see 4.4(b), 4.4(c) and 4.7 below) to the Environment Manager.

4.3   The Environment Manager shall, within 2 weeks of receipt of the copy of the completed questionnaire (or further information or other response), evaluate it in accordance with the Supplier Environmental Criteria (3.4).

4.4   The Environment Manager shall provide the Purchasing Manager with a copy of the completed Supplier Environmental Evaluation Form (3.5), requesting him to send the potential supplier one of the following:
       (a) An acceptance of the potential supplier (subject to other purchasing decisions), advising him of any potential requirement for the future enviromental audits if so indicated in the completed Supplier Enviromental Evaluation Form.

HIHF/EMS/Pro/WI23/v1.0/050694   **Page** 3 **of** 5

Figure 7.21 (cont.)

conducted as planned. This is more likely if care has been taken to ensure that the need for controls is understood, and that procedures and instructions are practicable, clear and accessible. The posting of notices, for example, on or next to the equipment to which they refer, and the labelling of waste bins according to their intended contents, are ways in which instructions can be made readily available at the point of use.

Line management should create a climate in which control is exerted effectively, and should routinely monitor the way in which procedures and work

(b) A request for further information on the points raised in the Supplier Environmental Evaluation Form.

(c) A rejection of the potential supplier on environmental grounds, enclosing the completed Supplier Environmental Evaluation Form, inviting the potential supplier to consider the evaluation and respond, if desired.

4.5   The Environment Manager shall file copies of the Supplier Questionnaire (or further information or response) and the completed Supplier Environmental Evaluation Form in accordance with the EMS Record Filing Procedure (3.6).

4.6   The Environment Manager shall incorporate any requirement for auditing in the Supplier Environmental Audit Programme (3.7).

4.7   On receipt of further information or other supplier response (see 4.4(b) and 4.4(c) above) the Purchasing Manager shall proceed as in 4.2 above.

5.0   VARIATIONS AND REVISION

5.1   The written authorization of the Environment Manager is required for any variation to this Procedure. He/she shall consider variation only in response to a written request from the Purchasing Manager giving the reasons for the variation requested.

5.2   The Environment Manager is responsible for maintaining this Procedure. He/she shall review its requirements and operation, and advise the Purchasing Director, in writing, if there is a need to change it.

Figure 7.21 (cont.)

instructions are implemented. The frequency of doing so should be based primarily on such factors as the environmental importance of the outcomes, the history of problems with particular procedures, the lengths of time for which they have been established, and the experience of their operators. However, monitoring also has the value of showing that correct implementation is considered important, and minimum frequencies of checking should take that fact into account.

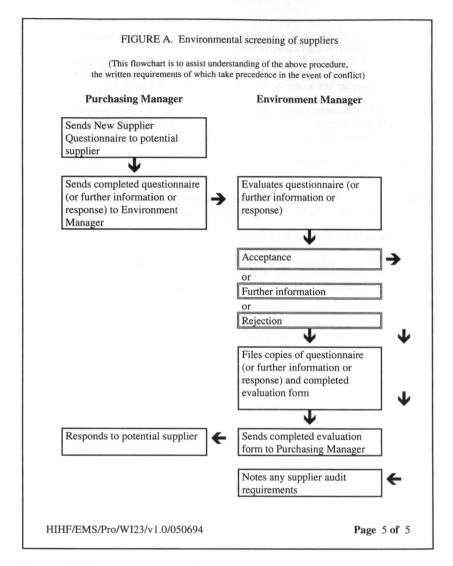

FIGURE A. Environmental screening of suppliers

(This flowchart is to assist understanding of the above procedure,
the written requirements of which take precedence in the event of conflict)

Figure 7.21 (conc.)

It is also important that monitoring of implementation should be seen to offer opportunities for 'catching people doing things right', as well as for spotting and correcting errors. Encouragement, motivation and reinforcement are important in ensuring that controls are correctly implemented, as is visible leadership from managers and supervisors in applying them personally.

7.14.8 Monitoring outcomes

Introduction

This discussion of monitoring refers to monitoring of outcomes of all kinds, whether undertaken within the site, at the site boundary or in the external environment. Thus, the term embraces such diverse activities as monitoring of:

- The quantities, flows and physical/chemical/biological compositions of effluents, emissions and wastes.
- The effects of releases on target organisms or ecosystems.
- Noise, dust, odour, litter and visual impact.
- Raw material, fuel and energy usage.
- The effectiveness of waste segregation and recycling measures.
- Complaints from neighbours.
- The effectiveness of information for consumers, e.g. concerning product use/disposal.

References 61–65 contain collections of measurement methods for various purposes.

Although there are obvious differences between these different kinds of monitoring activity, a requirement common to all is that they be carefully planned in order to achieve their objectives cost-effectively. The essential sequence of activities in planning any monitoring activity is summarized, as a set of key questions, in Figure 7.24. Each of these issues will now be considered in turn.

Stage 1 Providing a clear and quantified statement of the objectives is an essential first step in the design of any monitoring programme, without which subsequent steps may be prejudiced, resources wasted and control rendered ineffective.

The accuracy of the required information (i.e. the closeness of a measurement to the true value) must also be clearly stated at the outset, because if the data gathered are insufficiently accurate, the monitoring effort will have been wasted.[61] For example, if an effluent is to be monitored to check that the concentration of a particular determinand complies with a consent limit of 100 units, and the measured value is 80 units but the error associated with the measurement is ± 40 units, the measurement will have failed to provide adequate assurance that the limit is met. More accurate analysis is required in this instance, yet very often monitoring is conducted without the accuracy of the measurements ever being considered.

Stage 2 The location where measurements are made can have great bearing on the value of the data. To take an obvious example, there will be little or

---

DISPOSAL OF WASTES FROM PRODUCTION AREA A1

Production Staff - please remember that:
- Proper waste disposal is your responsibility
- It is important to put wastes in the **RIGHT PLACE**

Pallets - undamaged	Stack - area marked 'Undamaged Pallets'
Empty plastic drums - undamaged	Stand on pallets - area marked 'Undamaged Drums'
Empty plastic sacks - uncontaminated	Flatten - skip marked 'Clean Sacks'
Cardboard boxes - uncontaminated	Flatten - skip marked 'Clean Cardboard'
Damaged pallets and plastic drums - uncontaminated	Skip marked 'Damaged Pallets and Drums'
Any packaging contaminated with product or solvent	Skip marked 'Contaminated Packaging' in the fenced area of the yard marked 'Contaminated Waste'
Spilt or contaminated product	Place in plastic drum. Attach 'Contaminated Product' label (available from Production Area Office), having added details of any problems the waste poses, its area of origin, its name, and the process which produced it. Place labelled drum in the fenced area of the yard marked 'Contaminated Waste'

Please **PHONE** the Waste Disposal Supervisor on extension 4137 if you:
- Have any other type of waste
- Are not sure what to do
- Find that any waste area is full
- Find that the stock of labels or empty drums has run out

R.J.Morris
Waste Disposal Supervisor, 05/06/94   MI/Had/EMS/Pro/N13/v1.0/050694

Figure 7.22 Example of an instruction notice about the segregation of waste

no point in monitoring the occurrence of odours anywhere other than downwind of their source, but less obviously, simple considerations of atmospheric dispersion can predict how far downwind they might be detected, saving wasted monitoring effort applied in the wrong place. Even when a measurement is to be made within a confined effluent stream, the exact sam-

Mythological Industries plc

Title

PROCEDURE FOR COLLECTION AND DISPOSAL OF WASTE
AT THE HADES SITE

Document Number

MI/Had/EMS/Pro/035

Revision Status

Date	Revision	Description	Issued By	Checked By	Approved By
05/06/94	1.0	For Use	Ꝺℰℛ	GℵW	DℐT
18/05/94	0.0	For Comment	Ꝺℰℛ	-	-
			Environ Manager	Site Services Manager	Site Manager

MI/Had/EMS/Pro/035/v1.0/050694   **Page** 1 **of** 5

Figure 7.23 Example of a procedure for collection and disposal of waste. (Continued on pages 202–205)

pling position can be important. The measurement of particulate concentration in a gas stream, for example, needs to be conducted in a straight section of duct and a specified distance from any bends, to avoid, as far as possible, regions of turbulent gas flow.

List of Contents

1.0   PURPOSE
2.0   SCOPE
3.0   REFERENCES
4.0   DEFINITIONS
5.0   ACTIONS
6.0   VARIATIONS AND REVISION
7.0   DOCUMENTATION

Figure 7.23 (cont.)

On a more general note, the use to which monitoring data is to be put is fundamental in determining the level of detail, or disaggregation, which is required. Thus, centralized measurement of electricity consumption will obviously be unhelpful in monitoring the progress of individual units towards the achievement of local targets for energy saving. More importantly, it should not be simply assumed that centralized monitoring arrangements (e.g. for purchasing or vehicle fleet fuel use) do report the information which they

---

1.0   PURPOSE

1.1   To facilitate compliance with Waste Disposal Requirements under the Environmental Protection Act (1990).

2.0   SCOPE

2.1   This procedure shall apply to the collection and disposal of all wastes arising from the Hades Site.

3.0   REFERENCES

3.1   Procedure for Filing of Hades Site EMS Documents, MI/Had/EMS/Pro07.

4.0   DEFINITIONS

None

5.0   ACTIONS

Note: Actions and responsibilities assigned to the Waste Disposal Supervisor (WDS) shall, in his absence, be discharged by the Site Services Manager.

5.1   Production Area Managers are responsible for ensuring that their staffs dispose of wastes in accordance with instruction notices issued by the WDS.

5.2   The Duty Yard Supervisor shall ensure that, at least once a day:

(a) Undamaged pallets and empty plastic drums are collected from all production areas, and placed in the areas marked 'Pallets' and 'Plastic Drums' in the warehouse, for storage pending return to suppliers.
(b) All skips marked 'Clean Sacks', 'Clean Cardboard', 'Damaged Pallets and Plastic Drums' and 'Contaminated Packaging' are checked, and the Waste Disposal Supervisor advised when any is three-quarters full.
(c) Closed and fully-labelled drums of 'Spilt or Contaminated Product' are collected from all production areas, and placed in the 'Production Waste' section of the Waste Storage Area. Open or incompletely/illegibly labelled drums shall not be collected, and the relevant Production Area Manager shall be informed at once.

MI/Had/EMS/Pro/035/v1.0/050694   **Page** 3 **of** 5

Figure 7.23 (cont.)

are supposed to, in large organizations, particularly. The authors have found from experience that there are often parts of such organizations which operate autonomously, escaping centralized monitoring and control.

Stage 3   It is obvious that certain types of monitoring can be conducted on an essentially continuous basis: the monitoring of electricity consumption,

5.3 The WDS shall:

(a) Maintain the tidiness of the Waste Storage Area.
(b) Check that all drums of 'Spilt or Contaminated Product' delivered to the Waste Storage Area are securely closed, and have complete and legible labels.
(c) Reject any such drums deficient in these respects, arranging with the Duty Yard Supervisor for their return to the originating Production Area, and sending a consignment rejection note to the Site Services Manager and the relevant Production Area Manager.
(d) Record details of such drums received for storage in the Waste Storage Area log book.

5.4 The WDS shall also:

(a) Summon a licensed waste disposal contractor (see below) when a full load has accumulated (drums) or any skip is three-quarters full.
(b) Ensure that waste is packed safely prior to its removal from site.
(c) Ensure that waste is removed from the site *only* by licensed contractors, by consulting the quarterly list supplied by the Contracts Manager to identify such contractors, and checking the credentials of the contractor on arrival at the site. *Use of unlicensed contractors could result in prosecution.*
(d) Hand over to the contractor receiving the waste a description of it, and a signed copy of the transfer note.
(e) Keep a copy of the transfer note signed by the contractor, and file the note and the description of the waste in his/her office: see reference 3.1. *Only when 2 years old may these be discarded.*
(f) Record all details of waste leaving the site in the Waste Disposal log book, so that an up-to-date record is always available.

5.5 The WDS shall be responsible for checking that the requirements of this procedure are being met, and informing the Site Services Manager and Environment Manager of any persistent problems. Specifically, the WDS shall regularly check that drums and skips contain only the designated waste types.

MI/Had/EMS/Pro/035/v1.0/050694 **Page** 4 **of** 5

Figure 7.23 (cont.)

for example. In other cases, continuous monitoring may be desirable (e.g. aspects of effluent quality), but impracticable with current technology, or prohibitively expensive. In such cases decisions need to be made about the frequency and timing of sampling and analysis.

Prior information about the extent and time-scales of the variation to be expected (e.g. in an effluent stream) can be exploited to improve the efficiency of the sampling programme. Predictions may be possible from knowledge of plant operations and working patterns, but an initial period of intensive

6.0   VARIATIONS AND REVISION

6.1   The written authorization of the Hades Site Manager is required for any variation to this Procedure. He/she shall consider variation only in response to a written request giving the reasons for the variation requested.

6.3   The Site Services Manager is responsible for maintaining this Procedure, and shall keep its requirements and operation under review, and advise the Hades Site Manager, in writing, if there is a need to change it.

7.0   DOCUMENTATION

None

MI/Had/EMS/Pro/035/v1.0/050694   **Page** 5 **of** 5

Figure 7.23 (conc.)

monitoring may also be advisable. Then, as long as the plant continues to be operated in a similar way, monitoring effort can be concentrated on those periods of greatest interest: for example, when a maximum standard is most likely to be exceeded.

If such 'stratified' sampling is not possible, recourse will have to be made to random sampling, the power of which to provide assurance of compliance with, say, a maximum standard is explored in Table 7.23. These data, taken from

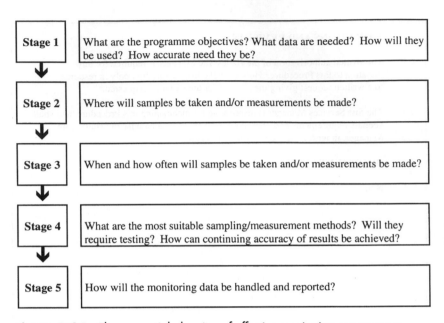

Stage 1	What are the programme objectives? What data are needed? How will they be used? How accurate need they be?
Stage 2	Where will samples be taken and/or measurements be made?
Stage 3	When and how often will samples be taken and/or measurements be made?
Stage 4	What are the most suitable sampling/measurement methods? Will they require testing? How can continuing accuracy of results be achieved?
Stage 5	How will the monitoring data be handled and reported?

Figure 7.24 The sequential planning of effective monitoring programmes

Table 7.23 The protection afforded by 100 per cent sample compliance, for (independent random) sampling schemes of different sizes

Number, (n), of samples, all of which comply	Risk (β) that the true percentage compliance is *lower* than the figure stated in the table		
n	$\beta = 1.0\%$	$\beta = 5.0\%$	$\beta = 10.0\%$
1	1.0	5.0	10.0
2	10.0	22.4	31.6
5	39.8	54.9	63.1
12	68.1	77.9	82.5
50	91.2	94.2	95.5

Ellis,[62] illustrate the degree of protection afforded by 100 per cent sample compliance, for random, independent sampling schemes of different sizes addressing a 'maximum' standard.

Thus, for example, if 12 (random independent) samples were taken during the period of interest, and all proved to be compliant, the statement made concerning compliance could only be of the following kind: 'We are confident, at the 99 per cent level, that true underlying compliance is no *worse* than 68.1 per cent'. Such statements would be likely to get short shrift from a director seeking to be assured that the company was 'compliant'.

Similar considerations apply to monitoring the segregation of wastes. Inspecting the contents of every skip is unlikely to be practical, and so some sampling strategy will need to be devised. This might mean, for example, one or both of the following:

- Concentrating effort on checking those skips filled at parts of the site where hazardous wastes are most likely to arise.
- Monitoring intensively for a period following the provision of instruction to the work-force, and less frequently thereafter.

Stage 4 Where alternative measurement methods exist, choice must be exercised. Of course it is essential that whatever method is chosen is capable of producing results of the accuracy required (specified in Stage 1), but thereafter the choice might be made on grounds of availability, convenience and cost. An advantage of clarifying accuracy needs in Stage 1 is that unnecessarily costly analyses can be avoided. If, on the other hand, the cost of obtaining the desired information is an unwelcome surprise, Stage 1 can be revisited before an unrealistic monitoring programme is initiated, and effort thereby wasted.

Appropriate quality control procedures will be required to ensure that routine monitoring results will continue to be of the required accuracy. The necessary disciplines are discussed in detail in Hunt and Wilson;[61] though dealing with water analysis specifically, the basic recommendations made therein will often be more widely applicable. Fundamentally, control of the quality of results requires that the measurement process be subjected to the same type of controls as are commonly applied to production processes (e.g. see discussion of Shewart and Cusum charts below), rather than reliance being placed solely on the inherent capability of the methodology to produce results of the required accuracy.

Stage 5 The handling and reporting of the data will be determined by the purpose for which they are collected. Simple comparison of results with a performance criterion may often be required, but more complex treatment of the data using appropriate statistical techniques may yield valuable results. Thus, for example, the use of Shewart (see Chapter 5) and Cusum control charts (developed initially for production quality control) can facilitate the detection of changes and trends.[66,67]

7.14.9 Corrective action

Corrective action is necessary when there is a non-compliance, that is, a failure in the planned operation of part of the EMS, or a failure to achieve an intended outcome, e.g. an objective not met or a performance criterion breached (see Figure 7.20). Corrective action has the objectives of:

- Restoring control as rapidly as possible
- Mitigating the consequences of the non-compliance
- Investigating and identifying root causes, and taking steps to prevent a recurrence

It is important to assign responsibilities for handling incidences of non-compliance, to ensure that these steps are taken. (The management representative (see Section 7.6) will need to be informed, and may participate in the subsequent investigation and remediation, but line management will usually be best placed to restore control and mitigate immediate consequences, and will need to be closely involved in identifying causes and modifying procedures to prevent recurrence.) Responsibilities should be defined *before* control is lost: when procedures are drawn up and performance criteria are determined.

In addition to the above objectives, there may be additional requirements, for example, to inform a regulatory agency if authorization conditions are breached, and work with it to mitigate consequences. Again, it is important to identify, and make plans to meet, such requirements when control procedures are under development.

In investigating incidences of non-compliance, and establishing their root causes, the Total Quality Management (TQM) technique of 'asking Why? 5 times' will often be helpful, to get beneath superficial causes and establish the real root of the problem. Suppose, for example, that neighbours complain about odours from a manufacturing plant; the line of enquiry might go something like this:

Q: 'Why do neighbours complain?'
A: *'Because they can smell materials used on site.'*
Q: 'Why do odorous vapours escape?'
A: *'Because the new tanks vent to atmosphere.'*
Q: 'Why do the new tanks vent to atmosphere?'
A: *'They were designed that way.'*
Q: 'Why was abatement equipment not included in the design?'
A: *'The designer didn't think of it.'*
Q: 'Why not?'
A: *'The procedure for designing new plant does not incorporate a mechanism for considering all environmental impacts.'*

Another aid to uncovering root causes used in TQM is the Ishikawa or fishbone diagram, a self-explanatory example of which is shown in Figure 7.25.

It is essential that when root causes have been identified, control arrangements and associated procedures are revised to take account of them and prevent recurrence of the non-compliance. However, such action is alone

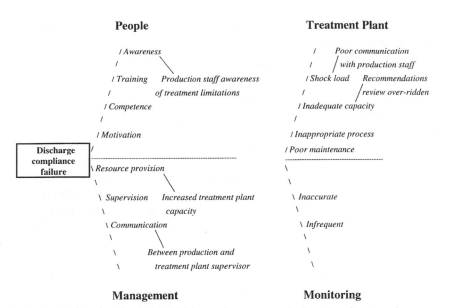

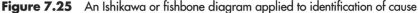

Figure 7.25 An Ishikawa or fishbone diagram applied to identification of cause

insufficient; the root cause of the problem, and the actions taken to prevent its repetition, need to be communicated to relevant staff, and appropriate monitoring arrangements put in place to check that the revised procedure is being effectively implemented. Corrective action cannot be considered complete until the effectiveness of the modification to the EMS has been proven.

7.14.10 Records

Records provide evidence that the management system has been operating, and indicate whether or not it has been successful in meeting objectives, targets and performance criteria. The information to be recorded may be quite extensive in scope and coverage; indeed, the majority of the elements of the EMS will probably have some associated recording requirement.

Examples include records of:

- Assigned roles and responsibilities
- Training needs identification, training provision, and training course success
- The environmental effects evaluation process and its results
- Communications from interested parties, and follow-up actions
- Progress towards objectives and targets
- Routine monitoring results, including any records thereof required by regulatory agencies

- Incidences of non-compliance, corrective actions taken, and their outcomes
- Audits and follow-up actions

Not included in this list are records of the costs and benefits of environmental management activities. Although monitoring and recording of these is not required by BS 7750 or EMA, many organizations will wish to ensure that their financial systems are capable of identifying environmental expenditure and benefits, when these can be quantified. Recording such information can help identify opportunities to achieve simultaneous environmental and financial benefits (see also Section 7.17).

Many of the detailed requirements relating to the legibility, control and secure storage of records are identical to those relating to documentation in general (see Section 7.13) and need not be repeated here. For particularly important records, e.g. those required by regulators, a duplicate set archived at a separate location may be prudent.

In the case of routine monitoring, the extent to which detailed data need to be stored, and for what period, will require careful consideration; continuous monitoring equipment can produce very large amounts of data. The use to be made of the data should determine the record-keeping arrangements, which should be decided and documented when monitoring plans are first developed. Routine control data will not normally be kept for an extended period: indeed, its reporting will often be on an 'exception' basis.

A related issue is the presentation of the results of monitoring, whether for internal management review or external reporting (see Section 7.18). In both cases, the overriding objective will be to offer concise and relevant *information*, rather than an indigestible mass of *data*. Unusual or problematic results will need to be clearly identified, and relevant comparisons, e.g. with objectives, regulatory limits and previous years' results, and interpretations facilitated by the use of appropriate diagrams.

7.15 Auditing

7.15.1 Introduction

As noted in Chapter 4, the 'Environmental Audit' — originally developed as a management tool to address concerns about corporate compliance with legislation and regulations — came to encompass a broad range of activities (including reviews, meaning the type of activity described in Section 7.3). The terms 'audit' and 'auditing' will be used in this section with reference to EMS audits, unless otherwise stated. In later parts of this section, we shall also consider performance/compliance audits and audits of an environmental statement.

Audits may be internal or external; internal audits are undertaken by the organization itself, external audits by others independent of the organization being audited. The term 'external audit' is here used to include activities such as assessment for BS 7750 compliance; see below. The nature of internal and external audits will differ somewhat, in keeping with their different objectives, but the general approach is the same. In this section, we shall describe auditing in general terms, but with particular emphasis on internal audits, noting where external auditing differs, as appropriate.

7.15.2 The purpose of EMS audits

Internal audits are an essential part of any management systems approach, providing the means by which the effective operation of the system can be checked, and remedial action taken if necessary. (Environmental Management Reviews, considered in the next Section, are higher level activities which check the continuing relevance of the environmental policy, update the evaluation of environmental effects, and check the efficacy of audits and follow-up actions.)

Internal audits are usually undertaken routinely, but they may also be undertaken in response to significant changes in the organization's EMS, activities, products or services, or by a need to follow up on corrective action. In general, therefore, internal audits are undertaken to give an organization an opportunity to improve its Environmental Management System, and thereby contribute to continual improvement in environmental performance.

External audits may be undertaken for a variety of reasons, including:

- Assessing the conformity of an organization's Environmental Management System to the requirements of a standard such as BS 7750, to permit its certification.
- Evaluating the environmental probity of an organization where there is a desire to establish or continue a contractual relationship, e.g. a company evaluating suppliers of raw materials, or a waste disposal contractor.
- Checking whether or not environmental management systems and practices meet specific regulatory requirements.

External audits, unlike internal audits, need also to address the effectiveness of the organization's Management Reviews.

7.15.3 Terminology

The term 'auditee' is used to refer to the organization whose operation is being audited, the term 'auditor(s)' or 'audit team' to those conducting the audit and the term 'client' to the organization commissioning the audit. Table 7.24 shows how these terms apply in different situations.

As noted above, this section will concentrate upon audits undertaken by the auditee organization itself for its own purposes, although many of the issues discussed will be applicable to all types of EMS audit. In this case, the client, auditee and auditor are all parts of the same organization although, of course,

Table 7.24 Types of EMS audit

Situation	Auditee	Auditor	Client	Audit description
A company (C) undertaking routine internal audits	C	C	C	Internal, first party
A retailer (R) undertaking audits of a supplier (S), using its (the retailer's) own auditing staff	S	R	R	External, second party
A company (C) commissioning audits of a waste contractor (W), by an auditing organization (A)	W	A	C	External, third party
A certification body (B) performing an assessment of a company (C) seeking certification to a standard	C	B	C	External, third party

the auditor(s) should wherever possible be independent of the part of the organization being audited. (In small organizations, such independence may be impossible to achieve, a fact recognized by BS 7750 which refers to the auditors being '. . . independent, so far as is possible, of the specific activities or areas being audited . . .'.)

In quality systems auditing, the term 'audit plan' is used to mean the proposed manner of carrying out a particular audit. The term was used in the first (1992) version of BS 7750 in a somewhat broader sense, however, to refer to a description of a continuing series of audits of an EMS *and* of the general manner in which they will be carried out; in the 1994 revision, the term 'audit programme' has been substituted. The term 'audit protocol' is also used in BS 7750, to refer to a generic description of the sequence of steps (actions to be taken by the auditor) for a specific type of audit. We shall follow BS 7750:1994 and use these terms with the following meanings:

- Audit programme: a description of a series of audits under an EMS.
- Audit protocol: a generic description of the steps for a specific type of audit.
- Audit plan: the proposed manner of carrying out a specific audit.

7.15.4 Audit programme and protocol

Under BS 7750, a programme of internal audits is to be established, defining the activities and areas to be audited, the responsibilities for doing so, and the frequency with which auditing is to be performed. Auditing frequency is to be decided on the basis of the actual or potential contribution of the activity or area to significant environmental effects, and the outcomes of previous audits. Under the EMA scheme, every part of a participating site is to be audited at least once in every 3 years. However, at least annual auditing will normally be appropriate for activities and areas having the potential to cause significant environmental harm.

BS 7750 also requires the organization to develop audit procedures and protocols which address, among other matters, audit methodology and reporting arrangements, and the selection of auditors. More detailed guidance on these issues may be found in ISO guidelines currently under development, as described below.

7.15.5 Sources of information on auditing

At the times when BS 7750 was being written and revised, there was no national or international standard on Environmental Management Systems Auditing, and it refers instead to the relevance to environmental management auditing of the *broad principles* of quality systems auditing, as expounded in the existing guideline standard BS 7229,[68] which, as ISO 10011, is also cited by the EMA Regulation.

Since that time (in July 1994) BSI has published, as Drafts for Public Comment (DPCs), three international (ISO) Committee Drafts of guideline standards on Environmental Auditing (see Chapter 8). One of these specifically addresses the conduct of EMS Audits,[69] the others address the general principles of environmental auditing,[70] and qualification criteria for *individual* auditors.[71] Further information on these and other ISO activities in the field of environmental management may be found in Chapter 8.

Among the many other texts and reports which contain useful information are those cited previously in Chapter 4. It should be noted, however, that the definition of, and approach to, auditing adopted in these texts often predates, and may in places differ from, that of BS 7750, EMA and the draft ISO standard. Texts on quality management systems and their auditing — for example, that by Sayle[72] can also be helpful.

7.15.6 EMS audits and the issues of environmental performance and EMS suitability and effectiveness

Environmental performance

There has been considerable debate about the role of the EMS audit in examining environmental performance. As detailed practices for accredited certification to BS 7750 and EMA registration are not yet in place, and International Standards have yet to be finalized, the following discussion can only summarize that debate and draw some general conclusions.

BS 7750 refers to the environmental management audit determining '. . . whether or not the environmental management system and the performance it achieves conform to planned arrangements . . .', and states that audit procedures shall deal, among other things, with 'environmental performance'.

The EMA Regulation refers to (internal) audits as addressing '. . . conformity with . . . policies and the site programme . . .', '. . . assessment of the factual data necessary to evaluate performance', and '. . . the objective of evaluating environmental performance at the site by determining whether the site meets the applicable standards and whether the system in place to manage environmental responsibilities is effective and appropriate'.

Thus both BS 7750 and EMA internal audits should examine performance data and information as *evidence* of the capability of the EMS, *as implemented*, to meet the requirements of the environmental policy and achieving the planned objectives. Thus, an EMS audit report may note that a particular objective has not been achieved, but as evidence of a non-conformity with the requirements of (say) BS 7750 regarding the environmental programme. The organization's management should certainly *not* regard the audit as a *primary means of performance control*, since to do so would undermine the fundamental importance of routine operational control and tend to transfer responsibility from local line management to the audit function.

The above discussion has focused on internal audits. The general conclusions regarding the role of performance observation would seem also to apply to certification assessments (third party audits by certification bodies). However, the position of verification activities (another form of external audit) undertaken by EMA verifiers is somewhat different.

The verifier is called upon to assess the Environmental Statement, and specifically to check '. . . whether the data and information in the environmental statement are reliable and whether the statement adequately covers all the significant environmental issues of relevance to the site'. Thus, it is arguable that verification involves auditing both of site performance — meaning an examination of those parts of the system producing performance data — and of the Environmental Statement itself (to check that it conforms to EMA requirements, and presents the performance information correctly).

Suitability and effectiveness

The role of EMS audits in examining the suitability and effectiveness of the EMS has also been much discussed, BS 7750 refers to (internal) audits determining '. . . whether or not the system is implemented effectively, and is suitable to fulfil . . . policy and objectives'. Likewise, the EMA Regulation refers to audits assessing '. . . the effectiveness of the environmental management system in fulfilling the company's environmental policy'. It is fundamentally unsound practice to restrict internal audits to examining the *implementation* of system elements, even if they are obviously unsuitable to their task (see below).

It has been argued, however, that management reviews, rather than audits, should address EMS suitability and effectiveness (and BS 7750 does refer specifically to this role of the management review). This implies it is the role of the top management — rather than external or internal auditors — to determine the suitability and effectiveness of the organization's environmental management arrangements.

Regarding external audits, two points may be made:

1 BS 7750 requires the environmental policy to be 'relevant' to the organization's activities, and its inherent 'suitability' is thus an issue to be considered by certifiers.
2 Certification will need to assess the conformity of the management review with the requirements of the standard. Thus, examining *evidence* of EMS 'suitability and effectiveness', which the review is charged to maintain, will be valid and necessary.

The reality should be that both audits *and* management reviews address suitability and effectiveness, albeit at different levels of detail and on different timescales.

7.15.7 Audit activities

The activities involved in carrying out EMS audits are shown in Figure 7.26. The detail of each of these activities will now be considered in turn.

Audit objectives and scope

Defining the objectives and scope of the audit is clearly essential to a successful outcome. While the overall objective will be to assess the suitability, effective operation and results of the EMS (or a part thereof), there can be a number of different reasons for making such an assessment, which may influence the scope of, and mode of conducting, the audit.

Thus, for example, if an audit is being undertaken non-routinely because of evidence (from previous audits) of frequent non-conformities in a particular area, or with a particular requirement (e.g. compliance with legislation and regulations), the scope of the audit may be restricted to that area, or its conduct focused upon that particular requirement. Of course, routine audits will seek to address all relevant environmental management activities, although the results of previous audits should be used (with other factors) in determining their frequency (as BS 7750 specifically requires).

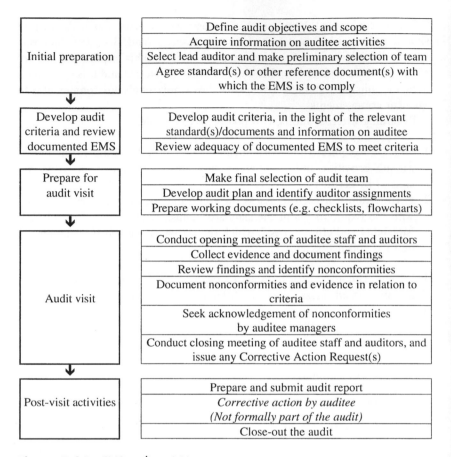

Figure 7.26 EMS audit activities

Background information

Background information on the auditee's activities may be gained from an advance visit (which may have been made at the outset when preliminary arrangements for the audit were discussed), and/or from an appropriately structured questionnaire to the auditee management, conveniently sent with a preliminary notice of the audit (see Figure 7.27). The types of information and documentation which may need to be examined prior to the audit visit (see below) are shown in Table 7.25. Precisely which items of EMS documentation and background information will be required in a particular case will depend upon such factors as the audit scope and the audit team's pre-existing knowledge of the auditee's activities.

Table 7.25 Examples of information which may be required

An annual report or similar general background documentation.

A description of the work carried out, including:
- Products and/or services.
- Manufacturing/operational processes and other activities (e.g. R&D, design).
- Schematic process/system diagrams, capacities and operating schedules.

Maps, aerial photographs, etc. showing:
- Features of environmental importance (e.g. manufacturing, storage, and waste handling/ treatment facilities, and discharge and emission points).
- Boundaries, topography and environs, including residential, industrial and other uses of land, water bodies, transport systems and sites of environmental significance.

Information on site history and usage, including periods prior to present occupation.

The Environmental Management Manual, emergency plans, procedures, work instructions and records.

The Legislation, Regulation and Policy Requirements Register and related documents such as authorizations, licences and consents and applicable Codes of Practice.

The Environmental Effects Register.

The Audit Programme and reports of previous audits and reviews, and of corrective (and other consequential) actions.

Information on participation in external environmental initiatives.

Information on expected/planned changes to any of the above.

Audit team and lead auditor

Selection of the audit team and lead auditor should be on the basis of the skills, expertise, training, qualification and temperament necessary for successful auditing and, as Sayle[72] emphasizes in the context of quality systems auditing, *not* on the basis of 'Who can we spare?'. Audits are expensive activities — not least in terms of the activities required of the auditee — and the potential return on that investment will not be realized if the audit team is less than optimally effective. While the lead auditor can be selected at this stage, only a preliminary selection of the whole audit team can be made because the lead auditor may discover the need for additional expertise (or simply for a larger team to meet planned time-scales) when the EMS documentation and other preparatory information is reviewed prior to the audit visit (see below). Auditor registration and development systems are operated by the Environmental Auditors Registration Association and Royal Society of Chemistry (see Appendix 2).

Specification of relevant document(s) and development of audit criteria

Agreement concerning the standard or model with which the EMS is intended to comply is necessary at an early stage in the audit process, so that appropriate audit criteria can be developed. These criteria consist of the requirements of the standard or model, and their ramifications in relation to the particular

Mythological Industries plc Central Audit Department	*Confidential*
Preliminary Notice of Audit Number *HSS/95/2*	

To: *Dr G. E. Ryon, Hades Styxside Site* **From:** *H. Ermes, MICAD* **Date:** *30/11/1994*

I am writing to advise you that, in accordance with *the Environmental Management Systems Audit Programme for Hades Styxside Site (HSS)*
Mythological Industries Central Audit Department (MICAD) wishes to conduct an Audit on *15 - 16 March 1995* as follows:

Auditee: *Hades plc Styxside Site*
Objective: *To assess EMS effectiveness and implementation in respect of monitoring systems*
Scope: *Effluent discharge to River Styx and incinerator emissions*
Basis: *BS 7750:1994, Clause 4.8.3*
                  HSS Environmental Management Manual, EM/4.1
Audit team: *Dr H. Ermes (Lead Auditor) and Ms D. E. Meter(subject to confirmation)*
Relevant documents will include: *The HSS Environmental Management Manual and relevant Procedures, Work Instructions and Records (including correspondence with Regulators)*

I should be grateful if you would confirm the suitability of the proposed audit date(s), and return a completed copy of the attached questionnaire to me by no later than:
7 January 1995.
I will then discuss further with you the relevant documents and the supply of copies to me in preparation for the audit visit. In the meantime, please contact me if you have any queries regarding the audit or questionnaire.

I shall look forward to hearing from you.

H. Ermes
Lead Auditor

Attachment(s):   *Pre-audit questionnaire (MICAD/EMSAQ)*

Distribution:
(1)   Dr G. E Ryon, Environment Manager, HSS
(1)   Dr P. Luto, Managing Director, HSS
(1)   Ms A. R. Temis, Group Environment Manager, Mythological Industries
(1)   Dr A. Pollo, Group Director - HSE, Mythological Industries plc
(1)   MICAD Audit Files

Form MICAD/NOA/v1.1 17/3/93   **Page 1 of 1**

Figure 7.27   Example of preliminary notice of audit

operation under audit, as revealed by the system documents and the background information obtained.

Review of the adequacy of the documented EMS for meeting the audit criteria

Having developed the audit criteria, the lead auditor (with assistance from other members of the team, if necessary) is in a position to review the adequacy of the *documented* EMS in relation to the audit criteria, and in the light of the auditee's activities. This will involve acquiring relevant EMS documentation, and reviewing it in relation to the criteria.

Should the review of the documented EMS reveal, or suggest, that the system is not adequate to meet the criteria, the relevant concerns should be taken up with the auditee management and resolved to the satisfaction of all parties before any further resources are expended on the audit.

However, one might argue that, if the EMS itself is deficient (because reliance cannot be placed on the system), the emphasis should then be on assessing in greater detail, and then strengthening where necessary, the EMS itself. Whether this is regarded as an audit or a review is perhaps a matter of semantics: it amounts to assessing the suitability, but not the effective operation and results, of the EMS. To that degree, we concur wholeheartedly with Greeno *et al.*[73] in their observation that '. . . it is unacceptable for environmental auditors to focus their examination on the functioning of an internal management system which they have assessed to be flawed in design'.

Development of audit plan and identification of auditor assignments

The audit plan should be reviewed and agreed with the client and communicated to the auditors and auditee. It should provide flexibility, to allow changes in emphasis based on information gathered during the audit, and to permit effective use of resources. The plan should address such matters as:

- Audit objectives and scope
- Reference documents (e.g. applicable EMS standard)
- Audit team members
- The language in which the audit is to be conducted, if this is not obvious
- Date and place where the audit is to be conducted
- Organizational units to be audited
- Expected time and duration for each major audit activity
- Arrangements for the opening meeting to be held with auditee management
- Any confidentiality requirements

An example of an audit plan is shown in Figure 7.28; care should be taken not to communicate specific details of the audit plan to the auditee, if their premature disclosure could compromise the collecting of objective evidence. If the auditee objects to any aspect of the audit plan, such objections should be passed to the lead auditor for resolution before the audit proceeds.

Preparation of working documents

The lead auditor selects and develops the detailed audit procedures, prepares working documents and briefs the audit team, though he/she may be assisted

---

Mythological Industries plc Central Audit Department   *Confidential*
Audit Plan   **Issued:**   3 February 1995

For Audit Number HSS/95/2 **of Hades plc Styxside Site on** 15-16 March 1995

Audit location:	143-148 Styx Avenue, Hades
Auditors:	Dr H. Ermes, Lead Auditor, MICAD
	Ms D. E. Meter, Auditor, MICAD
Audit language:	English
Confidentiality:	Normal Mythological Industries Group Audit Guide arrangements will apply (see document MICAD/AG)
Objective:	To assess EMS effectiveness and implementation in respect of monitoring systems
Scope:	Effluent discharge to River Styx and incinerator emissions
Departments:	Incineration, Effluent Treatment, Laboratory
Last audit:	None — first since Styxside Site EMS established
Basis of audit:	BS 7750: 1994 Environmental Management Systems; HSS Environmental Management Manual EM/4.1
Principal criteria:	Requirements of BS 7750:1994 (MICAD EMS Checklist 8 attached)

Tuesday 15 March

1400   Audit team arrives at HSS
1415   Opening meeting, including brief presentation on overall progress of EMS
       implementation by HSS staff
1500   Audit commences: Incineration Department
1700   Completion of day's auditing
1715   Audit team meeting

Wednesday 16 March

0850   Audit team arrives at HSS
0900   Audit resumes: Effluent Treatment Department
1100   Laboratory
1300   Lunch
1400   Audit team meeting
1500   Closing meeting and presentation of audit findings to HSS management
1630   Audit team departs

Form MICAD/AP(m)/v1.1 17/3/93   **Page 1 of 2**

Figure 7.28   Example of an audit plan

by others in these tasks. The documents required to facilitate the audit and report may include:

- Protocols/checklists used for evaluating EMS elements and/or auditee departments, normally prepared by the auditor(s) assigned to that specific element or department.

Audit Plan for Audit Number HSS/95/2 **(continued)**

The audit report will be issued no later than 23 March 1995, with the following distribution:

(4)	Dr G. E. Ryon	Environment Manager, HSS
(1)	Dr P. Luto	Managing Director, HSS
(1)	Ms A. R. Temis	Group Environment Manager, Mythological Industries plc
(1)	Dr A. Pollo	Group Director — HSE, Mythological Industries plc
(2)	MICAD Audit Files	

H. Ermes

H. Ermes
MICAD

3 February 1995

Attachment: MICAD EMS Checklist 8

Distribution:

(4)	Dr G. E Ryon	Environment Manager, HSS
(1)	Dr P. Luto	Managing Director, HSS
(1)	Ms A. R. Temis	Group Environment Manager, Mythological Industries plc
(1)	Dr A. Pollo	Group Director — HSE, Mythological Industries plc
(1)	Ms D. E. Meter	MICAD
(1)	Dr H. Ermes	MICAD
(1)	MICAD Audit Files	

Form MICAD/AP(c)/v1.1 17/3/93   Page 2 of 2

Figure 7.28 (conc.)

- Flowcharts, particularly useful for examining complex procedures with many decision points and transfers of control,[72] e.g. in solid waste handling.
- Forms for reporting audit findings and documenting supporting evidence.

Examples of a checklist and associated worksheet are shown in Figures 7.29 and 7.30, respectively; the use of such documents should not prejudice additional

Mythological Industries plc Central Audit Department		*Confidential*
EMS Audit Checklist No 8 *Verification, measurement and testing* BS 7750: 1994, clause 4.8.3	**Location** **Audit No.** **Scope** **Auditor** **Date**	**Audit Details** *Hades plc - Styxside Site* *HSS/95/2* *Effluent discharge to River Styx* *H. Ermes* *15/3/95*
Questions	**Yes/No**	**Remarks/Worksheet No.**
Are measurements to be made identified and documented?	✓	
Are all necessary measurements made to verify compliance with the requirements of:		
Legislation/regulations?	✓	
Corporate policy?	✗	*Policy to avoid harmful releases, but no toxicity check. 8/1*
Corporate objectives/local targets?	✓	
Programme/work instructions?	✓	
Is the accuracy required of the results specified?	✓	
Is the required accuracy set with due regard for the use to be made of the results?	✗	*Basis for requirements not clear for all determinands. 8/1*
Are locations and times of measurement specified and documented?	✓	
Are the locations and times set with due regard for the use to be made of the results?	✗	*No assessment of assurance from chosen frequencies. 8/1*
Are measurement procedures specified and documented?	✓	
Are measurement quality control procedures (including quality control charts) established, documented and maintained?	✗	*Control charts not maintained for all determinands. 8/1*
Are quality control records kept?	✗	*See previous remark.*
Are calibration records kept for measuring and test equipment?	✓	
Are acceptance criteria, and the action to be taken when measurements are unsatisfactory, established and documented?	✗	*Records show failure to meet Discharge Consent Condition for pH after failed follow-up. 8/1*
Is validity of previous results assessed and documented when measurement systems out of control or equipment out of calibration?	✗	*Not completely, because control charts not maintained for all determinands (see above). 8/1*
Are measurement and test facilities safeguarded from adjustments, damage or tampering which would invalidate the measurements or tests?	✓	
Are records kept of all monitoring results?	✓	
Form MICAD/ACL8/v1.3 5/4/94	Signed:	*H. Ermes 15/3/95* Page 1 of 1

Figure 7.29 Example of an audit checklist

audit activities or investigations which may become necessary as information-gathering proceeds. On completion, they should be filed until the audit report has been accepted by the auditee's management and they should be suitably safeguarded by the auditors to protect any confidential or proprietary information.

Mythological Industries plc Central Audit Department   *Confidential*

Audit Worksheet No. *8/1*   **Audit No.** *HSS/95/2*

Date *15/3/95* **Company/Site** *Hades - Styxside Site , Effluent discharge to River Styx*

Objective   *Assess EMS effectiveness and implementation in respect of monitoring*

People met   *Mr C. Haron*   *Treatment Plant Supervisor*
               Dr G. Riffolino   *Laboratory Supervisor*
               Dr G. E. Ryon   *Environment Manager*

Relevant   *Environmental Management Manual*   *EM/4.1*
documents   *Treatment Plant Operation Procedure*   *EP/TPO/3.3*
and records *Effluent Monitoring Procedure*   *EP/EM/3.1*
               Effluent Sampling Work Instructions   *EWI/ES/2.9*
               Effluent Analysis Work Instructions   *EWI/EA/2.6*
               Effluent Monitoring Records 1991-1993   *ER/EM/93, 92, 91*
               NRA correspondence with Hades   *ER/NRA*

Findings

The Environmental Policy commits Hades to eliminate all harmful releases to the environment, but the effluent is complex, and contains potentially toxic components for which no limit is set in the NRA Discharge Consent Condition, and is not subjected to monitoring of its overall toxicity.

The basis of the accuracy requirement for total mercury determination (total error not to exceed ± 2µg/ℓ), in relation to the Discharge Consent Condition limit (3µg/ℓ), is not clear and appears , prima facie, inadequately stringent.

No assessment has been made of the assurance of compliance provided by the chosen effluent sampling times/frequencies, although EP/EM/3.1 states that sampling frequencies will be based on statistical considerations.

Control charts not maintained for BOD and Suspended Solids, contrary to general commitment to do so in EWI/EA/2.6. Dr Riffolino cited the absence of standards for these determinands as the reason, but suitable materials are available.

File ER/NRA shows failure (not resulting in prosecution) to meet Discharge Consent Condition for pH on Monday 22 August 1994 after failure to follow up Hades monitoring results exceeding action limits on two occasions in the preceding week. The Works Manager was on leave at the time and, although EP/EM/3.1 requires the laboratory to inform Dr Ryon of such exceedences in his absence, Dr Riffolino has an outdated and uncontrolled copy which does not include this instruction.

The validity of previous measurement and test results for BOD and Suspended Solids cannot be assessed and documented when measurement systems are out of control because control charts not maintained for these determinands.

Form MICAD/AWS/v1.1 15/12/93   **Signed:** *H. Ermes 15/3/95*

Figure 7.30 Example of an audit worksheet

Conduct of opening meeting

The purpose of an opening meeting is to:

- Introduce the members of the audit team to the auditee's senior management.
- Review the scope and the objectives of the audit.

- Give a short summary of the methods and procedures to be used to conduct the audit.
- Establish communication links between the audit team and the auditee.
- Confirm that the resources and facilities needed by the audit team are available.
- Confirm the time and date for the closing meeting and any interim meeting of the audit team and the auditee's senior management.
- Clarify, if necessary, details of the audit plan.

Collection of evidence and documentation of findings

The concept of 'evidence' relates both to the elements of the EMS itself, and to the outputs of the system in terms of environmental performance. One may distinguish different ways of gathering evidence, for example:

- Examination of system documentation
- Enquiry by questionnaire or interview
- Observation of procedures in practice
- Observation of outputs and system hardware
- Measurement of outputs

The use of a questionnaire and examination of documentation prior to the audit visit has been discussed above, but documents and records will also be examined during the course of the visit itself, not only with respect to content, but also with regard to maintenance and availability at points of use, for example. However, during the audit visit, interviews and observations will be the mainstay of evidence-gathering.

It is beyond the scope of this text to provide detailed advice on the conduct of audit interviews, a subject which is in any case addressed thoroughly in texts relating specifically to auditing. Suffice it to say here that every effort should be made to put interviewees at ease and to ask open rather than closed questions ('Please take me through your checks of the pH meter' rather than 'Do you calibrate the pH meter every day using freshly-prepared pH4 and pH7 buffers at a known temperature?'), but also to be politely persistent in eliciting the information needed.

Direct measurement of outputs during the narrow time window of the audit itself is of very limited application, given the typically great temporal variability of typical environmental 'outputs' such as the quality and quantity of waste arisings, effluents and emissions to atmosphere. This issue has been adddressed in Section 7.14 above dealing with operational control and monitoring. Certain types of system 'output', e.g. dust, odour and litter, may be subject to direct observation by the auditors, without formal measurement. These are, however, subject to the same general considerations as measurements, in terms of temporal variability.

In a somewhat different category are such system 'outputs' as the storage of raw materials or of wastes, the state of the ground surface in areas of potential spillage, the general condition of the site and the specific condition of equipment or facilities relevant to environmental management, e.g. the condition of storage tanks, bunds, pollution control equipment and monitoring equipment.

These factors are typically subject to slower variation than those discussed previously, and may reveal the absence, or ineffective operation or maintenance, of equipment and facilities necessary to achieve corporate policy and objectives. To that degree, they may be usefully addressed by direct observation during the short period of an EMS audit. Thus, for example:

1 Inspection of storage facilities may reveal evidence of past spillages, even if containment is apparently satisfactory at the moment of audit.
2 The presence of long water hoses without trigger nozzles in drained areas will suggest that commitments to reducing water consumption are not being followed through.
3 The observation of a pH probe which is fouled or lacking reference electrode filling solution will indicate that pH records are of dubious validity, and that monitoring equipment maintenance in general will require especially careful examination.

It should be noted, however, that such observations, though useful, also suffer from the disadvantage that the factors concerned may be satisfactory at the time of audit — by chance or design — yet not be controlled effectively by the internal systems, such that their continued existence or correct application cannot be guaranteed.

Considerations of sampling programme design also apply to the examination of the company's own monitoring records, such as waste consignment notes or the records of an effluent monitoring programme. Thus, if the 'population' (in statistical terms) of all such notes or records numbers 200, inspection of 34 of them has been suggested[73] as the *minimum* necessary if the direct examination itself is 'extremely important' in assessing compliance, and/or if the environmental effect concerned is of 'critical concern'. The same authors suggest a minimum of 24 if the direct examination itself is to 'provide additional information to substantiate compliance or non-compliance', and/or if the environmental effect concerned is of 'considerable importance'. By contrast, they suggest a minimum of 12 samples if the purpose of the direct examination is to provide 'ancillary information' regarding the verification of compliance.

Table 7.26 shows further such examples. Suppose the auditor wishes to be 95 per cent confident that the true failure rate is no greater than a certain percentage. Having decided what failure rate is acceptable, statistical considerations show how many random samples of the records need to be examined. For a given total number of records (third column), the number of samples exam-

Table 7.26 Sampling requirements for specified failure rates

Number of independent random samples	True failure rate protected against with 95% confidence	Number of records in population	Corresponding 'worst-case' number of failures in population
9	28.3	10–15	1–2
10	25.9	16–25	2–5
13	20.6	26–50	3–8
20	13.9	51–90	5–11
32	8.9	91–150	6–11
50	5.8	151–280	7–14
80	3.7	281–500	8–16
200	1.5	501–1200	5–16
315	0.9	1201–3200	9–28
500	0.6	3201–10 000	17–58

ined (first column) will correspond to a small, but finite, number of failures (fourth column).

Here we see one of the reasons for, and benefits of, an EMS. If a well-documented procedure exists for completing and filing such notes or records, if the relevant up-to-date documents are found to be available at the point of use, and if the staff when interviewed show clear knowledge and understanding of the procedure and its requirements, much less effort need be expended on examining notes and records than suggested above.

But there are, of course, other factors relating to the examination of records. One may examine the recommended proportion, or even *all* of the records, and yet reach an erroneous conclusion if the data acquisition has itself been faulty. Again, for more lasting assurance — and more effective use of audit resources — one turns to the importance of the EMS, within which the auditor can seek documented evidence that the company has considered the above requirements, and in consequence developed appropriate monitoring systems and procedures. Thus, audits should examine not only the records of monitoring activities, but also the basis of the relevant sampling programme and the procedures for ensuring effective quality control of the sampling and measurement processes.

This discussion may prompt the reader to ask: 'Does the auditor need to be an expert in the design and execution of sampling programmes?' The answer is 'No', but the auditor does need sufficient general appreciation of the issues to make sensible decisions on the proportion of a record set to examine, and to ask the correct questions about the objectives, design and implementation of the company's monitoring programmes; and to make a general assessment of the adequacy of the answers! Of course, if complex and sophisticated monitoring is an important element of the overall EMS, it may be necessary to have recourse to suitable specialist expertise, but this may apply particularly to the initial assessment of system suitability, rather than to ongoing system auditing. Moreover, it is worth noting that many companies will be able to provide suitable statistical expertise from their (product) quality control departments.

It is important that auditors should not be hidebound by predetermined arrangements, but feel able to note, and investigate further, clues suggesting nonconformities even though they may not be formally covered by checklists, for example. It is also important that information gathered by one means should be checked, wherever possible, by others; thus, for example, the results of interviews should be tested by obtaining the same information from other independent sources, such as physical observation and records.

The lead auditor should have the freedom to make changes to the auditor's work assignments and to the detailed audit arrangements as the audit proceeds, if this is necessary for the optimal achievement of the audit objectives. Moreover, if it becomes apparent that the objectives cannot be achieved, the lead auditor should at once report the reasons to the auditee and client, and discuss further action with the latter.

Findings and nonconformities

All audit findings should be documented and reviewed with the responsible auditee manager with a view to obtaining acknowledgement of them. After all activities have been audited, the audit team should review all their findings to determine which are to be reported as nonconformities. The latter should be documented in a clear, concise manner, supported by evidence, and should be identified in terms of the specific requirements of the standard or model against which the audit has been conducted. Audit documents should be retained by agreement between the client, the auditor and the auditee.

Details of findings of conformity may also be documented, but care needs to be taken in doing so to avoid giving any absolute assurance of conformity based on an inevitably limited examination of the system and its implementation during the audit.

Conduct of closing meeting and issue of Corrective Action Request(s)

At the end of the audit visit, prior to preparing the audit report, the auditors should hold a meeting with the auditee's management and those responsible for the functions concerned. The main purpose of this meeting is to present audit findings and nonconformities with a view to ensuring that they are clearly understood and agreed, to clear up any misunderstandings on the part of the audit team and to issue any Corrective Action Requests (CARs): see Figure 7.31. Minutes of the closing meeting should be kept, and they should record any residual disagreements between audit team and auditee management.

| Mythological Industries plc | | *Confidential* |
| Central Audit Department Corrective Action Request **No.** | | *HSS/95/2/CAR1* |

Issued To: *Hades plc - Styxside Site* **By:** *H. Ermes, MI Central Audit* **Date:** *16/3/95*

Description of the nonconformity: *Failure to monitor toxicity of complex effluent discharged to R Styx, to meet Hades plc Environmental Policy commitment to eliminate all harmful releases to the environment.*
At variance with: *BS 7750:1994, Clause 4.8.3 Verification, measurement and testing*
Hades plc Environmental Policy EM/POL/1.3

| *H. Ermes* | *Lead Auditor* | *16/3/95* |
| Signature | Position | Date |

Auditee agreement with description of nonconformity: *I had thought that the NRA monitoring of "consented" determinands was sufficient, but accept that the corporate policy now requires toxicity assessment of this discharge.*

| *D. E. Ryon* | *Environment Manager* | *16 March 1995* |
| Signature | Position | Date |

Recommendation(s) for corrective action: *Instigation of a campaign of testing using a simple bacterial test to assess effluent toxicity. If significant levels of toxicity are found, potential sources should be investigated with a view to elimination.*

| *H. Ermes* | *Lead Auditor* | *16/3/95* |
| Signature | Position | Date |

Commitment to corrective action: *Assessment will be resourced from the central contingency budget. Further action will depend on the results.*

Date for completion of corrective action *31 July 1995 (Assessment)*

| *P. Luto* | *Managing Director* | *16 March 1995* |
| Signature | Position | Date |

Follow-up
Central Audit Department to conduct further audit of Hades Styxside Effluent Treatment and Monitoring systems (only) on 10 August 1995.

| *H. Ermes* | *Lead Auditor* | *16/3/95* |
| Signature | Position | Date |

Corrective action effective, CAR closed-out
As described in Audit Report AR/HSS/95/5

| *H. Ermes* | *Lead Auditor* | *10/8/93* |
| Signature | Position | Date |

| Form MICAD/CAR/ v1.2 29/03/94 | Page 1 of 1 |

Figure 7.31 Example of a corrective action request (CAR) form

In presenting their findings, the audit team should make clear the significance they attach to them, and their conclusions regarding the effectiveness of the EMS in ensuring that environmental management objectives will be met.

If agreed in the scope of the audit, the auditors may also make recommendations to the auditee for improvements to the environmental management

---

Mythological Industries plc   *Confidential*
Environmental Management System Audit Report
Number: AR/HSS/95/2   **Date of Issue:** 21 March 1995

Auditee:	Hades plc, Styxside Site (HSS)
Address:	143-148 Styx Avenue, Hades
Dates of Audit:	15 - 16 March 1995
Auditor:	Mythological Industries Central Audit Department (MICAD)
Last Audit:	None - first since Styxside Site EMS established
Standard:	BS 7750: 1994 Environmental Management Systems; Clause 4.8.3
Audit Scope:	Monitoring systems for effluent and gaseous releases only
Checklist used:	MICAD EMS Checklist 8

Staff met:	Mr C. Haron	Treatment Plant Supervisor, HSS
	Mr N. Imrod	Incinerator Supervisor, HSS
	Dr G. Riffolino	Laboratory Supervisor, HSS
	Dr G. E. Ryon	Environment Manager, HSS
	Dr P. Luto	Managing Director, HSS
Audit team:	Dr H. Ermes	Lead Auditor, MICAD
	Ms D. E. Meter	Auditor, MICAD

All of the above attended the Closing Meeting held on 16 March 1995.

Audit Results:

The audit resulted in the issue of four Corrective Action Requests (CARs), numbered HSS/93/1/CAR1 - 4, copies of which are attached. Three of the CARs relate to the effluent monitoring system for the discharge to the River Styx, and one relates to monitoring of the incinerator stack gases. At the closing meeting, HSS Managing Director Dr P.Luto undertook to ensure implementation of the recommended corrective actions within specified timescales, considered acceptable by the audit team, as described in the CARs.

Form MICAD/AP(m)/v1.1 29/03/94   Page 1 of 2

Figure 7.32 Example of an audit report. (Continued on page 230)

---

system. Recommendations are not binding on the auditee. It is up to the auditee to determine the extent, the way and means of actions to improve the environmental management system.

Preparation and submission of audit report

The lead auditor is responsible for preparing, signing and dating the audit report (Figure 7.32), and for sending it to the client within the agreed time

---

Audit Report for Audit Number HSS/95/2 **(continued)**

At the closing meeting, the audit team also recommended that Mr Haron attend a course on statistical aspects of effluent monitoring. Mr Haron and Dr Ryon responded that this training need had already been identified by existing EMS procedures, and a request for attendance had been sent to Dr Luto on 6 May 1993. Dr Luto stated that he had authorized the request on 13 May 1993.

MICAD Position Statement

Based on the evidence presented and with the exception of the matters in respect of which Corrective Action Requests have been issued, the Hades Styxside Site monitoring systems for effluent discharges and gaseous emissions meet the requirements of BS 7750: 1994 Environmental Management Systems, Clause 4.8.3.

Acknowledgement

The assistance of all HSS staff involved in the audit, and the prompt response of HSS senior management to the recommendations made, is appreciated by the audit team. Their enthusiasm for the newly-established EMS at Styxside, and commitment to achieving BS 7750 certification by end 1995, is clearly evident.

H Ermes
H. Ermes (Dr)
Lead Auditor
MICAD

21 March 1995

Attachments: Corrective Action Requests (CARs), numbered HSS/95/2/CAR1 - 4

Distribution

(4)	Dr G. E. Ryon	Environment Manager, HSS
(1)	Dr P. Luto	Managing Director, HSS
(1)	Ms A. R. Temis	Group Environment Manager, Mythological Industries plc
(1)	Dr A. Pollo	Group Director - HSE, Mythological Industries plc
(2)	MICAD Audit Files	

Form MICAD/AP(m)/v1.1 29/03/94   Page 2 of 2

Figure 7.32 (conc.)

period. The client is responsible for providing the auditee's senior management with a copy of the audit report, and for any additional distribution (subject to any prior agreement between the parties). Care should of course be taken by all parties to safeguard any confidential or proprietary information.

In the case of internal audits, the client may conveniently be the management representative, who will be responsible for forwarding the report to the management of the audited function or department.

Audit reports may contain some or all of the following elements, depending on the audit scope and on prior arrangements made between the parties:

1 The scope and objectives of the audit, including identification of the specific organization/function/department audited.
2 Details of the audit plan, and identification of audit team members, auditee's representative, and audit dates.
3 Identification of the standard or model against which the audit was conducted.
4 Findings and nonconformities.
5 The audit team's judgement of the extent of the auditee's compliance with the applicable environmental management system standard and related documentation, and of the system's ability to achieve defined environmental management objectives.
6 If within the scope of the audit, the audit team's comments on aspects of environmental practices and performance which, though they are not system nonconformities, represent possible opportunities for improvement.

The audit is normally considered to be complete when the audit report has been submitted to the client.

Follow-up corrective action and close-out

Corrective action is the responsibility of the auditee, and is not part of the audit itself. If such action is taken during the course of the audit visit after a nonconformity has been acknowledged by auditee management, and is considered by the auditor satisfactorily to address the nonconformity, the Corrective Action Request may be closed out at the closing meeting. Otherwise, and if within the agreed scope, subsequent confirmation of the implementation of corrective action, and close-out, will be undertaken by the auditors. This may involve, depending on the nature and significance of the nonconformity concerned, examination of changes to written procedures or a further visit to the audited site or facility.

7.16 Reviewing and Revising

7.16.1 Introduction

The Environmental Management System, once established, should contain mechanisms for its own maintenance (note the number of times the phrase 'establish and maintain' is used in BS 7750 in connection with procedures, systems, etc., about 20; the EMA Regulation also uses it extensively). The system should, then, be inherently flexible and subject to a degree of continuous revision at appropriate levels. Some of this revision will result from procedures described earlier in this chapter under 'corrective action' or 'auditing'. But other elements of the system should contain their own mechanisms for revision. For instance, procedures to identify training needs should be capable of identifying *new* training needs, and similarly, identifying *new* means of meeting training needs. In these ways, an effectively implemented and maintained EMS should be able to keep the organization progressing along the route of continual improvement upon which it has set out.

Sometimes, however, this *route*, or the rate of travel along it, may need to be changed, and examining such needs is a role which can only be undertaken by senior management. This is because, as explained in Section 7.4, environmental issues should be considered in conjunction with all the other factors influencing the future of the organization and the outlook for the business. Only the most senior management will have a sufficiently broad view of these factors. In practice, this means they may commission others (e.g. the environmental management representative, consultants) to gather the information they need and point out its implications, but senior mangement have the responsibility for ensuring the review is undertaken and for making the necessary decisions. It is this examination which is meant by a review of the EMS.

It should be noted that the EMA Regulation uses the word review in a different sense, to mean the preparatory review of BS 7750. However the EMA does require an activity equivalent to the review of BS 7750, because its Annex 1, Section B, calls for the periodical review, and revision as appropriate, of environmental policy, objectives and programmes.

7.16.2 Updating the scenario

Section 7.4 described the development of a future scenario in preparation for establishing an EMS, but of course such a scenario will begin to date almost as soon as it is completed. Examples of the kinds of changes which may have occurred were given in Chapter 2 and Section 7.4. It should never be necessary to commence its preparation again; it can be updated on a continuous basis. This is not to imply that a whole new activity needs to be set up; pre-existing management systems, or those for environmental management, can be used to gather the necessary information.

An obvious example is the maintenance of the register of legislative, regulatory and other requirements. This should, in any case, be detecting future requirements long before they reach the statute book.

Similarly, marketing personnel will be monitoring competing products and consumer preferences for all product or service attributes, not only environmental ones. The 'future environmental scenario' has a separate existence only in that it draws together all these items of information, which otherwise may be scattered throughout the organization, so that they may be succinctly presented to senior management.

7.16.3 Audit follow-up

Section 7.15 described EMS audits and the requests for corrective action which might follow from them. As an unsatisfactory response to such requests might not be detected until the next audit, and repeatedly unsatisfactory audit reports would imply some underlying problem, a mechanism for addressing the outcomes of audits is needed. The EMS review provides such a mechanism.

7.16.4 Ensuring continuing suitability and effectiveness

Section 7.15 pointed out that while EMS audits should consider the suitability of the system, reviews should also look at its suitability, but at a different level. To summarize the difference, audits should examine the suitability of components of the system to meet a stated purpose (e.g. whether a measurement instrument is capable of providing data of sufficient accuracy) whereas the review should examine the suitability of the policy and objectives to meet business needs.

This is where the updated scenario has its use, but it may not be only *external* pressures which have changed. The organization might have, for example:

• Made acquisitions or divestments
• Itself been taken over
• Reduced or increased its product range
• Opened new sites
• Closed sites
• Bought its own premises, where previously renting
• Sold premises, and become a tenant
• Integrated vertically, and taken over its suppliers or outlets

Thus the changing needs of the business need to be considered in the light of the updated scenario.

The consequences might be revisions to policy, but policy statements are usually written in broad terms such that only the most major internal or external changes will prompt their revision. Changes to objectives are more likely; partly because some may have been completed and the organization will wish to set new ones to ensure continual improvement, but also because changing circumstances (both external and internal) will change the appropriateness of certain objectives.

If, for instance, there is a policy commitment to reduce resource consumption, it may be appropriate to set new or more stringent objectives to save energy, for one or more of the following reasons:

• New, less energy-intensive processes are becoming available.
• Old plant is due for replacement.

- Increasing energy prices have shortened the payback times to be expected from energy saving investments.

7.16.5 Documenting reviews

Reviews should be documented in order to provide a record of their deliberations and findings. The reason(s) for their conduct should be recorded: they may be routine or they may have been triggered by specific circumstances, whether internal or external to the organization, as described above. The documentation need not be lengthy; its purpose is to avoid the same issues being needlessly re-examined at a later date, and to ensure that the review's recommendations are followed up.

7.17 Assessing Costs and Benefits

7.17.1 Introduction

It is not uncommon for companies to express concern about the costs of implementing the EMS concept: this is an understandable reaction, particularly in time of economic recession when businesses are hard-pressed. However, it is also recognized that environmental probity is essential to satisfy the expectations of interested parties, and to avoid fines, liabilities and damage to corporate reputation.

It is also being increasingly realized, as examples are publicized, that substantial cost savings can also result from improved management of environmental matters. While it would be wrong to suggest that the implementation of an EMS will always bring a net financial benefit, this is sometimes the case. In other cases the benefits may be of a different kind, i.e. real enough, but not readily assigned a financial value (see Chapter 1). This section looks at the costs likely to be incurred in establishing and maintaining an EMS, and identifies some of the ways in which financial benefits may result.

7.17.2 What does an EMS cost?

The costs of implementing, and then maintaining, an EMS vary according to such factors as the organization's:

- Size
- Activities, products and services
- Environmental effects
- Existing general management arrangements and systems

Thus, one can consider as extremes:

1 A very small company, operating on a single site, making one product or product range, using a simple process, having very limited environmental effects, and already operating a well-developed management system.
2 A very large company, operating on many sites in different countries, providing a wide range of products and services, operating complex processes, with a large network of suppliers, having many significant environmental effects, but with diverse and poorly developed management systems at its different sites.

Moreover, there is the additional complicating question: what costs can validly be assigned to the EMS itself, when many of its components and activities are those that an organization may need to have in place, and perform, in order to comply with legal and regulatory requirements? Put in another way, the greater *potential* costs of an EMS in an organization having many significant, *regulated* effects will often be offset by the fact that such an organization should already have much of the EMS in place.

Again, for organizations which use considerable resources (raw materials, energy, fuel, water), and/or produce large quantities of wastes, the costs of such use will be high. One might therefore expect existing management arrangements to be well developed, to ensure that usage is efficient and associated costs kept under close scrutiny. To the extent that this is so, the costs of introducing and maintaining an EMS will be lower. Conversely, if the necessary management systems are but poorly developed, the costs of EMS introduction will be higher, but the scope for offsetting savings through enhanced efficiency in the use of resources, and reduced waste, will also be higher, and the argument will be stronger, that the associated costs should be assigned to general, rather than environmental, management. (It is interesting that companies appear to find, surprisingly frequently, that cost-savings — even those requiring little or no capital outlay — are identified by 'environmental' thinking, when they have eluded traditional management scrutiny!)

Thus, there is no simple answer to the question 'What does an EMS cost?' No simple formula or readily representative figures can be given for the costs of establishing and running an EMS across such a spectrum of situations, and it is not easy even to say what the question truly means, in terms of assignable costs.

Nevertheless, to the extent that introduction and maintenance of an EMS involves formalization of arrangements for handling environmental issues, there are clearly costs involved even in organizations with an excellent record of legal compliance, and efficient in their use of resources, and in limiting waste. All that can reasonably be stated is that the costs of implementing an EMS vary from perhaps several thousands of pounds sterling in a small, simple organization with very limited effects, to tens of thousands of pounds in a medium-sized enterprise with a number of significant effects, to hundreds of thousands of

Table 7.27 Format for developing EMS cost estimates

Activity	Effort			
	EMS establishment (total)		EMS maintenance (p.a.)	
	Staff (man-days)	Other costs* (£)	Staff (man-days)	Other costs* (£)
Overall planning and monitoring				
Conducting an initial review				
Establishing a policy				
Organizing and assigning responsibilities				
Education and training				
Evaluating environmental effects				
Awareness of legislation and regulations				
Objectives and programme				
Control and documentation				
Auditing				
Reviewing				
Total staff costs (at £ ___ per man-day) Total costs (£)				
Total cost of EMS establishment Total cost of EMS maintenance	£		£	p.a

*Other costs can be itemized separately, and may include training materials, document production, external expertise, dedicated computer systems, etc. Items necessary for normal, legal operation (e.g. abatement equipment) should not be included.

pounds in a large and complex organization, operating complex processes with many significant effects, over many different sites.

The annual costs of maintaining an EMS, relative to the costs of its initial establishment, will again vary according to the circumstances of the particular organization. It is likely, however, that they will in many cases be roughly a quarter of the set-up costs, assuming that environmental management is well integrated (as it should be) with pre-existing general management arrangements.

Those charged with considering the likely costs within a particular organization may find it helpful to develop their estimates using a format similar to that in Table 7.27. In developing such estimates, a number of points should be borne in mind:

1   Certain activities can often be incorporated with other management activities so that the marginal cost is much reduced, even negligible. For example, in the area of training, new recruits should be briefed on a company's environmental policy within an existing induction programme, and a company handling hazardous materials could incorporate environmental aspects in existing safety training at limited cost. Again, updating EMS procedures may be carried out as part of the normal management system maintenance, and EMS auditing may perhaps be incorporated with health and safety, quality or general management auditing.

2   The normal costs of complying with legal and regulatory requirements, in terms of abatement equipment for example, should not be assigned to the EMS itself as such expenditure would be incurred whether or not a formal EMS was implemented.

3   In assessing the costs of internal auditing, it should be borne in mind that there will be staff costs for the audited facility, in addition to the effort of the auditors themselves.

7.17.3 Quantifiable financial benefits

Table 7.28 shows some examples of reported cost savings (taken variously from references 74–77) across a wide range of industrial and commercial sectors, which illustrate what can be achieved by a sound, proactive attitude to environmental management.

In addition to savings from improved cost control, financial benefits can accrue to the business through product/service differentiation leading to

Table 7.28 Examples of savings achieved by good environmental management

Sector	Actions	Savings (£)
Printing material manufacture	Acid recovery and re-use	12 000 p.a.
	Improved effluent pH control	12 000 p.a.
	Substituting scrubber liquor for acid	44 000 p.a.
Beverage manufacture	250 waste minimization opportunities	2 000 000 p.a.
Surfactant manufacture	Effluent improvement (no capital outlay)	83 000 p.a.
Coating manufacture	Improved process water management	50 000 p.a.
Retailing	Computerized energy management system	1 700 000 p.a.
Car manufacture	Various, including improved insulation, recycling and recovery systems	260 000 p.a.
Chemical manufacture	Container recycling	30 000 p.a.
Insurance	Computer heat recovery system	2 yr payback
Brewing	Renewed lighting system (£75 000 outlay)	2 yr payback
Accountancy	Renewed/reduced lighting system	32 000 p.a.

improved market share and/or margins. Detailed information on such issues is, for obvious reasons, much less readily available. However, the reader will no doubt be able to think, for example, of a number of companies which have successfully differentiated their products, services and activities on environmental grounds, with significant benefits to growth and profitability.

7.17.4 Financial penalties to be avoided

Financial penalties resulting from environmental offences and/or damage can be very large. Thus, for example, fines of up to £20 000 can be imposed for certain offences even in magistrates' courts (see Chapter 3), and the greatest fine yet imposed in the UK for a pollution incident has been £1 000 000. Fines can, however, be dwarfed by damages awarded in civil actions, and by the costs of clean-up imposed by regulators. Additionally, environmental considerations — both in terms of liabilities from past activities, and of future commercial prospects — are increasingly important in business acquisitions.

7.17.5 Non-quantifiable benefits

In addition to benefits and penalties which may readily be quantified financially, there are numerous less-readily quantified benefits potentially to be gained from sound handling of corporate environmental affairs (and, as a corollary, potential penalties to be suffered by their neglect). These have been identified in Chapter 1, and include: enhanced image and attractiveness as both supplier and employer, better relationships with regulatory agencies, avoidance of diversion of management time on 'fire-fighting' activity, and improved confidence of insurers and investors.

Finally, as has been pointed out by the senior managements of many companies, particularly those in environmentally 'vulnerable' sectors, sound environmental management is an essential feature in maintaining the confidence of society at large, and continuing to receive from it a 'licence to operate', using that term in its broadest sense.

7.17.6 Conclusions on costs and benefits

The costs of establishing and maintaining an EMS, and the benefits which may be achieved from doing so, can only be assessed in relation to the individual company concerned, and may both be difficult to quantify completely. It should be borne in mind, however, that although the costs will generally be higher in companies with more numerous or serious environmental effects, so too will the potential benefits, both direct and indirect. In such companies, the costs of systems to ensure basic legal and regulatory compliance may themselves be considerable. Moreover, the additional costs of a more extensive, formal EMS may be heavily offset by improved cost control through more effective use of resources and avoidance of waste, whether of raw materials, fuel and energy, or of scarce management time.

7.18 Environmental Reporting and Communication

7.18.1 Introduction

Published environmental policy statements are now a commonplace. As declarations of principles and intent they are to be welcomed, but interested parties increasingly expect companies to give substance to their promises and claims by also publishing details of environmental performance, compliance failures and quantified objectives, and progress towards achieving them.

Of course, reporting of environmental performance data may be required by regulators (e.g. the HMIP and NRA registers in the UK), but we are here concerned with voluntary reporting going beyond, and addressing issues not covered by, regulatory requirements. Just a few years ago, many would have greeted with surprise such voluntary reporting of the 'warts and all' picture. Today, however, while not exactly common, comprehensive and frank reporting of corporate environmental performance is increasingly being practised by leading companies, across a range of sectors.

Examples of those publishing some form of freestanding environmental performance report include: BA, British Gas, Body Shop, BP and BP Chemicals, BT, Dow Europe, ICI, Monsanto, National Westminster Bank, Norsk Hydro, Northumbrian Water, Severn Trent Water, Shell Canada, Waste Management International. Others, including Bayer, BASF, BMW, Reckitt and Colman, Sainsbury and Volvo include environmental sections within their Annual Reports.

A number of UK business organizations have encouraged the practice of corporate environmental performance reporting, including the Confederation of British Industry, the Hundred Group of Finance Directors and the Chartered Association of Certified Accountants, the last of which has established an Environmental Reporting Awards Scheme (ERAS) which was won in 1991 jointly by BA and Norsk Hydro, and in 1992 and 1993 by BT.

Finally, it should be noted that specific reports, either freestanding or in the corporate Annual Report, are only one of many means by which organizations communicate with their interested parties on environmental matters. Other channels used to communicate corporate performance and other environmental information include meetings, newsletters, press releases and advertisements; in a large and complex organization, many or all of these may be used to take a wide range of messages about environmental aspects of performance, products and plans to disparate groups of interested parties.

7.18.2 The potential benefits of voluntary environmental reporting

Voluntary reporting demonstrates the organization's commitment to environmental probity, and underpins its published policy, bringing potential advantage through:

- Better communication with all interested parties.
- Enhanced confidence of investors, shareholders and regulators.
- The approval of customers and consumers.
- Increased employee satisfaction.

In certain sectors of high perceived environmental vulnerability, reporting on performance is increasingly likely to be seen by the public as part of a company's 'licence to operate', using that term in the general, rather than the legal-regulatory, sense. Additionally, companies which have committed considerable effort and expenditure to environmental performance enhancement will increasingly want to show what has been achieved, and many will also seek competitive advantage thereby, or, at the least, seek to demonstrate that their performance is as good as that of their competitors.

Voluntary 'warts and all' reporting also provides a most effective stimulus for the maintenance of good corporate environmental management, and can provide the dominant 'engine' of the 'virtuous circle' shown in Figure 7.33.

**Reporting
and Consultation**

**Monitoring and
Auditing**

Objective setting

Implementation

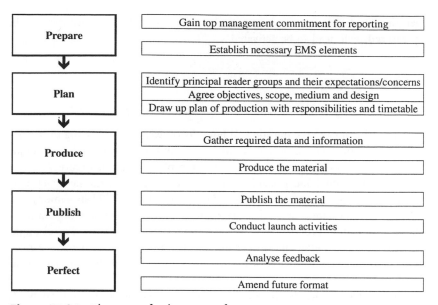

Figure 7.34 The steps of voluntary performance reporting

7.18.3 The reporting process

A logical approach to the process of voluntary environmental performance reporting is shown in Figure 7.34; each of the steps is examined in more detail.

7.18.4 Preparation

Top management commitment

The first essential for environmental performance reporting is top management commitment; this is not just commitment to the reporting concept, but to environmental probity, to continual improvement of performance and to 'warts and all' disclosure (since other approaches to reporting will not in future be seen to indicate genuine commitment).

Establishment of EMS elements

An Environmental Management System should also be in place, or under development. An EMS in complete conformity with a standard need not be operating before the reporting process starts, but at least those elements which permit sound objectives to be set, and progress towards meeting them to be monitored, will need to be activated.

7.18.5 Planning

Identification of principal reader groups and their expectations/concerns

In seeking to answer the question 'Whom do we wish our reporting to reach?', it is helpful to devise a profile showing the importance attached to reaching different groups of interested parties: an example is given in Figure 7.35.

Having identified and prioritized the key reader groups, the next step is to identify their expectations, interests and concerns; Table 7.29 lists some typical sources of information on such matters. In a large and complex organization, the identification process may be undertaken formally—by, for example, representative consultations and/or market research—but for many organizations it will suffice to consider carefully the known and likely concerns of the key groups.

Thus, for example, shareholders and financiers are likely to be particularly interested in such matters as responses to environmental threats to core technologies, environmental liabilities, maintenance of reputation, and avoidance of

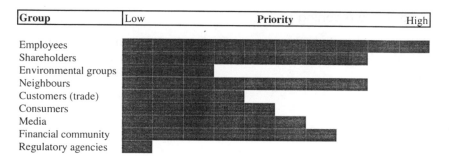

Figure 7.35 Example of key reader group profile

Table 7.29 Some sources of information on reader group expectations and concerns

Employees:	line management; meetings; suggestion boxes
Neighbours:	local press; meetings; complaints; local representatives
Shareholders:	issues raised at AGMs and other shareholder contacts
Consumers:	market surveys (own, sector or general); consumer publications
Financial:	meetings; financial press
Pressure groups:	publications and campaigns; meetings; consultations; media coverage

environmentally vulnerable acquisitions. By contrast, neighbours are likely to be most concerned about such matters as potential major hazard scenarios and emergency response plans, and nuisance factors such as noise, dust and odours. It is of course prudent to remember readership groups which may not be specifically targeted, but which may have an interest in, and specific expectations of, any reporting undertaken.

Agreement of objectives, scope, medium and design

Having identified the key readers and their expectations, the next step is to consider the scope and detailed objectives of the reporting, i.e. to consider what the organization wishes to communicate, in terms of such factors as:

- Coverage of the reporting:
  - site or country specific
  - company-wide
  - subsidiaries
- Background information on corporate activities
- Environmental commitment and policy
- Environmental management arrangements
- Legal compliance record
- Emergency plans
- Significant effects of activities, products and services, including resource usage
- Specific environmental advantages of products and services
- Specific complaints and issues of concern to interested parties
- Corporate environmental objectives
- Improvement programmes to achieve objectives
- Progress towards achievement of objectives
- Financial aspects of environmental programmes
- Environmental liabilities
- Environmentally relevant research and development activities
- Involvement in external environmental initiatives
- Longer-term issues and goals
- Mechanisms to communicate with, and receive feedback from, interested parties

Particular attention will obviously be paid to those issues identified as being of concern to the key reader groups, and to those matters which the organization itself particularly wishes to address: whether to report progress, to correct what it may consider to be misunderstandings and oversimplifications, or to extol the environmental benefits of new processes, products or services.

Any organization seeking registration under the EU EMA scheme will need to ensure that its reporting conforms to its requirements regarding the

'Environmental Statement'. The regulation stipulates that it should be designed for the public, be concise and comprehensible, and contain:

- A description of site activities
- An assessment of significant issues
- Summary data on:
  - pollutant emissions
  - waste
  - use of raw materials, energy and water
  - noise and other significant effects
- Information on other factors regarding performance
- A presentation of policy, programme and the EMS
- The deadline for the next Statement
- The name of the accredited verifier

When issues of content have been addressed, attention can be turned to the 'how' of reporting, with the goal of matching the medium to the message and target readership. Table 7.30 indicates the broad suitability of different media for different messages and readerships; it is certainly not a definitive statement: not least because it cannot reflect the interaction between the message and the audience — but it provides a starting point for consideration of suitable report-ing mechanisms.

The choice of medium must be made in each specific case, in relation to individual circumstances and conditions, but for general, regular (e.g. annual)

Table 7.30 Suitability of different reporting media to different messages and readers

	Medium of Reporting					
	Special Report	Annual Report	Newsletter	Meeting	Press release	Advert
Nature of message						
Overall performance	***	***	*	*	**	**
Progress on all/long-term goals	***	**	**	*	*	*
Progress on local/short-term goals	*	*	***	**	*	*
Product/service benefits	*	*	**	**	**	***
Specific development/response	**	*	**	**	***	**
Target readers						
Employees	***	**	***	***	*	*
Shareholders	**	***	*	*	*	*
Pressure groups	***	**	**	***	*	*
Neighbours	**	*	**	***	**	**
Customers (trade)	*	*	***	**	**	***
Consumers	*	*	*	*	**	***
Media	**	**	*	**	***	**
Financial community	**	***	*	**	**	*
Regulatory agencies	**	*	**	***	*	*

reporting a stand-alone environmental performance report or a section in the corporate Annual Report are most suitable. Choosing the former does not mean that a full version has to be produced every year; if appropriate, full reports can be issued every 2 or 3 years, with updates in between. The EMA scheme requires a full report to be published at the end of each audit cycle: a maximum of 3 years. If the audit cycle is not annual, a simplified annual statement may be produced, containing only the summary data in the above list.

With regard to design, apart from the choice between using in-house resources, or an external agency, the major decision will relate to general aspects of style, e.g. at one end of the spectrum a simple, low-key approach without photographs or, at the other, a glossy but 'green' image. The former has the merit, in some eyes, of conveying serious intent and distancing 'warts and all' performance reporting from documents which may be perceived as 'greenwashes'.

Whatever view is taken, the report itself should be clearly laid out and accessible to the non-technical reader, with sections devoted to each major topic area. Quantitative information and time-scales should be given for both objectives and progress towards meeting them, but the readers should be presented with summary *information* rather than with ranks of numerical data. Simple diagrams and charts, e.g. bar charts comparing different years, should be used in preference to tables whenever possible, and effort made to present complex or unusual information in a comprehensible manner. Thus, for example, figures for fuel or energy consumption may be compared with national usage (see Section 7.8) and, where appropriate, large consumption and production figures may be made more readily understood by comparison with the domestic situation.

If there is perceived to be a need to present detailed data, for example, to avoid the risk of appearing to 'massage' data by summarizing, this should be done in appendices, called up in the main text of the report.

Thought should be given at the design stage to the mechanism for encouraging feedback on the report. A reply-paid card with suitable questions, and a contact name and address, can be included with the report itself, and attention drawn to the desire for comment from readers in any covering letter. Finally, the distribution and launch of the report require careful consideration and this is discussed below.

Drawing up plan of production with responsibilities and timetable

In a large or dispersed organization, considerable effort may be needed to produce an environmental performance report, and large numbers of people may be involved at various sites or in different countries. There may also be a need to involve outside organizations, e.g. in design, data collation and printing (and for verification of the report, if required: see below). There will certainly also be an ultimate deadline to meet, for example, if the report is to be co-ordinated with, or a part of, the corporate Annual Report. These requirements and activities need careful planning, to ensure that all involved are aware of their reponsibilities and the timetables to be met.

7.18.6 Production

Gathering required data and information

This may often be the most lengthy stage of the reporting process, and the time to gather, check and process the data to produce comprehensive, yet concise and comprehensible, information should not be underestimated, particularly if the report is to cover many facilities, subsidiaries and/or countries of operation.

Organizing the gathering, processing and checking of the data and information required may present considerable demands on the organization, but will obviously be made easier if a comprehensive EMS is well established. External assistance may be obtained to cope with the peak demands of data collation and checking and report drafting.

Production of the material

Depending on the nature, size and intended distribution of the report, it may be produced in-house or by an external printer. Care should be taken to ensure that it conforms to corporate policy requirements, e.g. in terms of the paper used.

7.18.7 Publication

Publication of the material

Report distribution will, of course, be determined by the target readership and the organization's knowledge of its interested parties. If a freestanding environmental performance report is produced, it may not be thought appropriate to include a copy with each corporate Annual Report, particularly if there are a large number of shareholders and other recipients, but the Annual Report may usefully note the existence of the environmental report, and indicate how copies of it may be obtained.

Conduct of launch activities

Depending on such factors as the target reader groups and the objectives of reporting, the organization may choose to publicize the availability of the report through press releases and/or advertisements. Attention should also be given to making copies of the environmental report available to the staff at the time of distribution, together with information on how to handle enquiries about it which they may receive subsequently.

7.18.8 Perfecting

Analyse feedback

Any feedback and comments obtained should be analysed, and written recommendations made for amendments to future reporting to address them.

Amend future format

The planning of any future reports should include early consideration of any recommendations made in the light of feedback from readers.

References

1 The Oil Industry Exploration and Production Forum, *Guidelines for the Development and Application of Health, Safety and Environmental Management Systems*, Report No. 6.36/210, E&P Forum, London, 1994.

2 Coopers & Lybrand Deloitte, Business in the Environment, *Your Business and the Environment. A D-I-Y Review for Companies*, Legal Studies & Services (Publishing) Ltd, London, 1991.

3 G. Winter, *Business and the Environment. A Handbook of Industrial Ecology with 22 Checklists for Practical Use*, McGraw-Hill, Hamburg, 1988.

4 HASTAM, *Environment Audit*, Mercury Books, London, 1991.

5 J. L. Greeno, G. S. Hedstrom and M. DiBerto, *Environmental Auditing: Fundamentals and Techniques*, revised edition, Arthur D. Little, Cambridge MA, 1988.

6 Confederation of British Industry, *Narrowing the Gap. Environmental Auditing Guidelines for Business*, CBI, London, 1990.

7 B. W. Marguglio, *Environmental Management Systems*, Marcel Dekker, New York, 1991.

8 International Chamber of Commerce, *ICC Guide to Effective Environmental Auditing*, ICC Publication No. 483, ICC, Paris, 1991.

9 J. Argenti, *Systematic Corporate Planning*, Van Nostrand Reinhold, Wokingham, 1983.

10 M. J. Morris, *The First Time Manager*, Kogan Page, London, 1988.

11 P. Brimblecombe, *Air Composition and Chemistry*, Cambridge Environmental Chemistry Series, Cambridge University Press, Cambridge, 1986.

12 M. J. Silvester, *Chemistry in Britain*, March 1993, 215–218.

13 D. S. Pugh, D. J. Hickson and C. R. Hinings, *Writers on Organisations*, Penguin Books, Harmondsworth, 1985.

14 C. Martin, 'Investor Relations — Considerations of Environmental Statements', presented at a conference on The European Commission's Proposed Pan-European Environmental Auditing Scheme, London, September, 1992.

15 *New Scientist*, 8 February 1992.

16 Her Majesty's Stationery Office, *Secretary of State's Guidance — Compression Ignition Engines, 20–50MW Net Rated Thermal Input*, PG1/5(91), HMSO, London, 1991.

17 Royal Commission on Environmental Pollution, Twelfth Report, *Best Practicable Environmental Option*, HMSO, London, 1988.

18 CBI, *Corporate Environmental Policy Statements*, CBI, London, 1992.

19 Dewe Rogerson Limited, personal communication.

20 IChemE, *Training Package E05. Environmental Management Systems*, Institution of Chemical Engineers, Rugby, 1994.

21 The Electricity Association, *BS 7750 Environmental Management Systems Sector Application Guide — Electricity Transmission and Distribution*, The Electricity Association, London (undated).

22 T. Kletz, *Hazop and Hazan. Identifying and Assessing Process Industry Hazards*, 3rd edition, Institution of Chemical Engineers, London, 1992.

23 A. Hyde (Ed.), *Central Statistical Office Monthly Digest of Statistics*, HMSO, London.

24 Her Majesty's Inspectorate of Pollution, *Consultation Paper on Environmental, Economic and BPEO Assessment Principles for Integrated Pollution Control*, HMIP, London, April 1994.

25 R. Wilson and B. Jones, *The Phosphate Report*, Landbank Environmental Research and Consulting, January 1994.

26 News article, Euphoria Postponed Once More, *Chemistry in Britain*, June 1993, 455.

27 G. Handl (Editor-in-chief), *Yearbook of International Environmental Law*, Graham & Trotman/Martinus Nijhoff, London, vol. 1, 1990; vol. 2, 1991; vol. 3, 1992.

28 Commission of the European Communities, *European Community Environment Legislation*, The Commission, DG XI, Brussels, 1993.

29 T. Handler, *Regulating the European Environment*, Baker and McKenzie, London, 1993.

30 L. Murley (Ed.), *NSCA Pollution Handbook*, National Society for Clean Air and Environmental Protection, Brighton, UK, 1994.

31 Freshfields Law Group (Eds), *Tolley's Environmental Handbook. A Management Guide*, Tolley Publishing Company Limited, Croydon, 1994.

32 S. Ball and S. Bell, *Environmental Law*, Blackstone Press, London, 1992.

33 J. R. Salter, *Corporate Environmental Responsibility: Law and Practice*, Butterworths, London, 1992.

34 S. Tromans, *The Environmental Protection Act 1990*, Sweet and Maxwell, London, 1991.

35 J. Garbutt, *Waste Management Law. A Practical Handbook*, Chancery Law Publishing, London, 1992.

36 W. Howarth, *Wisdom's Law of Watercourses*, W. Shaw & Sons, London, 1992.

37 Masons in association with the Centre for Environmental Law, University of Southampton: *Water Law: A Practical Guide to the Water Act 1989*, Woodhead-Faulkner, New York, 1990.

38 W. Howarth, *The Law of the National Rivers Authority*, The National Rivers Authority/Centre for Law in Rural Areas, Aberystwyth, 1990.

39 Clifford Chance, *Environmental Law Guide*, Clifford Chance, London, 1992.

40 Denton Hall, *A Guide to Environmental Registers*, Denton Hall, London, 1993.

41 *Barbour's Health, Safety and Environmental Index*, Barbour Index plc, London.

42 *Croner's Environmental Management*, Croner Publications Ltd, Kingston upon Thames.

43 *Croner's Waste Management*, Croner Publications Ltd, Kingston upon Thames.

44 J. F. Garner, D. J. Harris, H. McN. Henderson and I. G. Doolittle, *Garner's Environmental Law*, Butterworths, London.

45 C. Cross (Ed.), *Encyclopedia of Environmental Health Law and Practice*, Sweet and Maxwell, London.

46 N. Haigh (Ed.), *Manual of Environmental Policy; the EC and Britain*, Longman, London.

47 *European Environment Law for Industry*, Agra Europe, London.

48 Enflex Info, ERM, London.

49 Silver Platter, Microinfo Ltd, Alton, Hampshire.

50 *Environment Business*, Information for Industry Ltd, London.

51 *The ENDS Report*, Environmental Data Services Ltd, London.

52 *Environment Information Bulletin*, Industrial Relations Services, London.

53 *Environmental Law Monthly*, Monitor Press, Sudbury, UK.

54 *European Environmental Law Review*, Graham & Trotman/Martinus Nijhoff, London.

55 R. Wade-Smith (Ed.), *Environmental Law Reports*, Sweet and Maxwell, London.

56 S. Battersby (Ed.), *Environment Law Brief*, Legal Studies and Services (Publishing) Ltd, London.

57 L. Stebbing, *Quality Assurance. The Route to Efficiency and Competitiveness*, 2nd edition, Ellis Horwood, Chichester, 1989.

58 E. Gowers (revised by S. Greenbaum and J. Whitcut), *The Complete Plain Words*, 3rd edition, Penguin, London, 1987.

59 Health and Safety Executive, *Successful Health and Safety Management*, HMSO, London, 1991.

60 Oil Industry Exploration and Production Forum, *Guidelines for the Development and Application of Health, Safety and Environmental Management Systems*, Report No. 6.36/210, E&P Forum, London, July 1994.

61 D. T. E. Hunt and A. L. Wilson, *The Chemical Analysis of Water. General Principles and Techniques*, 2nd edition, The Royal Society of Chemistry, London, 1986.

62 J. C. Ellis, *The Sampling Handbook*, Report NS 29, WRc, Medmenham, 1989.

63 Her Majesty's Stationery Office, *Index of Methods for the Examination of Waters and Associated Materials 1976–1992*, HMSO, London, 1992.

64 American Public Health Association and others, *Standard Methods for the Examination of Water and Wastewater*, 18th edition, APHA, Washington, 1992. (See also Supplement to the 18th edition, 1994.)

65 Air and Waste Management Association and others, *Methods of Air Sampling and Analysis*, 3rd edition, Lewis Publishers, Chelsea, Michigan, 1989.

66 O. L. Davies and P. L. Goldsmith, *Statistical Methods in Research and Production*, 4th edition, Longmans Group Limited for ICI, London, 1977.

67   R. O. Gilbert, *Statistical Methods for Environmental Pollution Monitoring*, Van Nostrand Reinhold, New York, 1987.

68   British Standards Institution, *BS 7229: Guide to Quality Systems Auditing*, BSI, London, 1991.

69   British Standards Institute, *ISO/CD 14011/1. Guidelines for Environmental Auditing — Audit Procedures*. Part 1: *Auditing of Environmental Management Systems*, BSI, London, June 1994.

70   British Standards Institute, *ISO/CD 14010. Guidelines for Environmental Auditing — General Principles of Environmental Auditing*, BSI, London, June 1994.

71   British Standards Institute, *ISO/CD 14012. Guidelines for Environmental Auditing — Qualification Criteria for Environmental Auditors*, BSI, London, June 1994.

72   A. J. Sayle, *Management Audits: the Assessment of Quality Management Systems*, 2nd edition, Allan J. Sayle Ltd, 1988.

73   J. L. Greeno, G. S. Hedstrom and M. DiBerto, *Environmental Auditing: Fundamentals and Techniques*, revised edition, Arthur D. Little, Cambridge MA, 1988.

74   ENDS Report 221, June 1993.

75   *Environment Risk*, May 1993.

76   J. Elkington and P. Knight, with J. Hailes, *The Green Business Guide*, Victor Gollancz, London, 1991.

77   Energy Efficiency Office, *Introduction to Energy Efficiency: Factories and Warehouses*, DoE, London, 1994.

8

Current and Future Developments

8.1 BS 7750 and the EU Eco-Management and Audit Regulation

The development of the EU Eco-Management and Audit (EMA) Regulation is described in Chapter 4. The relationship between the Regulation and BS 7750 is in principle quite simple. The EMA Regulation requires participants to implement an EMS, but additionally they must publish quite extensive detail about their environmental performance and management system, whereas BS 7750 requires publication only of the policy and objectives. Thus compliance with BS 7750 may be regarded as a stepping-stone towards participation in the EMA scheme. BS 7750 compliance should certainly not place any burdens on a company beyond the requirements of the EMA Regulation, but it will help a company establish its EMS and remedy any deficiencies, prior to meeting the publication requirements of the EMA scheme.

There are, however, some differences in scope between the two initiatives. Firstly, BS 7750 was written with the intention that it should be applicable to any organization, whereas the EMA scheme is intended for industry, specifically:

- Mining and quarrying, including oil and gas extraction
- Electricity, gas, steam and hot water production
- Recycling or treatment of waste
- Destruction or disposal of waste
- Manufacturing, of any type

This industrial bias is reflected in the language of the EMA Regulation, although other sectors may participate in the scheme, at the discretion of the Member States, on an 'experimental' basis. (Thus, for example, a UK initiative by the Department of the Environment and local government organizations has resulted in the scheme being opened to local authority operations.) Secondly, the EMA scheme is site-based. This means that registration will be awarded to sites, rather than to their operating companies. While BS 7750 certification could be awarded to individual sites of a multi-site organization, it could also be awarded to the organization as a whole.

Despite the apparently simple relationship between BS 7750 and the EMA scheme, this has yet, at the time of writing (May 1995) to be formally acknowledged. The Regulation states that:

> 'Companies implementing … standards for environmental systems and audits and certified … as complying with those standards shall be considered as meeting the corresponding requirements of this regulation …'

provided that both the standard itself and the certification procedure have been officially recognized.

BS 7750 was worded with regard to the wording of the EMA Regulation (which, in turn, used much of the language and many of the concepts of early versions of the standard: see Chapter 4). There is one instance where a discrepancy appears to exist, but in practice this should not cause any difficulty.

The EMA Regulation describes an environmental review (meaning the activity called a preparatory review in BS 7750) as essential for a company to participate in the scheme. In BS 7750, of course, the preparatory review is only described in guidance, not the specification, because some companies have long-established environmental management systems, and if they ever formally conducted a preparatory review, it would be of historical interest only. In any case, the information gained in a preparatory review should subsequently be updated by the operation of the EMS itself, especially the conduct of the environmental effects evaluation.

It is notable that during the evolution of the EMA Regulation, its authors seem to have decided that the detailed specification of an EMS was beyond its scope, and that this was better addressed by standards-making bodies. Consequently the Regulation now refers to national, European and international standards (see Section 8.3), and the material relating to Environmental Management Systems is mainly confined to several annexes and is descriptive rather than specific. Its language lacks the precision of that used in standards; for instance, references to the establishment and maintenance of systems are inconsistent. An organization seeking EMA registration is likely to find the clearer structure and language of a standard helpful, whether or not it seeks certification to that standard.

8.2 Certification and Verification

8.2.1 Certification to BS 7750

In developing BS 7750, it was always the intention of BSI that the new standard would support a certification scheme, in the way that the quality management system standard, BS EN ISO 9000, does. Such certification has the advantage of demonstrating to third parties that an independent assessor considers the organization to be in compliance with the standard.

While certification may be accredited or non-accredited, the remainder of this section will be concerned only with accredited certification. (Note that *accreditation* is awarded to a certifying body; this body conducts *assessments* and awards *certification*.)

In the UK, the National Accreditation Council for Certification Bodies (NACCB) has the role of awarding accreditation to organizations wishing to be certification bodies for BS 5750. Such accreditation (indicated by a crown accompanying the logo of the certification body) provides assurance that the certifying body is competent to carry out assessments of quality management systems. Government has invited the NACCB to perform an equivalent role in respect of BS 7750, which it proposes to undertake by:

- Requiring certification bodies to comply with BS 7512 (EN 45012) General Criteria for Bodies Operating Quality System Certification (with some adaptations).
- Auditing certification bodies at least once a year.
- Performing a complete reassessment every fourth year.

The NACCB uses the term 'assessment' to mean any initial third party examinations of either a company's or a certification body's management system. Follow-up inspections are called 'audits'. These assessments and audits should ensure that the certification body possesses the organizational structure, expertise, systems and procedures to enable it to undertake assessments of environmental management systems. The NACCB's existing expertise has been supplemented with an Environmental Accreditation Panel, to enable it to undertake this new role.

In 1994, the NACCB undertook a trial, involving about 20 intending certifying bodies, to test its proposed approach to accrediting such organizations. It has subsequently produced its criteria, and accreditation became available from March 1995. Some of the important areas addressed by its criteria are considered below; aspects of the development of these are discussed in ENDS Report 238.[1]

Separation of certification and consultancy activities   This is a normal requirement for certification bodies (e.g. in the quality field), which NACCB will waive for BS 7750 for an initial period of 2 years, to allow interchange of expertise.

Scope of certification bodies   This will be established in relation to understanding of activities and associated environmental effects, rather than by industrial sector.

Effects evaluation It is made clear that the organization, not the certifier, makes the decision on what constitutes a significant effect, but that the certifier must be satisfied that the procedure used by the organization is appropriate. Again, with respect to indirect effects, the certification body is not to prescribe the extent — upstream and downstream — to which such effects are evaluated, but is to use relevant knowledge to test system suitability and effectiveness.

Regulatory compliance Certification bodies are required to ensure that the EMS records, and takes corrective action to address, any regulatory non-compliances.

Continual improvement This is seen as a fundamental factor in certification, and objectives and targets must be soundly set, in the light of a proper evaluation of effects.

Relation to quality system certification Simultaneous assessment of both quality and environmental management systems is catered for. However, the criteria make it clear that there are major differences between environmental and quality management, and that initial assessment of an EMS should be a separate activity.

Minimum level of EMS readiness Before certification, the organization must have established a fully designed and documented EMS, given appropriate training to key staff, and commenced performance monitoring.

Routine surveillance This will be undertaken every year after initial certification, at a minimum, with a full reassessment every 3 years (or enhanced routine surveillance, twice yearly, such that every system element is reassessed every 3 years).

Competence of assessment teams The criteria address both individual and team competence, and emphasize that the team must be able to identify omissions from the EMS, in relation to the organization's activities, as well as failures to implement the EMS as it is documented.

8.2.2 Verification for the EU EMA Regulation

The EMA Regulation requires not only third party verification of the management system, but also validation of the published environmental statement, to ensure the data and information it contains are reliable, and that it covers all the significant environmental issues of relevance to the site.

The accreditation requirements for EMA verifiers are listed in Annex III of the Regulation. The rules of the scheme are such that accreditation will establish the competence of the verifier both to verify environmental management systems and validate environmental statements; it will not be possible for an organization to seek accreditation for one of these activities and not the other.

In practice an EMA verifier will take one of two approaches to verification, because an organization which has achieved certification to an EMS standard will not be subject to detailed scrutiny of its EMS. This is subject, of course, to the EMS standard being approved by the EU, and the certification being awarded by an accredited certifying body. In such a case the verifier's role would be to establish these facts, assess any requirements not covered by the EMS standard (e.g. the preparatory review) and validate the statement.

In order to maximize the efficient use of resources the UK Government has arranged for accreditation for the EMA scheme and BS 7750 to be awarded by the same body, the NACCB. The NACCB criteria include the requirement that EMA verifiers be able to validate the environmental statement, as well as perform the tasks required of a BS 7750 certification body.

8.2.3 The European situation

All the Member States are required to provide accreditation arrangements meeting the requirements of the EMA Regulation's Annex III. Once accredited, a verifier may operate in any Member State, but when performing verification activities in a Member State other than that where it is accredited, it must notify the accreditation organization of that Member State. In these circumstances, an accredited verifier may be subject to spot checks by the local accreditation organization.

8.3 European and International Standards Development

8.3.1 Introduction

Since BS 7750 was first published early in 1992, related developments elsewhere have proceeded apace. Several other countries, including Canada, France, Ireland and South Africa, have been working on their own national standards.

Meanwhile the International Organization for Standardization, ISO, set up a Strategic Advisory Group on the Environment (SAGE), to work on various aspects of environmental management. This work has been taken over by Technical Committee TC 207 on Environmental Management.

Table 8.1 Sub-committees of TC 207 and their working groups

Sub-committee and secretariat	Subject	Working groups of the sub-committees[*]	
SC 1 UK	Environmental Management Systems	1	Specification and guidance
		2	General guidance
SC 2 Netherlands	Environmental auditing	1	General principles
		2	Audit procedures
		3	Qualification criteria for auditors
SC 3 Australia	Environmental labelling	1	Guiding principles (programmes and systems)
		2	Type II labelling
		3	Basic principles of all environmental labelling
SC 4 USA	Environmental Performance Evaluation	1	Generic performance evaluation
		2	Industry sector performance evaluation
SC 5 France	Life Cycle Assessment	1	General principles and procedures
		2	Inventory (general)
		3	Inventory (specific to manufacturing operations)
		4	Impact assessment
		5	Life cycle improvement assessment
SC 6 Norway	Terms and definitions	None	

[*] There is also a working group of TC 207 itself, addressing environmental aspects in product standards, for which Germany provides the secretariat.

The European Standards body, CEN, is following the development of the ISO EMS standard (ISO 14001) to assess whether or not it will meet the requirements of the EMA Regulation. If it does not, CEN will need to produce a European standard to complement the Regulation, as it is mandated to do by the EU.

8.3.2 The work of ISO Technical Committee TC 207

Background

SAGE was set up in 1991 to advise ISO on the need for environmental management standards. SAGE did not itself have the power to produce standards, but TC 207 does, and, through a number of sub-committees (SCs), is now developing standards covering a range of environmental management issues, as listed in Table 8.1. The activities of these sub-committees are described below.

Sub-committee 1: Environmental Management Systems

The work of SC 1 is being undertaken within two working groups (WGs). WG 1 is producing a Specification which prescribes only those elements of an EMS which may be audited, together with guidance on the use of the Specification.

WG 2 is drafting more general guidance, to include details of good EMS practice, and the facilitation of management culture change.

The outcomes (at the time of writing, May 1995) have been Committee Drafts (published as BSI Drafts for Public Comment) of the EMS Specification with Guidance,[2] considered further below, and of the General Guidelines.[3]

Both WGs have considered the particular needs of small and medium sized enterprises, but it does not appear that there will be a separate standard for such organizations.

Sub-committee 2: Environmental Auditing

SC 2 has established four WGs. The first is addressing general principles, the second audit procedures, the third, qualification criteria for environmental auditors and the fourth environmental site assessment.

WGs 1, 2 and 3 have each produced one Committee Draft.[4,5,6] These drafts are now (May 1995) being developed further in the light of comments received.

Sub-committee 3: Environmental Labelling

There are three WGs (see Table 8.1). WG 1 on guiding principles for labelling certification programmes addresses such issues as:

- Operation of criteria-based, Third Party certification schemes
- Development and review of product category criteria
- Consultation mechanisms allowing interested parties to participate
- Roles of ecological and performance criteria
- Relationship of labelling to Life Cycle Assessment

The work of WG 2 considers issues of relevance to self-declaration (First Party) environmental claims relating to the supply of goods and services. It addresses both general criteria (e.g. concerning the relevance and meaningfulness of claims) and specific terms used in environmental claims (e.g. relating to the use of recycled material, and to energy efficiency).

WG 3 deals with the development of general principles applicable to *all* types of environmental labelling, addressing such issues as truthful and non-deceptive labelling, the incorporation of life-cycle thinking, transparency and accessibility of labelling schemes, communication, and avoidance of barriers to trade.

Sub-committee 4: Environmental Performance Evaluation

Environmental Performance Evaluation (EPE) is the process of measuring, analysing, assessing and describing an organization's environmental performance against agreed criteria for appropriate management purposes. The work of SC 4 therefore has particularly important links with the work of SC 1 on EMS and SC 2 on Environmental Auditing, and the goal is to provide assistance to organizations in the design and implementation of their own performance evaluation.

The intention is to identify effective, efficient and appropriate means of performance evaluation, applicable to all organizations, in all countries and regions. The over-arching, initial work addresses such issues as:

- Purposes for which EPE is undertaken
- Areas/categories in which performance indicators may be needed
- General types of performance indicator which may be used
- Selection of performance indicators

and subsequent activity will further develop performance indicators, both general and sector-specific.

Sub-committee 5: Life Cycle Assessment

The work of WG 1 of SC 5 on general principles and practices is addressing such issues as:

- Applications of Life Cycle Assessment (LCA)
- Definition of LCA goals and scope
- Inventory analysis, including data quality issues
- Impact assessment
- Presentation and interpretation of results
- Critical review process

Other WGs are addressing specific issues in greater detail. There is already substantial international agreement on the quantification aspects of Life Cycle Analysis. However, WG 4 of SC 5 has recognized the difficulty of defining state-of-the-art assessment techniques, as subjective judgements are involved and are the subject of ongoing research. For the time being, therefore, it will develop guidelines rather than specifications.

Sub-committee 6: Terms and Definitions

The purpose of this Sub-Committee is to develop a self-consistent set of terms and definitions within the Environmental Management area. SC 6 is collecting information from the other Sub-Committees to identify the terms needing definition, and maintaining a database of definitions. This will be developed and refined through iterative consultation with the other Sub-Committees.

Working Group on environmental aspects in product standards

This is a Working Group of TC 207 itself, which aims to provide guidance to those writing product standards, by addressing such matters as:

- Raising awareness of the environmental effects of standards' requirements.
- Helping avoid negative environmental impacts from requirements.
- Recommending appropriate methodologies.

8.3.3 Comparison of draft ISO EMS standard (ISO 14001) with BS 7750 and EMA

It is understood that there has been considerable debate within TC 207 SC 1 WG 1 concerning, in particular, the degree of detail to be incorporated in an ISO EMS Specification. Efforts have been made to resolve significant differences of approach through detailed discussions of individual requirements, as the potential value of an agreed world-wide EMS Specification is widely recognized.

There are subtle differences of wording between the Committee Draft[2] of ISO 14001 and BS 7750 in a number of areas, but the fundamental EMS model is essentially the same in both documents, and in the EMA Regulation. Some areas of difference are discussed below.

Continual improvement

BS 7750 and EMA explicitly require an organization to make a commitment to continual improvement in *environmental performance*. More specifically, EMA and BS 7750 refer to reducing adverse environmental effects to '... levels not exceeding those corresponding to economically viable application of best available technology' (or EVABAT for short).

As one might expect, national or regional concepts such as BATNEEC and EVABAT have not found their way into ISO/CD 14001, which defines continual improvement in terms of enhancing the environmental management system with the purpose of achieving improvements in overall environmental performance.

Definition of 'organization'

EMA defines the organization to which it applies in terms of a site; BS 7750 allows for a multi-site organization. ISO/CD 14001 defines an organization so that this may be a single 'operating unit', even if this occupies only part of a site, formally recognizing what may have to be acknowledged in practice in the implementation of both BS 7750 and EMA.

Environmental effects evaluation

ISO/CD 14001 has adopted the word 'impacts', with essentially the same meaning as 'effects' in BS 7750, and a new term 'aspects' referring to components of a company's activities, products and services which are likely to interact with the environment.

BS 7750 specifically requires procedures for identifying, examining and evaluating all effects, both direct and indirect, but in its 1994 revision has added the guidance that the evaluation of indirect effects should include all those which it can control, or could reasonably be expected to influence. The EMA Regulation does not so specifically refer to indirect effects in general, though its Annex D of 'good management practices' refers to 'any significant impact on the environment in general' and to advice to customers on the handling, use and disposal of products.

The current ISO approach requires identification of 'aspects' of the organization's activities, products and services that it can control or could be reasonably expected to influence, and a determination of those which have (or could have) significant impacts (i.e. effects).

ISO/CD 14001 appears to make less specific mention of contractors (in BS 7750 and EMA) or suppliers (in BS 7750), and of covering the consequences of past, as well as of current and future, activities (covered explicitly by both BS 7750 and EMA): although these aspects are not excluded by the definition of 'environmental impact'.

Registration of environmental effects/impacts

BS 7750 and EMA require the organization to maintain an internal register of significant environmental effects. The ISO approach to date calls for a procedure to identify environmental aspects to determine which have significant impacts; it does not, however, call for them to be recorded.

Registration of legislative and regulatory requirements

BS 7750 and EMA require a record to be kept of all applicable environmental legislation and regulations. ISO/CD 14001 requires a procedure to 'identify and have access to' such material, but not to record it.

Time-scaled objectives

BS 7750 and EMA refer to objectives quantifying (wherever practicable) the commitment to continual improvement over defined time-scales. ISO/CD 14001 retains the quantification requirement (with the practicability qualification), but refers to timeframes in relation to the environmental management programme devised to meet the objectives.

Public availability of objectives

BS 7750 requires that objectives should be publicly available, and to facilitate this, the revision of 1994 also added that policy statements should tell the reader from where the objectives can be obtained. EMA appears likewise to require that objectives be made publicly available. This is not stated explicitly, but seems to be implied by a combination of elements in Articles 1, 3 and 5.

ISO/CD 14001 shares with BS 7750 the requirement to establish, maintain and document objectives (and targets); currently, however, it does not appear that it would require objectives to be made publicly available.

Monitoring and measurement

All three documents — BS 7750, EMA and ISO/CD 14001 — differ in this area. BS 7750 is most detailed, referring (among others) to specification of requirements, monitoring procedures and quality control procedures. The EMA Regulation refers to requirements and monitoring procedures, and ISO/CD 14001 refers to establishing monitoring procedures and calibrating equipment, which is only a part of measurement quality control.

8.3.4 Timetables for implementation

While many of the differences between the current ISO approach and the EMA Regulation may be considered minor, others (including some touched upon above) may not, and might therefore result in an eventual ISO EMS Specification which would not obtain European Commission approval for EMA use. Such an outcome could result in CEN producing a European EMS standard, to satisfy the EMA requirement.

Conversely, if the final version of ISO 14001 were considered to meet EMA requirements, the prospect of a separate European standard would disappear.

At the international level, the earliest that ISO could produce ISO 14001 as an agreed EMS standard is about one and a half years after agreement of a Committee Draft, so late-1996 is probably the earliest date possible. A similar timetable would apply to associated ISO Standards on EMS auditing.

When a CEN standard is introduced, separately or by acceptance of an ISO standard, individual European countries will be obliged to withdraw any corresponding national standards.

8.4 The Future

Reference has already been made to the fact that BS 7750 and the draft of ISO 14001 both have certain management system concepts and approaches in common with the ISO 9000 series of quality system standards. Similarly, it has been noted that environmental management systems and health and safety management systems have (arguably greater) commonalities, and guidelines for the joint handling of Health, Safety and Environmental Management have been developed in at least two major industry sectors. These are the Chemical Industries Association *Responsible Care* programme,[7] and the upstream oil and gas industry's HSEMS Guidelines, produced by the Exploration and Production Forum[8] with assistance from the authors' Consultancy.

The obvious question arises: 'Can we expect an ISO Standard providing a generic Management System (MS) specification, with associated subspecifications or guidelines for the application of such a specification to quality, environment, health and safety and (perhaps) other matters?' The best answer that can be currently given is: 'Possibly, but not for a long time.'

The ISO Technical Committees responsible for quality management and environmental management, TC 176 and TC 207, are liaising. However, the issues involved are complex, and the progress of international standards development is inevitably relatively slow. These factors seem likely to ensure that the production of such a generic 'umbrella' MS standard, with suitable revision of the existing quality management standards and draft environmental management standards, is many years away. Nevertheless, the way forward is pointed by the recent (October 1994) production of a draft ISO Standard specifically for the offshore petroleum and natural gas industries, dealing jointly with Health, Safety and the Environment, based on the HSEMS Guidelines of the Exploration and Production Forum.[8]

The lack of an overall management systems standard may seem unfortunate, particularly to those organizations operating to, or developing systems in conformity with, the ISO 9000 series, *and* BS 7750/EMA or the draft of ISO 14001. As already noted, an organization has just one management system, and the advantages of operating to a single MS model may be considerable. However, the existence for some time to come of separate standards is likely to pose few *real* problems, for a number of reasons:

- Existing standards (e.g. BS 7750 and the ISO 9000 series) are already compatible in those areas where common or related system requirements exist.
- The UK National Accreditation Council for Certification Bodies (NACCB) has stated that it will expect such bodies to take into account areas of commonality in their certification assessments.
- There are, in any event, many important areas of difference between the handling of quality and environment, which no ultimate 'umbrella' standard could (or should) seek to bridge.

Companies and other organizations wishing to develop and implement an EMS in conformity with a recognized model are also often concerned that the existence of both BS 7750 and EMA, and the ongoing development of ISO 14001, presents possibilities of wasted effort. Again, the authors believe that such concerns, while understandable, can be much exaggerated: the compatibility of EMA and BS 7750 has been noted throughout the text, and the draft of ISO 14001, though different in a number of respects, follows the fundamental pattern established by BS 7750.

But in conclusion, we would again emphasize the wider potential benefits to be gained by any organization from the application of a systematic approach to environmental management, whether or not formal recognition of the resulting system to a national or international model is sought.

Development and implementation of an EMS is, simply, the application of well-established management concepts, principles and practices to the organization's handling of environmental matters; and good environmental management is itself, simply, good business.

References

1 ENDS Report 238, November 1994, 35.
2 British Standards Institution, Draft BS ISO 14001: *Environmental Management Systems — Specification with Guidance for Use*, BSI, London, October 1994.
3 British Standards Institution, Draft BS ISO 14000: *Environmental Management Systems — General Guidelines on Principles, Systems and Supporting Techniques*, BSI, London, October 1994.
4 British Standards Institution, *ISO/CD 14010. Guidelines for Environmental Auditing — General Principles of Environmental Auditing*, BSI, London, June 1994.
5 British Standards Institution, *ISO/CD 14011/1. Guidelines for Environmental Auditing — Audit Procedures*. Part 1: *Auditing of Environmental Management Systems*, BSI, London, June 1994.
6 British Standards Institution, ISO/CD 14012. *Guidelines for Environmental Auditing — Qualification Criteria for Environmental Auditors*, BSI, London, June 1994.
7 Chemical Industries Association, *Responsible Care*, CIA, London, 1992.
8 Oil Industry Exploration and Production Forum, *Guidelines for the Development and Application of Health, Safety and Environmental Management Systems*, Report No. 6.36/210, E&P Forum, London, July 1994.

Appendix 1

The WRc alert EMS Self-assessment Questionnaire

Note to user

The uses and limitations of this questionnaire are described in Section 7.1. In use, it should be given — with the italicized rubric — to representative staff within the organization. Their attention should be drawn to the answer recording table at the end, which they should be asked to return to you. It should be emphasized to them that completion should not take more than about 15 minutes: the first choice of answer they make is likely to be the most accurate.

Interpretation of the answers is straightforward. A predominance of A answers indicates a rudimentary EMS, and a predominance of E answers one which is well-developed; B, C and D answers represent intermediate positions. The *pattern* of answers to the questions (easily seen from the answer recording table, without further treatment) is in many respects of more significance and value than the absolute level. It shows at a glance which EMS elements are most, and which least, well developed, and where effort is therefore most necessary.

WRc alert EMS Questionnaire

Your help in completing this questionnaire is appreciated. It will help in assessing the current position and, through repeated use, progress towards establishing an Environmental Management System (EMS).

Under each of a number of headings you will find five options (labelled A–E) to complete the opening words. Please choose just the ONE statement per item which best describes the position in the company, as you see it, and tick that choice in the separate marking table provided. Please do not take more than about 15 minutes (about 40 seconds per question): the first choice of answer you make is likely to be the most accurate.

Note that none of the options offered is a definitive statement of the requirements of BS 7750, EMA or any other EMS model. They are simply general descriptions of possible corporate positions on different issues, from which a very broad assessment of readiness to comply such models can be made.

1 Commitment

With regard to the environment as a business issue, my company's top management is:

A sceptical about its importance to us.

B waiting to see what others in the sector will do.

C interested and active when specific threats or needs arise.

D conscious of the need to address environmental issues proactively.

E fully committed, with a main board director responsible for, and active in, environmental matters.

2 Review

In assessing the company's current position on the environment, we have:

A not done anything formal as yet.

B reviewed production impacts, at departmental discretion.

C performed structured reviews of all production impacts.

D performed structured reviews of impacts of all activities/products/services.

E undertaken structured reviews of all impacts *and* of our environmental management system and practices.

3 Policy

My company's written environmental policy:

A is being drafted.

B is incomplete in its coverage of major impacts, but is publicly available (though not given to all company staff).

C has good coverage of major impacts, but is not publicly available (though it is available to staff).

D has good coverage, is publicly and internally available, and is backed by some (unpublished) objectives.

E has good coverage, is publicly available, and is backed by tough but achievable objectives (quantified and publicly available).

4 Organization and personnel

In my company, environmental responsibilities:

A are not really defined.

B are known to those who perform basic control measures.

C are defined in most departments.

D are defined and documented in most departments.

E are defined, documented and understood in all departments.

5 Verification activities

In my company, environmental monitoring and verification activities:
A are undertaken when we have a problem with the regulators.
B are carried out by departments as they see fit, from their resources.
C are defined and documented in most departments.
D are defined and documented in all departments.
E are defined, documented and fully resourced in all departments.

6 Management representative

Our environmental management co-ordinator has:
A yet to be/been appointed.
B responsibilities which are not really clear.
C clear responsibilities, but lacks the necessary authority.
D clear responsibilities and authority, but conflicting interests.
E clear responsibilities and authority, and proven effectiveness.

7 Communication with staff

Our communications with staff on environmental matters are:
A non-existent or haphazard.
B restricted to those managers and supervisors who need to know.
C undertaken by line managers, at their discretion.
D intended to make sure everybody is aware of the potential environmental effects of their work, and of their responsibilities.
E carried out effectively through well-established systems, to ensure that everybody is aware of the importance of complying with our policy and objectives, of the potential environmental effects of their work, of their responsibilities, and of the importance of agreed working procedures.

8 Identifying and addressing training needs

Environmental training needs in my company:
A have yet to be assessed.
B are being assessed in some departments.
C have been assessed in all departments, and addressed in some.
D have been assessed and addressed in all departments.
E have been assessed and addressed in all departments, and systems are in place to update the training as necessary in future.

9 Recording regulatory and policy requirements

My company:

A has yet to check formally its environmental obligations.

B has checked some of the environmental requirements of regulators.

C has checked all of the regulatory requirements, and some of the requirements arising from our environmental policy.

D has checked all regulatory and policy requirements.

E has established systems to check and update records of both types of requirement.

10 Communication with interested parties

My company:

A responds as necessary to communications from regulators.

B has established communication channels with our regulators.

C has established communication channels with regulators, and responds as necessary to other queries.

D has established communication channels with most interested parties (regulators, neighbours, customers, pressure groups, etc.).

E has established documented communication channels of proven effectiveness with all interested parties.

11 Examination and assessment of environmental effects

With regard to the assessment of its environmental effects, my company:

A has yet to do it.

B has assessed the effects of production processes.

C has assessed the effects of all its activities/products/services.

D has assessed the effects of all its activities/products/services — under normal, abnormal and emergency conditions.

E has assessed the effects of all its activities/products/services under all conditions, and has procedures in place to update all such assessments.

12 Environmental objectives and targets

My company:

A does not have specific environmental objectives, just a general policy.

B has identified some broad objectives.

C has developed some quantitative objectives.

D has quantitative objectives and departmental targets for all main impacts, which commit us to continual improvement.

E has quantitative objectives and departmental targets for all main impacts, which commit us to continual improvement; it also has procedures in place to update environmental objectives and targets.

13 Manual

My company:
A has yet to develop any kind of environmental manual.
B has an outline manual in preparation.
C has a detailed manual covering some of its activities.
D has a detailed manual covering most of its activities.
E has a detailed manual covering all of its activities, and has procedures for updating, controlling distribution, and ensuring the manual's use.

14 Documentation

With regard to formal environmental documents:
A we do not really have any.
B local management prepares them as needed, and copies go to, or are taken by, whoever needs them.
C they are available for most activities having significant environmental impacts, and copies go to, or are taken by, whoever needs them.
D they are comprehensive, dealing with all activities having significant environmental impacts, and are distributed according to agreed circulation lists.
E they are comprehensive, reviewed/revised periodically, approved for distribution by authorized personnel, distributed to agreed lists, available at all sites of need and properly removed when obsolete.

15 Operational control responsibilities

Responsibilities for operational control/monitoring activities relevant to our environmental performance are:
A obvious from custom and practice.
B on job descriptions/files in the personnel department, if defined.
C defined in most areas and known to the individuals concerned.
D defined and documented for all areas.
E fully defined and documented, and co-ordinated across the company.

16 Operational control

Activities, functions and processes which affect, or may affect, the environment are:
A currently being identified.

B known, and written work instructions are being produced.

C all subject to written work instructions, for in-house work.

D all subject to written work instructions, for in-house work, monitoring, procurement and contracted work, and approval of planned processes/equipment.

E all subject to written work instructions, for the above activities, and include criteria for environmental performance.

17 Verification

With regard to verification of compliance with requirements:

A we leave it up to local management discretion.

B we have identified the information needed.

C we have documented both the information needed and the procedures to obtain it.

D we have documented the information needed, the procedures to obtain it, the acceptance criteria *and* the action to be taken when these are not met.

E we have documented the information needs, procedures, acceptance criteria, action to be taken *and* implemented systems to assess and document the validity of verification information when systems are found to be malfunctioning.

18 Corrective action

With regard to investigation and corrective action:

A it is up to line management.

B responsibility for initiating it is defined.

C responsibility is defined and procedures are in place to investigate, plan and take action.

D responsibility is defined and procedures are in place to investigate, plan and take action, *and* to assess the effectiveness of that action.

E responsibility is defined and procedures are in place to investigate, plan and take action, assess effectiveness *and* change procedures as a result.

19 Environmental management records

Environmental records in my company are kept:

A locally at line managers' discretion.

B for most major effluents, emissions and wastes.

C for all activities with significant environmental impact.

D according to a defined system for all environmental management activities (including training, audits and reviews), covering all objectives/targets.

E according to a defined system (covering storage, maintenance and retention times) for all environmental management activities, covering all objectives/targets, addressing procurement and contracted work, with established policies on internal and external availability.

20 Environmental management audits

The situation regarding auditing of the environmental management system and/or environmental performance in my company is that:
A we are planning to do one.
B we have carried out an audit (or was it a review?) of our impacts.
C line managers do a compliance audit of their area about once a year.
D our environmental manager does a regular audit of each area to an agreed procedure.
E we have a defined plan and protocol for independent, internal or external, auditing of each area, covering both environmental effects and environmental management systems.

21 Environmental management reviews

With regard to environmental management reviews:
A we do not have any.
B the environment manager presents to the board every year.
C the environment director visits all sites every year.
D the environment manager makes a review of our system every year.
E the board makes a thorough annual review of the relevance and effectiveness of our EMS, taking into account the results of the audits.

Please give answers on the Recording Sheet.

WRc alert EMS Questionnaire: Recording of Answers

Please tick the appropriate box for each question.

Question	A	B	C	D	E
1					
2					
3					
4					
5					
6					
7					
8					
9					
10					
11					
12					
13					
14					
15					
16					
17					
18					
19					
20					
21					

Appendix 2

Sources of Information and Useful Addresses

Directories

Civil Service Yearbook 1994, HMSO, London, 1994

Councils, Committees and Boards, CBD Research Ltd, Beckenham, Kent, 1993

Directory of British Associations, CBD Research Ltd, Beckenham, Kent, 1994

Directory of Environmental Consultants 1992/93, 3rd edition, Environmental Data Services Ltd, London, 1992

Environment Business Directory 1994, Information for Industry Ltd, London, 1994

Environment Industry Yearbook 1993, The Environment Press, London, 1992

Municipal Yearbook 1994, Municipal Journal Limited, London, 1994

Waste, Recycling and Environmental Directory 1993, Thomas Telford, London, 1992

Who's Who in the Water Industry, Turret Group plc for the Water Services Association, London, 1994.

The European Union

The European Commission

Rue de la Loi 200
B-1049 Brussels
Belgium
00 32 2 235 1700

London Information Office

Jean Monnet House
8 Storey's Gate
London
SW1P 3AT
0171 973 1992

Directorate-General XI — Environment, Nuclear Safety and Civil Protection

Rue de la Loi 200
B–1049 Brussels
Belgium
00 32 2 299 11 11

UK Government

Department of the Environment (DoE)

2 Marsham Street
London
SW1P 3EB
0171 276 3000

Energy Efficiency Office

2 Marsham Street
London
SW1P 3EB
0171 276 6200

DoE Regional Offices

North East
Wellbar House
Gallowgate
Newcastle-Upon-Tyne
NE1 4TD
0191 201 3300

Yorkshire and Humberside
City House
New Station Street
Leeds
LS1 4JD
0113 243 8232

North West
Sunley Tower
Piccadilly Plaza
Manchester
M1 4BE
0161 832 9111

West Midlands
5 Ways Tower
Frederick Road
Edgbaston
Birmingham
B15 1YT
0121 626 2000

East Midlands
Cranbrook House
Cranbrook Street
Nottingham
NG1 1EY
01602 476121

Eastern
Herron House
49–53 Goldington Road
Bedford
MK40 3LL
01234 363161

South West
Tollgate House
Houlton Street
Bristol
BS2 9DJ
0117 921 8230

South East
Charles House
375 Kensington High Street
London
W14 8QH
0171 217 3000

Department of the Environment for Northern Ireland

Clarence Court
10–18 Adelaide Street
Belfast
BT2 8GB
01232 540540

Scottish Office

New St Andrew's House
Edinburgh
EH1 3TG
0131 556 8400

Welsh Office

Crown Building
Cathays Park
Cardiff
CF1 3NQ
01222 825111

Department of Trade and Industry (DTI)

151 Buckingham Palace Road
London
SW1W 9SS
0171 215 5000

DTI Environmental Helpline

0800 585794

Department of Transport

2 Marsham Street
London
SW1P 3EB
0171 276 0800

Ministry of Agriculture Fisheries and Food (MAFF)

Whitehall Place
London
SW1A 2HH
0171 270 8080

Regulatory Agencies

Her Majesty's Inspectorate of Pollution (HMIP)

Central Office
Romney House
43 Marsham Street
London
SW1P 3PY
0171 276 8061

East Office
Howard House
40–64 St John's Street
Bedford
MK42 0DL
01234 272112

West Office
Highwoods Pavilions
Jupiter Road
Patchway
Bristol
BS12 5SN
0117 931 9653

North Office
First Floor
Stockdale House
Headingley Business Park
8 Victoria Road
Headingley
Leeds
LS6 1PF
0113 278 6636

Her Majesty's Industrial Pollution Inspectorate (HMIPI) (Scotland)

27 Perth Street
Edinburgh
EH3 5DW
0131 244 3062

The Health and Safety Executive (HSE)

Baynards House
1 Chepstow Place
Westbourne Grove
London
W2 4TF
0171 243 6000
Public Enquiry Point 0114 2 892345

National Rivers Authority

Rivers House
Waterside Drive
Aztec West
Almondsbury
Bristol
BS12 4UD
0117 962 4400

Eastbury House
30–34 Albert Embankment
London
SE1 7TL
0171 820 1010

Anglian Region
Goldhay Way
Orton
Goldhay
Peterborough
PE2 0ZR
0733 371811

Northumbria and Yorkshire Region
Rivers House
21 Park Square South
Leeds
LS1 2QG
0113 2 440191

North West Region
PO Box 12
Richard Fairclough House
Knutsford Road
Warrington
WA4 1HG
01925 53999

Severn Trent Region
Sapphire East
550 Streetsbrook Road
Solihull
West Midlands
B91 1QT
0121 711 2324

Southern Region
Guildbourne House
Chatsworth Road
Worthing
Sussex
BN11 1LD
01903 820692

South West and Wessex Region
Manley House
Kestrel Way
Sowton
Exeter
EX2 7LQ
01392 444000

Thames Region
Kings Meadow House
Kings Meadow Road
Reading
Berkshire
RG1 8DQ
01734 535000

Welsh Region
Rivers House
St Mellons Business Park
Cardiff
CF3 0LT
01222 770088

Scottish River Purification Boards

Clyde River Purification Board
Rivers House
Murray Road
East Kilbride
Glasgow
G75 0LA
01355 238181

Forth River Purification Board
Clearwater House
Heriot Watt Research Park
Avenue North
Riccarton
Edinburgh
EH14 4AP
0131 449 7296

Highland River Purification Board
Strathpeffer Road
Dingwall
Inverness
IV15 9QY
01349 62021

North East River Purification Board
Greyhope House
Greyhope Road
Torry
Aberdeen
AB1 3RD
01224 248338

Solway River Purification Board
Rivers House
Irongray Road
Dumfries
DG2 0JE
01387 720502

Tweed River Purification Board
Burnbrae
Mossilee Road
Galashiels
TD1 1NF
01896 2425

Department of the Environment for Northern Ireland — Water Service

Northland House
3 Frederick Street
Belfast
BT1 2NS
01232 244711

Eastern Division
1 College Square East
Belfast
BT1 6DR
01232 328161

Southern Division
Marlborough House
Central Way
Craigavon
Co Armagh
BT64 1AD
01762 341144

Western Division
PO Box 8
Altnagelvin
Belt Road
Londonderry
BT47 2LL
01504 46211

Northern Division
Academy House
121A Broughshane Street
Ballymena
BT43 6EE
01266 653655

Local authorities

For Local Authority Air Pollution Control (LAAPC) for Part B processes under the Environmental Protection Act 1990, and for Noise and Nuisance, the Regulatory Agencies are:

- District councils (including boroughs)
- Metropolitan councils
- Islands councils (Scotland)

For Waste Regulation under the Environmental Protection Act 1990, the Regulatory Agencies are:

- County councils
- Metropolitan councils and statutory waste regulatory authorities
- District and islands councils (Scotland)
- District councils (Wales)
- Environment service (Northern Ireland)

Local authority adddresses and telephone numbers may be obtained from several of the directories listed above.

Sewerage Undertakers

Water utilities (England and Wales)

Anglian Water plc
Anglian House
Ambury Road
Huntingdon
Cambridgeshire
PE18 6NZ
01480 443000

Dwr Cymru Cyfyngedig/Welsh Water plc
Plas y Ffynnon
Cambrian Way
Brecon
Powys
LD3 7HP
01874 623181

North West Water Group plc
Dawson House
Great Sankey
Warrington
WA5 3LW
01925 234000

Northumbrian Water Group plc
Regent Centre
Gosforth
Newcastle Upon Tyne
NE3 3PX
0191 284 3151

Severn Trent plc
2308 Coventry Road
Birmingham
B26 3JZ
0121 722 6000

Southern Water plc
Southern House
Yeoman Road
Worthing
West Sussex
BN13 3NX
01903 264444

South West Water plc
Peninsula House
Rydon Lane
Exeter
Devon
EX2 7HR
01392 446688

Thames Water plc
14 Cavendish Place
London
W1M 9DJ
0171 636 8686

Wessex Water plc
Wessex House
Passage Street
Bristol
BS2 0JQ
0117 929 0611

Yorkshire Water plc
2 The Embankment
Sovereign Street
Leeds
LS1 4BG
0113 2 343234

For sewerage services in Scotland, the relevant bodies are the regional and islands councils.

For sewerage services in Northern Ireland, the relevant body is the water service, addresses for which are given under 'Regulatory Agencies' above.

Other Organizations

Governmental

Advisory Committee on Business and the Environment (ACBE)
Department of Trade and Industry
151 Buckingham Palace Road
London
SW1W 9SS
0171 215 1042

Countryside Commission
John Dower House
Crescent Place
Cheltenham
Gloucestershire
GL50 3RA
01242 521381

Countryside Council for Wales
Plas Penrhos
Ffordd Penrhos
Bangor
Gwynedd
LL57 2LQ
01248 370444

English Nature
Northminster House
Northminster Road
Peterborough
PE1 1UA
01733 340345

National Radiological Protection Board
Chilton
Didcot
Oxfordshire
OX11 0RQ
01235 831600

Royal Commission on Environmental Pollution (RCEP)
Church House
Great Smith Street
London
SW1P 3BZ
0171 276 2080

Scottish Natural Heritage
12 Hope Terrace
Edinburgh
EH9 2AS
031 447 4784

United Kingdom Ecolabelling Board (UKEB)
7th Floor
Eastbury House
30–34 Abbott Embankment
London
SE1 7TL
0171 820 1199

General

British Standards Institution
2 Park Street
London
W1A 2BS
0171 629 9000

BSI Environment Office
Linford Wood
Milton Keynes
Buckinghamshire
MK14 6LE
01908 220022

Business in the Environment
8/9 Stratton Street
London
W1X 5FD
0171 629 1600

Centre for Environment & Business in Scotland (CEBIS)
58/59 Timber Bush
Edinburgh
EH6 6QH
0131 555 5210

Council for Environmental Education
University of Reading
London Road
Reading
RG1 5AQ
01734 756061

Environment Council
21 Elizabeth Street
London
SW1W 9RP
0171 824 8411

Groundwork Foundation
85–87 Cornwall Street
Birmingham
B3 3BY
0121 236 8565

Institute for European Environmental Policy
158 Buckingham Palace Road
London
SW1 9TR
0171 824 8787

National Accreditation Council for Certification Bodies
13 Palace Street
London
SW1H 5HX
0171 233 7111

Scottish Environmental Education Council
University of Stirling
Stirling
FK9 4LA
01786 467867

Professional bodies

Environmental Auditors Registration Association (EARA)
The Old School
Fen Road
East Kirkby
Lincolnshire
PE23 4DB
01796 763613

Institute of Energy
18 Devonshire Street
London
W1N 2AU
0171 580 7124

Institute of Environmental Assessment
The Old School
Fen Road
East Kirkby
Lincolnshire
PE23 4DB
01796 763613

Institute of Environmental Managers
58/59 Timber Bush
Edinburgh
EH6 6QH
0131 555 5334

Institute of Wastes Management
9 Saxon Court
St Peter's Gardens
Northampton
NN1 1SX
01604 20426

Institution of Chemical Engineers
Davis Building
165–171 Railway Terrace
Rugby
Warwickshire
CB21 3HQ
01788 578214

Institution of Environmental Sciences
14 Princes Gate
London
SW7 1PU
0181 766 6755

Institution of Water and Environmental Management (IWEM)
15 John Street
London
WC1 2EB
0171 831 3110

Royal Society of Chemistry
Thomas Graham House
Millbrook Business Park
Milton Road
Cambridge
CB4 4WF
01223 423622

United Kingdom Environmental Law Association (UKELA)
c/o Bates, Wells and Braithwaite
61 Charterhouse Street
London
EC1M 6HA
0171 251 1122

Industry organizations

International Chamber of Commerce (ICC)
14–15 Belgrave Square
London
SW1X 8PS
0171 823 2811

Confederation of British Industry (CBI)
Centre Point
103 New Oxford Street
London
WC1A 1DU
0171 379 7400

Interest groups

Association for the Protection of Rural Scotland
3rd Floor
Gladstone's Land
483 Lawnmarket
Edinburgh
EH1 2NT
0131 225 7013

British Trust for Conservation Volunteers
36 St Mary's Street
Wallingford
Oxfordshire
OX10 0EU
01491 39766

Council for the Protection of Rural England
Warwick House
25 Buckingham Palace Road
London
SW1W 0PP
0171 976 6433

Campaign for the Protection of Rural Wales
Ty Gwyn
31 High Street
Welshpool
Powys
SY21 7JP
01938 552525

Friends of the Earth
26–28 Underwood Street
London
N1 7JQ
0171 490 1555

Green Alliance
Second Floor
49 Wellington Street
London
WC2E 7BN
0171 836 0341

Greenpeace
Canonbury Villas
London
N1 2PN
0171 354 5100

Marine Conservation Society
9 Gloucester Road
Ross-on-Wye
Herefordshire
HR9 5BU
01989 66017

National Society for Clean Air and Environmental Protection (NSCA)
136 North Street
Brighton
BN1 1RG
01273 326313

National Trust
36 Queen Anne's Gate
London
SW1H 9AS
0171 222 9251

National Trust for Scotland
5 Charlotte Square
Edinburgh
EH2 4DU
0131 226 5922

Royal Society for the Protection of Birds (RSPB)
The Lodge
Sandy
Bedfordshire
SG19 2DL
01767 680551

Tidy Britain Group
The Pier
Wigan
Greater Manchester
WN3 4EX
01942 824620

Transport 2000
Walkden House
10 Melton Street
London
NW1 2EJ
0171 388 8386

Watt Committee on Energy
40 Grosvenor Place
London
SW1X 7AE
0171 235 2565

World Wide Fund for Nature
Panda House
Weyside Park
Catteshall Lane
Godalming
Surrey
GU7 1XR
01483 426444

Index

Note: the Appendices are not covered by the Index,